Field Guide to the Coastal Environments of Northern Ireland

Edited by
Jasper Knight

2002

ISBN 1 85923 158 6

Contents

Background

Introduction – *Jasper Knight and Andrew Cooper* 1-2

Physical and geological setting of Northern Ireland's coast – *Jasper Knight* 3-6

Glaciation of Northern Ireland's coast – *Jasper Knight and Marshall McCabe* 7-10

Relative sea-level changes – *Peter Wilson and Julian Orford* 11-15

Human use and management of the Northern Ireland coast – *Suzanne McLaughlin and Eric Bann* 16-25

Low Energy Coasts

Late Devensian glacial events and environmental change around Strangford Lough – *Marshall McCabe and Jasper Knight* 29-37

Maritime archaeology in Greyabbey Bay, Strangford Lough – *Thomas McErlean, Wes Forsythe and Rosemary McConkey* 38-45

Strangford Lough: environmental setting and management issues – *Gonzalo Malvarez and Fatima Navas* 46-49

The ecology of Strangford Lough – *Alex Portig* 50-53

Strangford Lough management – *Eric Bann* 54-57

Murlough dunes – *Julian Orford and Joanne Murdy* 58-67

Dundrum Bay: coastal processes and modelling – *Fatima Navas and Gonzalo Malvarez* 68-73

Coastal zone management at Newcastle, County Down – *Joanne Hanna* 74-79

Contents

High Energy Coasts

Quaternary events and history on the northern coastal fringes of Ireland – *Marshall McCabe* . 83-104

Shelf sediments and stratigraphy – *Andrew Cooper* *105-108*

Offshore archaeology of the north coast – *Colin Breen, Wes Forsythe and Rory Quinn* *109-114*

Onshore archaeology and human habitation in the coastal zone – *Peter Wilson* *115-122*

Lough Foyle – *Andrew Cooper and Jeremy Gault* *123-131*

Native oysters – a problem for fisheries and conservation in Europe – *Tony Andrew* *132-138*

Magilligan Foreland – *Peter Wilson* *139-145*

Bann estuary dunes – *Peter Wilson and John McGourty* *146-151*

Nearshore sediment dynamics of the River Bann estuary: some preliminary results –
Lyn McDowell, Jasper Knight and Rory Quinn *152-156*

Basalt cliffs and shore platforms between Portstewart (Co. Derry) and
Portballintrae (Co. Antrim) – *John McKenna* *157-164*

Management of Co Antrim's sandy beaches – *Andrew Cooper and Derek Jackson* *165-168*

Runkerry beach – *Derek Jackson* *169-171*

The volcanology of the Tertiary lavas of the Giant's Causeway, Co Antrim – *Paul Lyle* *172-177*

Coastal habitats – *Alan Cooper* *178-183*

References *187-203*

Contributors

Tony Andrew, School of Biological and Environmental Sciences, University of Ulster, Coleraine, Co Londonderry, Northern Ireland, BT52 1SA (te.andrew@ulst.ac.uk)

Eric Bann, School of Biological and Environmental Sciences, University of Ulster, Coleraine, Co Londonderry, Northern Ireland, BT52 1SA (ee.bann@ulst.ac.uk)

Colin Breen, School of Biological and Environmental Sciences, University of Ulster, Coleraine, Co Londonderry, Northern Ireland, BT52 1SA (cp.breen@ulst.ac.uk)

Alan Cooper, School of Biological and Environmental Sciences, University of Ulster, Coleraine, Co Londonderry, Northern Ireland, BT52 1SA (a.cooper@ulst.ac.uk)

Andrew Cooper, School of Biological and Environmental Sciences, University of Ulster, Coleraine, Co Londonderry, Northern Ireland, BT52 1SA (jag.cooper@ulst.ac.uk)

Wes Forsythe, Centre for Maritime Archaeology, University of Ulster, Coleraine, Co Londonderry, Northern Ireland, BT52 1SA (w.forsythe@ulst.ac.uk)

Jeremy Gault, School of Biological and Environmental Sciences, University of Ulster, Coleraine, Co Londonderry, Northern Ireland, BT52 1SA (jr.gault@ulst.ac.uk)

Derek Jackson, School of Biological and Environmental Sciences, University of Ulster, Coleraine, Co Londonderry, Northern Ireland, BT52 1SA (d.jackson@ulst.ac.uk)

Jasper Knight, School of Biological and Environmental Sciences, University of Ulster, Coleraine, Co Londonderry, Northern Ireland, BT52 1SA (j.knight@ulst.ac.uk)

Paul Lyle, School of the Built Environment, University of Ulster, Jordanstown, Co Antrim, Northern Ireland, BT37 0QB (p.lyle@ulst.ac.uk)

Gonzalo Malvarez, School of Biological and Environmental Sciences, University of Ulster, Coleraine, Co Londonderry, Northern Ireland, BT52 1SA (g.malvarez@ulst.ac.uk)

Marshall McCabe, School of Biological and Environmental Sciences, University of Ulster, Coleraine, Co Londonderry, Northern Ireland, BT52 1SA (m.mccabe@ulst.ac.uk)

Contributors

Rosemary McConkey, Centre for Maritime Archaeology, University of Ulster, Coleraine, Co Londonderry, Northern Ireland, BT52 1SA (ra.mcconkey@ulst.ac.uk)

Lyn McDowell, School of Biological and Environmental Sciences, University of Ulster, Coleraine, Co Londonderry, Northern Ireland, BT52 1SA (jl.mcdowell@ulst.ac.uk)

Thomas McErlean, Centre for Maritime Archaeology, University of Ulster, Coleraine, Co Londonderry, Northern Ireland, BT52 1SA (tc.mcerlean@ulst.ac.uk)

John McGourty, School of Biological and Environmental Sciences, University of Ulster, Coleraine, Co Londonderry, Northern Ireland, BT52 1SA (jf.mcgourty@ulst.ac.uk)

John McKenna, School of Biological and Environmental Sciences, University of Ulster, Coleraine, Co Londonderry, Northern Ireland, BT52 1SA (j.mckenna@ulst.ac.uk)

Suzanne McLaughlin, School of Biological and Environmental Sciences, University of Ulster, Coleraine, Co Londonderry, Northern Ireland, BT52 1SA (sm.mclaughlin@ulst.ac.uk)

Joanne Murdy, School of Geography, Queen's University, Belfast, Northern Ireland, BT7 1NN (j.murdy@qub.ac.uk)

Fatima Navas, School of Biological and Environmental Sciences, University of Ulster, Coleraine, Co Londonderry, Northern Ireland, BT52 1SA (f.navas@ulst.ac.uk)

Julian Orford, School of Geography, Queen's University, Belfast, Northern Ireland, BT7 1NN (j.orford@qub.ac.uk)

Alex Portig, School of Biology and Biochemistry, Queen's University, Belfast, Northern Ireland, BT9 7BL (a.portig@qub.ac.uk)

Rory Quinn, School of Biological and Environmental Sciences, University of Ulster, Coleraine, Co Londonderry, Northern Ireland, BT52 1SA (rj.quinn@ulst.ac.uk)

Peter Wilson, School of Biological and Environmental Sciences, University of Ulster, Coleraine, Co Londonderry, Northern Ireland, BT52 1SA (p.wilson@ulst.ac.uk)

Background

Background

Introduction

Jasper Knight and Andrew Cooper

This field guide accompanies the excursion component of the International Coastal Symposium (ICS), hosted by the Coastal Research Group of the University of Ulster at Coleraine, Northern Ireland, 25-29 March 2002. The Northern Ireland coast shows great diversity in coastal regime and environment, from the high-energy, rocky north coast, open to the Atlantic Ocean, to the low-energy, high tidal-range southeast coast of Northern Ireland which fronts the Irish Sea. Coastal environments include estuaries and sea loughs, rocky shore platforms, coastal dunes, embayments and forelands. The scientific and aesthetic quality of the Northern Ireland coast is also shown by its many Blue Flag beaches (awarded for beach cleanliness and management), Marine Nature Reserves, and the statutory protection of much of the coast as 'Areas of Outstanding Natural Beauty' and 'Areas of Special Scientific Interest'. Additionally, the columnar basalt formations exposed at the coast at the Giant's Causeway are designated as a UNESCO World Heritage Site.

The Northern Ireland coast has also developed in symbiosis with human activity. Some of the earliest archaeological evidence for human settlement in Ireland (dated to the Mesolithic, ~ 7000 BP) is found at Mountsandel, 4 km south of the Coleraine campus of the University, at approximately the tidal limit of the River Bann. Additionally, coastal sand dunes throughout the north of Ireland show human activity in the coastal zone since 3000-4000 BP.

It is currently an exciting time in coastal science at the University of Ulster. The Coastal Research Group conducts research into themes including coastal morphodynamics, Quaternary environmental change, and coastal zone management. In recent years it has expanded in size dramatically and has diversified its research interests into high-resolution coastal surveying and monitoring, offshore marine geophysics and maritime archaeology. It is now one of the largest coastal science groups in the UK and has a range of postgraduate programmes (MSc and PhD level). A new Centre for Coastal Science (cost over £1.5m) is currently being built at the Coleraine campus and a new undergraduate degree programme in Marine Science is being developed (first intake in October 2002). These augur well for the continued development and expansion of coastal science at the University of Ulster, and continued high-quality teaching and research centred around the natural laboratory that is the Northern Ireland coast. During the ICS, we hope to demonstrate aspects of our work to our international colleagues and to showcase our diverse coastal environments.

This field guide is organised into three main sections. The first section outlines the geological and physical setting of the Northern Ireland coast, including the effects of glaciation and sea-level change. The second section on low-energy coasts accompanies the two half-day field excursions to the coast of Co. Down (Strangford Lough,

Background

Newcastle/Dundrum). The third section on high-energy coasts accompanies the full-day excursion to the north coast of Northern Ireland (north Co. Londonderry, Co. Antrim). The routes undertaken on these field excursions are shown on the inserted figure.

We would like to thank the following organisations for sponsorship of the ICS at the University of Ulster: Industrial Reseach and Technology Unit (IRTU), Belfast Harbour Commissioners, Marine Institute, Dublin, and University of Ulster.

Physical and geological setting of Northern Ireland's coast

Jasper Knight

Introduction and coastal physical characteristics

The island of Ireland is located on the mid-latitude NE Atlantic on the continental shelf of NW Europe (50-60°N) (Fig. 1). It lies adjacent to the climatically-sensitive North Atlantic from which it derives its mild climate. The coastline of Ireland (total 6300 km long) can be classified as paraglacial (Carter, 1990) and is highly variable in terms of its wave climate and energy, geomorphic development during the late Pleistocene and Holocene, and present-day morphology and coastal dynamics (Carter and Orford, 1988). Much of this dynamic

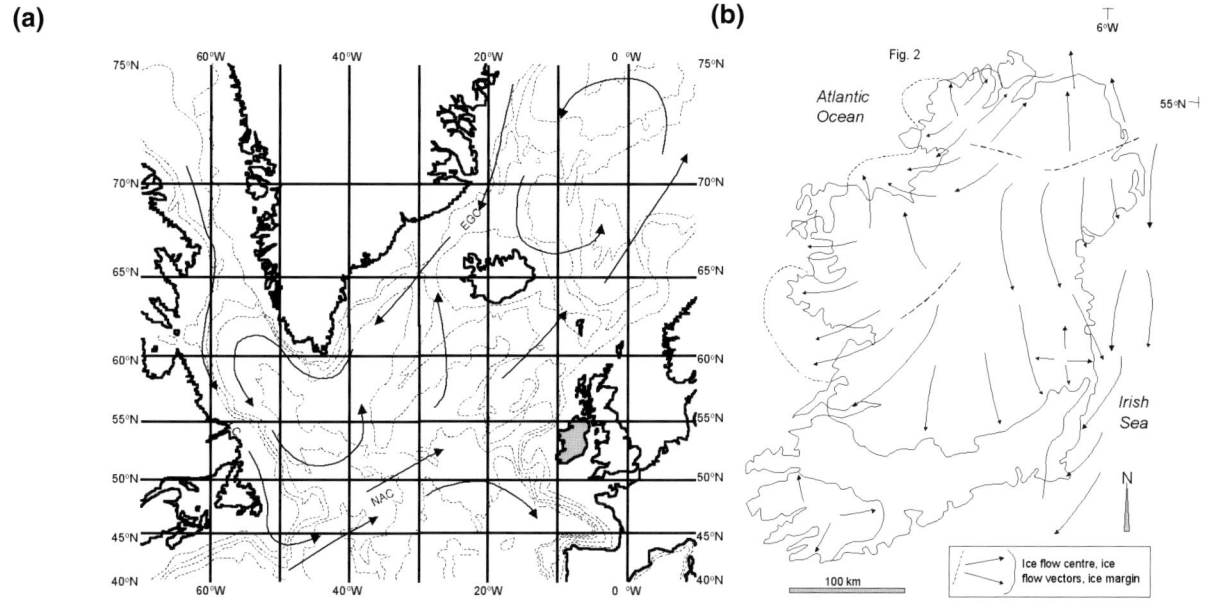

Fig. 1. (a) Location of Ireland (shaded) in the northeast Atlantic, showing generalised bathymetry and surface water currents. LC = Labrador Current, EGC = East Greenland Current, NAC = North Atlantic Current. (b) Ice flow centres, flow vectors and ice margins in Ireland during the late Devensian glaciation (after McCabe, 1985), and the location of the study area in the north of Ireland (boxed).

Background

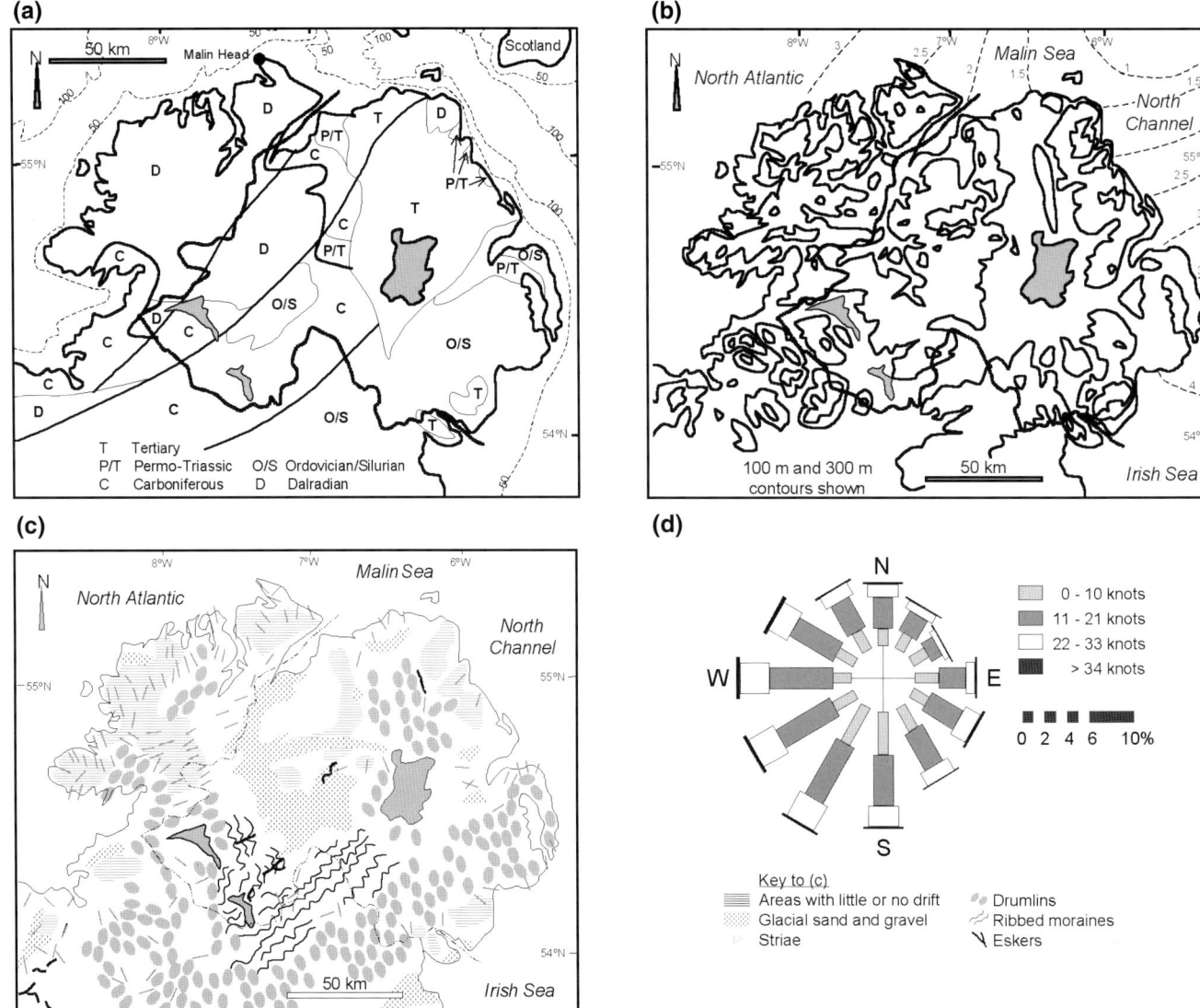

Fig. 2. (a) Bedrock geology (after Wilson, 1972) and bathymetry of the north of Ireland. (b) Topography of the north of Ireland (100 m and 300 m contours shown) and tidal range (metres at mean springs) across the Northern Ireland coast (Berne et al., 1997). Note data are not shown for Republic of Ireland coasts. (c) Distribution of glacial landforms in the north of Ireland (after McCabe, 1985; McCabe et al., 1999). In maps a-c the Province of Northern Ireland is shown by the dotted and dashed line. (d) Hourly wind speeds by speed band and direction, 1956-1996, Malin Head (location shown in (a).

nature is due to the influence of late Pleistocene glaciation and the effects of changing relative sea-level due to ice unloading (Carter, 1982a).

The north and northeast coast of Northern Ireland comprises steep rock cliffs and headlands which are separated by smaller sandy embayments (Fig. 2). The eastern and southeastern coast of Northern Ireland is of lower relief and fronted mainly by glacial sediments which give rise to sandy and muddy beaches and embayments. Estuaries and sea-loughs are found on both coastal types, including Lough Foyle and Belfast Lough. The range of coastal types and their different characteristics (whether bedrock or drift-dominated) also results in highly diverse coastal features and unique ecological habitats (Berne et al., 1997). The 'hard' and 'soft'-rock coasts of Northern Ireland have been described by Carter et al. (1992) and Carter and Bartlett (1990) respectively. According to Carter (1990), macroscale controls on coastal evolution include tectonic setting, sea-level history, sediment availability and wave/tide regime. In Northern Ireland, these components are both highly variable across the coast, and have changed markedly over time. Aspects of these are discussed in more detail below and in other sections of this fieldguide. General information on physical coastal environments in Northern Ireland is given in Barne et al. (1997) and British Geological Survey offshore reports by Jackson et al. (1995) and Fyfe et al. (1993).

Bedrock geology

Coastline shape and geometry are controlled broadly by bedrock type and the presence of certain geological structures including faults and bedrock strike which generally follow northeast southwest-aligned Caledonian lineaments (Stephens, 1970; Wilson, 1972; Pendlebury and Dobson, 1976). Rocks of varying ages (Dalradian to Recent) outcrop along the Northern Ireland coast (Fig. 2). The area around Lough Foyle is underlain by Carboniferous, Triassic and Jurassic rocks which occupy a depression in the Precambrian basement. These rocks are generally overlain by glacial sediments and by Holocene blown sand around Magilligan. The north coast is generally fronted by Tertiary basalts which are underlain mainly by the Cretaceous Ulster White Limestone. The Giant's Causeway (a World Heritage Site) is developed in tholeiitic basalts exposed at the coast. Sandy beaches are present at some localities such as Benone and Portstewart. In northeastern and eastern Northern Ireland Permo-Triassic rocks rest unconformably on Dalradian rocks, and both are sometimes cut by Tertiary dikes. The southeastern coast of Northern Ireland comprises northeast southwest-trending Ordovician and Silurian rocks which give the coastline a low relief. The Mourne Mountains are cored by Tertiary granites. Glacial sediments are common and Holocene dunes are well-developed around Dundrum.

Offshore bathymetry, substrates and physical oceanography

The north coast of Northern Ireland fronts the Malin Sea (Fig. 2). Between Lough Foyle and Portrush the bathymetry slopes shallowly offshore and surficial sediments mainly comprise planar sand (Pendlebury and Dobson, 1976). East of Portrush the bathymetry is steeper (both immediately offshore and north of Rathlin Island) and outcrops of chalk and basalt are present. Surficial sediments include asymmetric sand waves and ridges (amplitude < 12 m) and sand ripples, and planar gravel, sandy gravel and sand (Pendlebury and

Dobson, 1976). Further offshore, planar gravel substrates are overlain by sand ribbons (Pendlebury and Dobson, 1976). The North Channel, located between the coast of northeast Ireland and southwest Scotland, is characterised by steep bedrock slopes and isolated submerged peaks and islets. This area, between Rathlin Island and Larne, is subject to strong tidal switching and very rapid currents (Knight and Howarth, 1999). Bedforms in this area comprise gravel dunes with coarse bioclastic and boulder lags, and tidal sand waves (Pendlebury and Dobson, 1976).

The Irish Sea coast of Northern Ireland (south of Larne) is characterised by steep offshore gradients developed in bedrock in the north of the area, shallowing to the south where sediment cover is more common. Nearshore sand is present around Dundrum Bay, and Strangford Lough has a flat, muddy to sandy substrate. Bedforms are poorly developed but include tidal sand ridges and ribbons (Belderson, 1964).

Wind, wave and tidal patterns

Northern Ireland's coast fronts seas with different bathymetries, energy levels and tidal regimes. These impact on the physical processes operating along these coasts (Carter and Orford, 1988). The western and northern Ireland coasts, exposed to the Atlantic, are dominated by long-period swell- and storm-waves with a potential fetch of several thousand kilometers from the west and southwest which is the direction of the prevailing wind (Fig. 2). The eastern Ireland coast borders the epicontinental, semi-enclosed Irish Sea which is fetch-limited. Here, tidal processes are of greater importance in coastal dynamics (Ramster and Hill, 1969). Tidal range increases outwards from an amphidromic point located offshore southwest Scotland, and varies from macro- to mesotidal across the coast of Northern Ireland (Fig. 2). Between the two coastal regimes (wave dominated on the north coast, tide dominated on the east coast), tidal switching in the North Channel is a dominant feature affecting sediment distribution patterns and offshore bedforms (Knight and Howarth, 1999). Wind records from Malin Head, north coast of Ireland, show dominant westerly and sounthwesterly winds, especially during winter (Fig. 2).

Impacts on present-day coastal processes

The physical setting of the Northern Ireland coast, outlined above, provides the background for evaluating mesoscale coastal dynamics and changes in coastal systems under scenarios of changing climate or through human alteration of the coast. For example, present-day coastal erosion varies markedly according to whether coasts are fronted by bedrock or glacial sediment (Carter *et al.*, 1992) and by overall energy regime of the coast, as imparted by waves and tides (Carter and Bartlett, 1990). The rate of coastal erosion has a direct impact on sediment budgets, beach nourishment and the maintenance of coastal sand dunes, salt-marshes and mudflats. Changes in coastal processes, resulting from a range of human and physical forcing factors, may therefore have profound effects on sediment system dynamics and coastal stability.

Glaciation of Northern Ireland's coast

Jasper Knight and Marshall McCabe

Introduction

The aim of this account is to summarise how Northern Ireland's diverse landscapes were shaped during the last glaciation, and the direct and indirect effects of glaciation on Northern Ireland's coasts in the postglacial period (the Holocene). The surficial geomorphology of most (> 90%) of the north of Ireland and its coast is largely a relict of glacial processes which operated during the late Devensian (Weichselian) period (~ 25,000-13,000 years BP), also known in Ireland as the late Midlandian (Mitchell *et al.*, 1973). During this period glacial ice covered the northernmost part of the British Isles, generally spreading from source areas in lowland Ireland, upland Scotland and northern England (Boulton *et al.*, 1985; McCabe and Eyles, 1989). In the western British Isles ice drained generally southwards through the Irish Sea which acted as the main outlet glacier for ice on the surrounding land masses (McCabe and Eyles, 1989). Ice sourced from Ireland was sensitive to changes in the strength of the Irish Sea glacier, which sometimes penetrated into Irish coastal lowlands in periods when Irish ice was relatively inactive and restricted in extent.

During the late Devensian, ice flowed from inland centres of accumulation (Co. Tyrone, Sperrin Mountains, Lough Neagh) outwards towards ice margins which were located mainly around the position of or offshore from present-day coasts (Fig. 1b). Ice activity in this period can be inferred from the spatial patterns and directional components of glacial landforms and sediments found onshore (e.g. McCabe *et al.*, 1999), and from borehole and seismic evidence offshore (Fyfe *et al.*, 1993; Jackson *et al.*, 1995). Some of this evidence is described below. Age control on these ice events comes from the use of two methodological approaches: relative age assessment of cross-cutting and superimposed glacial bedforms inland, and absolute age assessment (through radiometric dating) of marine muds within the glacial sediments themselves. Broadly, this evidence shows that activity of the Irish ice sheet occurred in tempo with very rapid (centennial to millennial-scale) changes in North Atlantic climate, and generally matches with the climate shifts observed in other North Atlantic marine and ice-core records (McCabe and Clark, 1998; McCabe *et al.*, 1998; Knight, submitted).

This account briefly outlines the geomorphic and sedimentary evidence for ice flow direction, characteristics and timing, and the effects of glaciation on the Northern Ireland coast. For more detail, the reader is referred to McCabe (1985, 1987, 1993), McCabe and Eyles (1989), McCabe *et al.* (1999) and Knight *et al.* (in press).

Glacial morphosedimentary evidence and the dating of ice events

Glacial erosion and deposition resulted in the formation of distinctive upland and lowland landform assemblages in the north of Ireland. These are described in turn.

Upland areas (> 150 m OD), nearest to or adjacent to the former ice centres, include the Sperrin Mountains, Mourne Mountains, Antrim hills, and Donegal mountain ranges. These areas are relatively drift-poor and comprise glacially-sculpted, streamlined and striated bedrock surfaces and other erosional features such as roches moutonneés, meltwater channels and, occasionally, corries. In these upland areas, glacial landforms are strongly controlled by bedrock structures including bedrock strike and fault orientation. For example, glaciated valleys in the Sperrins and Donegal take their alignment from the NE-SW-trending Caledonian lineaments. In contrast, glaciated surfaces in the Antrim hills reflect the subhorizontal basalt bedding, and rounded non-aligned surfaces and corries in the Mourne Mountains are due to the crystalline granite substrate. During the last glacial maximum (LGM; ~ 22-18 kyr BP) the highest mountain peaks in the Sperrins (< 678 m OD) and Mournes (< 850 m OD) were overtopped by ice.

Ice thinning, however, led to increased topographic control over time. Ice action on mountain tops therefore took place mainly during early and maximal stages of the glacial cycle. Few constraining radiometric dates are available from upland areas, but some cosmogenic ^{36}Cl ages from Ireland record the timing of exposure of bedrock surfaces or large erratic boulders (Phillips et al., 1996). Glacial depositional features in upland areas are found mainly within glacial valleys and reflect topographic control during ice retreat. Landforms found here include cross-valley moraines, deltas and kame terraces. For example, ice-marginal deltas and meltwater channels found around the margins of the Sperrin Mountains record stages of ice retreat away from upland flanks. Lowland ice sheets impounded glacial lakes between the ice margin and bedrock uplands, leading to deltas and terraces of various heights linked to meltwater channels (e.g. Dardis, 1986).

In contrast, lowland areas (< 150 m OD) are drift-dominated and comprise mainly depositional landforms including ribbed (Rogen) moraines, drumlins, eskers and ice-marginal (end) moraines (Fig. 2c). Bedforms in lowland areas are generally morphologically complex and were formed at various periods throughout the late Devensian. For example, ribbed moraines composed of subglacial diamicton (till) were likely formed around the time of the LGM when basal ice thermal regimes were changing, permitted the moulding and preservation of the ribbed moraine shape (Knight and McCabe, 1997; McCabe et al., 1999). Streamlined drumlins are often developed on ribbed moraine crests, and therefore postdate the formation of these bedforms (Knight et al., 1999). Sediments within the drumlins include massive to stratified subglacial diamicton, leeside and channelised sand and gravel, and interbeds of all these components (Dardis and McCabe, 1983; Dardis et al., 1984; McCabe and Dardis, 1989). Dating control on periods of drumlinisation is achieved through AMS ^{14}C dating of cold-water marine microfaunas (the Arctic foraminifera *Elphidium clavatum*) found *in situ* within marine muds on coastal lowlands. These faunas are found hosted within mud beds within ice-marginal morainal banks which are considered coeval with periods of drumlin formation up-ice (McCabe, 1996). Dates from marine molluscs in western (McCabe et al., 1986), and *E. clavatum* tests in eastern Ireland (McCabe, 1996; McCabe and Clark, 1998), show that ice activity waxed and waned in a millennial-scale rhythm between ~ 19-

15 kyr BP (McCabe and Clark, 1998). In addition, marine-based ice streams in eastern Ireland acted to rapidly draw ice towards tidewater margins in the Irish Sea (McCabe et al., 1999; Knight et al., 1999). Such ice streams acted to destabilise the ice sheet, leading to *in situ* mass wastage around ice margins (stagnation zone retreat; SZR) and onshore ice retreat. End moraine assemblages are often found marking the termini of drumlin fields inland, such as on the Mourne Plain, Co. Down coast (McCabe et al., 1984, 1987).

Evidence for stages of deglaciation inland comes mainly from patterns of outwash spreads, eskers and deltas which are located adjacent to bedrock uplands. In some lowland areas there are well-developed esker systems, such as the Glarryford esker (Bann valley) and Colebrook esker (Clogher valley). These indicate the organisation of subglacial meltwater locally into discrete channels. However, end moraines are generally absent from these lowland areas, supporting the argument that SZR was an important process of overall ice mass wastage, possibly related to elevational changes of the firn line above the level of the remnant lowland ice sheets.

Timing of glacial events

Evidence for dated and undated ice advance and retreat stages, outlined above, can be built into a chronostratographic model which describes the sequence of glacial events from the LGM onwards (Table 1). Detailed explanation of this scheme is given in McCabe et al. (1999) and Knight et al. (in press). Six substages within the late Devensian period are identified. The boundaries between these substages are interpreted to be coeval with shifts seen in reconstructed sea-surface temperature, lithic and faunal abundance observed in North Atlantic marine cores offshore Ireland (e.g. Kroon et al., 1997, 2000), and with the pattern of stadial (cool) and interstadial (warm) events observed in the Greenland GRIP $\delta^{18}O$ ice core record (Björck et al., 1998). Collectively, these records show that the northeast Atlantic region in particular experienced very rapid and near synchronous changes in climate during the last deglaciation, and that the British ice sheet (of which the Irish ice sheet was part) responded to this external climatic forcing.

Direct and indirect effects of glaciation on the Northern Ireland coast

Direct effects of glacial erosion and deposition processes are manifested on the Northern Ireland coast. Bedrock surfaces have usually been stripped bare of surficial sediment and bedrock slopes are often oversteepened such as along the northern, eastern and western margins of the Antrim basalt plateau. In the Antrim glens (eastern side of the plateau) and around the hilltop of Binevenagh (northwestern side of the plateau) this has led to instability and landsliding. Glacial erosion has also been focused along and has overdeepened pre-existing valleys, such as the Foyle, Lower Bann and Lagan river valleys. For example, the Foyle valley is overdeepened to -30 m OD (Bazley et al., 1997). Glacial sediment which was carried offshore by ice is vitally important in the formation and maintenance of present-day beaches and dunes. Part of this sediment body was reworked onshore during late Pleistocene and Holocene sea-level rise. Glacial sediment still found offshore is an important potential resource for sand and gravel aggregate, and provides spawning and feeding habitats for fish (Sweeney, 1989). Onshore, glacial sediments are generally confined to coastal lowlands where they

Background

Table 1: Characteristics of glacial-climate substages within the late Devensian glacial stage in the north of Ireland

Substage	Time period (uncalibrated ^{14}C kyr BP)	Geological signatures	Climate events	Coastal events
Nahanagan Stadial	11.0-10.5	Cold-climate processes; corrie glaciers in the Mourne Mountains	Younger Dryas period; return to cool, wet climate	Start of isostatic sea level recovery
Woodgrange Interstadial	11.8-11.0	Late-glacial organic sequences in some lowland areas	Bölling/Allerød (warm) climate oscillation	Marine transgression in eastern and northern Ireland
Rough Island Interstadial	13.0-11.0	Marine mud drape and stagnation zone retreat in eastern (Rough Island) and northern Ireland (Bann valley)		
Killard Point Stadial	15.0-13.0	Activity of ice streams; streamlining of ribbed moraines and drumlins; formation of offshore morainal banks in eastern Ireland	Heinrich event 1 in North Atlantic; hemispheric cooling	Incursion of Scottish ice into north Co. Antrim
Cooley Point Interstadial	17.0-15.0	Marine mud drape and intertidal boulder pavement formation in eastern Ireland		Ice retreat onshore in eastern Ireland
Belderg Stadial	18.0-17.0	Formation of drumlin assemblages in western and eastern Ireland	Start of climate warming and ice retreat from southern Britain	Ice retreat northwards through the Irish Sea
Glenavy Stadial	25.0-18.0	Formation of ribbed moraines	Last Glacial Maximum	Confluence of ice from Irish and Irish Sea sources

are susceptible to erosion, contributing in a minor way to beach nourishment and coastal agriculture.

Indirect effects of glaciation include changes in relative sea-level (RSL), continuing at the present time, as a result of ice loading and unloading. Raised beaches found across Northern Ireland provide evidence for these isostatic effects during the Holocene (Carter, 1982a), and these may be added to or help mitigate future RSL changes. These will impact closely on the sediment dynamics and stability of the coastal zone (Carter, 1991a).

Relative sea-level changes

Peter Wilson and Julian Orford

That there have been significant changes in Late Pleistocene and Holocene relative sea level (RSL) along the coast of Northern Ireland has been recognised for a long time, but the temporal and spatial magnitudes of change are not fully resolved. Early studies (e.g. Portlock, 1843; Bell, 1891; Symes *et al.*, 1888; Praeger, 1893, 1897; Stewart, 1897; Coffey and Praeger, 1904) described deposits of estuarine clay, marine shells, and/or beach sands and gravels, with a fauna somewhat different to that of adjacent shorelines. These deposits, at elevations above and below the present high water mark, were regarded as evidence for RSL changes. Jessen's work on pollen and plant macro-fossils from buried peats at sites in the Bann estuary and at Portrush (Jessen, 1949) enabled him to propose marine activity to an elevation of at least 5 m OD at the close of the Atlantic stage (c. 5000 years BP). Between 1960 and 1980 RSL changes figured in several studies (e.g. Stephens, 1963; Stephens and Synge, 1965; Dresser *et al.*, 1973; Singh and Smith, 1973; Stephens *et al.*, 1975). During the same interval reports by Officers of the Geological Survey recorded the presence of raised marine features - rock platforms, beach sediments and caves - some of which were inferred to have developed in association with Late Pleistocene and Holocene RSL highstands (Wilson and Robbie, 1966; Manning, *et al.*, 1970; Wilson and Manning, 1978; Griffiths and Wilson, 1982).

Fig. 3: Sea-level curves for the east (A) and north (B) coasts of Northern Ireland, after Carter (1982a)

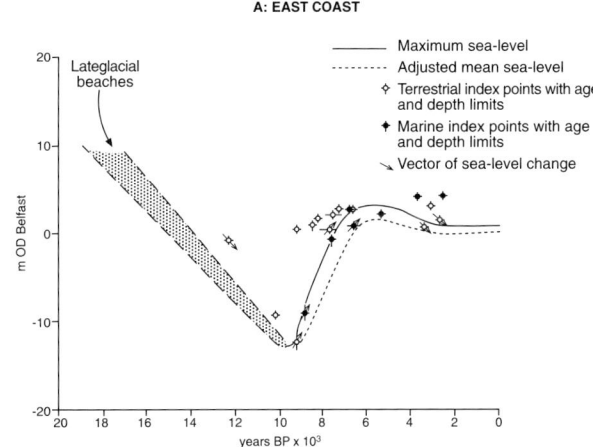

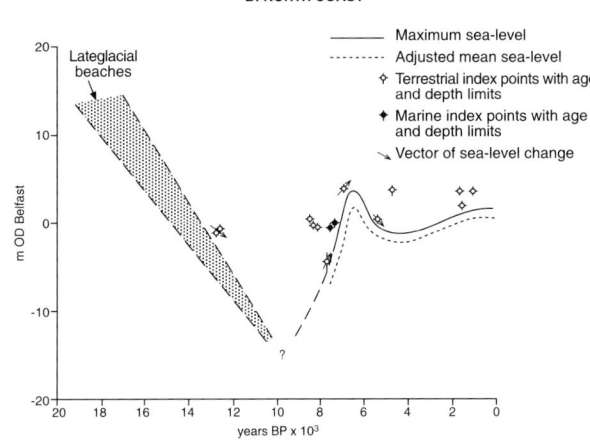

From data contained in these and other studies, the late Bill Carter constructed RSL curves for the east and north coasts of Northern Ireland (Fig. 3; Carter, 1982a). Although this was the first time that formal curves had been presented, Carter noted that "the record is fragmentary and should be treated with caution". For the period prior to 9000 ^{14}C years BP the RSL curves were based primarily on morphological evidence for Late Pleistocene raised beaches, with very few constraining ^{14}C dates. Many more ^{14}C dates from coastal stratigraphies were available for the last 9000 ^{14}C years BP, but lack of precision in some sample altitudes contributed to uncertainties in the position of the curves. Nevertheless, the general pattern recognised was one of Late Pleistocene high RSL of 15-20 m OD at 18,000-16,000 years BP followed by a rapid fall to c. -30 m OD at 11,000-10,000 years BP (Fig. 3). The Holocene rise in RSL on the east coast peaked c. 5500 years BP at c. 1-3 m OD with a subsequent fall to present datum. On the north coast, RSL peaked at c. 6500 years BP at c. 2-4 m OD and then fell rapidly to below 0 m OD by 5500 years BP, since when it has risen to its present-day level.

Both the timing and impact of the mid-Holocene higher-than-present sea level on Northern Ireland are debatable and Carter's (1982a) statement that "there is considerable scope for further investigations of sea-level changes" has not been ignored. In the last 20 years much additional pertinent data has been obtained. On the north coast, Late Pleistocene (c. 18,000-17,000 years BP) glaciomarine sediments have been described at 100 m OD in the Carey Valley (McCabe and Eyles, 1988) and at 10-20 m OD at Portballintrae (McCabe et al., 1994). A gravel barrier with crest height of 10 m OD developed on Rathlin Island between 13,000-12,000 years BP (Carter, 1993), and recent offshore geophysical data has been used to infer a RSL lowstand of -30 m OD between 12,000-9000 years BP (Cooper et al., 1998). In and near the estuary of the River Bann, Wilson and McKenna (1996) presented ^{14}C dates that indicate RSL was at least -6 m OD at c. 9000 years BP and peaked at c. 6000 years BP, although the height reached by this transgression was not established. Soon after this peak (c. 500 years), RSL had fallen to below 0 m OD (Hamilton and Carter, 1983).

On the east coast, recent studies concerning Late Pleistocene RSL have produced significantly different interpretations. Model predictions of Lambeck (1996) indicate low (-60 m OD) RSL around 15,000 years BP. In contrast, stratigraphic and AMS ^{14}C dating evidence presented by McCabe (1997) demonstrates high RSL of 20-25 m OD between 16,000-13,000 years BP.

Field investigations of RSL around the west (Carter et al., 1989) and northwest (Shaw and Carter, 1994) Irish coast have only confirmed the general gradient of an RSL structure identified by Carter (1982a). The relative elevation of the mid-Holocene deceleration event appears to fall towards the west of Ireland, to a position in northwest Ireland (Donegal) that is below present OD. There is also an inferred structural change in the tendency of the RSL post-deceleration. Whereas in the east, there is a maximal peak and inferred regressive phase, in the west there is no maximal peak, rather a deceleration in the transgressive tendency that has persisted to the present-day. Thus the presence of a Holocene highstand was restricted to northeast Ireland. In the past decade, the crustal modelling work of Lambeck (1996) has re-opened the issue of the highstand around the north of Ireland. His model specifies a distinctive mid-Holocene highstand for both north and northeast Ireland peaking between 5-6 m OD at c. 6000 years BP. The subsequent regressive limb of the highstand is pronounced in time beyond Carter's extrapolation, and thus could be a more prominent forcing component of late-Holocene coastal deposition.

A test of this extent might be observed in the elevation/chronology framework of coastal deposition around the north and northeast coasts of Ireland. Murdy (2001) and Orford et al. (in press) have used IRSL dating to determine the 2000-3000 year age of the seaward edge of regressive sand and gravel beach ridges that underlie a large Holocene dunefield at Murlough, Co Down (east coast). Though the dated ridges *per se* are not accurate sea-level indicators, their elevation is marginally higher than the present day beach ridge. The dated ridges form the lowest unit to a diachronous prograded beach ridge series whose landward higher beach ridges underlie dunes with included organic-rich horizons dated to 2000-4500 years BP. These data collectively are seen as indirect evidence for a prolongation and slow decline of the mid-Holocene highstand, as opposed to Carter's view of a rapid decline. Such a slow decline is also recognised by Lambeck's recent modelling (Lambeck and Purcell, 2001). This long decline in RSL during the late Holocene may help to explain the presence of apparently stranded beach ridges at the rear of coastal re-entrants along the east coast of Northern Ireland from Cushendun in the north to Carlingford Lough in the south.

In the absence of dating evidence constraining the age of raised marine sediments considerable care needs to be exercised in attributing them to RSL change. Carter (1983) argued that supra-elevation of water levels as a result of extreme storms may cause sediment deposition several metres above present high water. Such sequences may be interpreted, incorrectly, as products of a mid- to late Holocene RSL highstand. McKenna (1990) provided an example of such sediments at sites on the north coast. In a number of coastal embayments vegetated sediment terraces at c. 6-8 m OD receive surface veneers of sand and gravel as a result of contemporary storm-wave activity. These supra-tidal terraces consist of crudely laminated coarse marine sands and rounded gravel clasts, suggesting discrete depositional events. They are regarded as the accumulation over many years of storm-wave sedimentation at contemporary sea level.

Modern (i.e. 20th century) determinations of RSL change for Northern Ireland are ambiguous given the short time base of data from available tide gauges. The principal data are from Malin Head (north coast) and Belfast Harbour (east coast) while Portrush (north coast) and Bangor (east coast) are very recent installations (Table 2). Gauges overlap in time but record access is patchy and data are only now being converted to digital form. All contemporary available analyses for Malin and Belfast are based on High and Low water positions. Orford (2001) has reviewed the variable data sets and treatments. The main problem has been that short data windows have not allowed for nodal detrending and the initial estimates of changes in mean sea level (MSL) from Malin and Belfast by Carter (1982b) may be overestimated. Table 2 shows the annual RSL change rates for both raw and detrended data from Malin Head (1958-1992: 12 years extension beyond Carter's data set) and Belfast Harbour (1918-1980). Nodal-detrended

Background

Table 2: Data sources and RSL change rates around Northern Ireland (mm yr⁻¹) in the 20th century.

Tide-Gauge Location Data source	Start	Finish	Annual RSL change rate (mm yr^{-1})	Annual RSL change rate using nodal detrend method (mm yr^{-1})
Malin Head				
a) High and low water analysis. Some gaps in period 1988-92	1958	1992	**-0.19**	**-0.01**
b) Carter (1982b)	1958	1980	**-2.40**	Not available
Portrush	1995	2000	**+1.30**	Not available
Belfast Harbour				
a) Belfast Harbour Commissioners. High and low water analysis	1918	1963	**-0.16**	**-0.02**
b) Carter (1982b)	1918	1980	**-0.20**	Not available
Bangor	1996	2000	**+2.49**	Not available

Malin Head and Belfast Harbour RSL change rates show negative tendency, although the strength diminishes the more the time series includes post-1980 data. Carter (1982b) thought his estimate of -2.4 mm yr⁻¹ for Malin reflected the last vestiges of isostatic uplift from the last glacial maximum, while the downward shift in Belfast might have been related to the expansion of the port facilities down stream from the gauge and hence some variable filtering of extreme tidal levels towards the end of the data period.

When the longest Malin and Belfast records are detrended, the remaining RSL change signal (<-0.02 mm yr⁻¹) shows a virtual absence of any negative tendency. The best estimate of Malin Head's detrended negative RSL change (-0.01 mm yr⁻¹) reflects the possibility of a much reduced isostatic signal than hitherto identified. However, there is still the possibility of an accelerating rise in MSL that is now masking a remnant but significant 20th century isostatic signal. Carter (1982b) also identified RSL change of -0.2 mm yr⁻¹ for Belfast. This is close to the current analysis (-0.16 mm yr⁻¹). Variation between these two estimates is probably due to the longer record then available to Carter, but no longer available at the time of nodal detrending.

The Bangor and Portrush tide gauges are included to show recent positive trends in RSL change. Their short record precludes definitive analysis, so they cannot be relied on as evidence of long term change. Unfortunately the RSL change record from Malin and Belfast is not yet available to allow a time-comparable analysis with these two new sites. Malin has shown periods of change comparable with Portrush, while Bangor's rapid contemporary RSL rise is comparable to that recorded at Belfast Harbour in both the early 1920s and early 1940s. Although the result of nodal detrending suggests that there is little if any long-term isostatic difference between Malin and Belfast MSL in the middle of the 20th century, the difference between Portrush and Bangor's MSL in the 1990s might indicate an isostatic differential still working in reducing Portrush relative to Bangor.

Human use and management of the Northern Ireland coast

Suzanne McLaughlin and Eric Bann

Human uses of the coast

Human influence on the coastline of Ireland can be traced back to the hunter-gatherer societies of at least 5,000 years ago (Mitchell, 1976). As the population of Ireland increased in pre-famine times, immense pressure was put on coastal areas in the exploitation of land for agricultural purposes and through the cutting of marram grass for thatching. During this period there are several accounts of severe episodes of sand erosion and engulfment of properties along the Irish coast (Quinn, 1977; Murphy, 1980). From post-famine times (1840s) to the present man has continued to influence the coastal environment. Activities such as the removal of beach material for agricultural, commercial or recreational purposes (Conroy and Mitchell, 1971; Bradshaw *et al.*, 1991), reclamation of land for agriculture (Orford, 1988; Carter, 1989), engineering works such as seawalls and harbours (Carter and Bartlett, 1990; Carter and Mulrennan, 1985) and recreation and tourism (Carter, 1980; Carter *et al.*, 1993) have all played a part in influencing the contemporary physical coastal environment.

One example of where direct human impact has caused the degradation of the coastal zone is the removal of sediment from beaches by farmers which has, in the past, had an important influence on coastal erosion. Historically, farmers were given rights by estates to remove sand from certain beaches to use on their land. This was not a problem in the past as the contemporary technology ensured that only small amounts were taken. However now farmers are using bulldozers and tractors to remove sand in much greater quantities and this is causing problems. An early study by Oldfield *et al.* (1973) estimated that over the period 1950-1969 100,000 m^3 of sand was removed from the western end of Portrush East Strand. A later study by Bradshaw *et al.* (1991) also highlighted these sand removal problems on the beaches of the north-east coast of Ireland.

Other problems on the coast of Northern Ireland have been due to a lack of understanding of coastal processes, for example the implications of hard defence structures such as seawalls built to secure the shoreline position and provide a means of access. At Portrush West Strand and Carnlough Carter and Bartlett (1990) noted a lowering of the beach surface by over a metre in 25 years following seawall construction. The construction of harbours and jetties can also affect the coastal area, for example, the construction of a new concrete jetty at Portballintrae (to replace an older wooden structure), caused the beach sediment to move offshore to deeper water where it was lost to the system (Carter and Bartlett, 1988; Carter, 1991) (Figs. 4, 5).

Pressure is also being put on coastal areas by increasing populations. The population of Northern Ireland is presently approximately 1.6 million with the greatest concentration being in the east around the Greater Belfast area (Atkins, 1997). Carter (1988) noted that many coastal populations are expanding faster than national populations. This pattern of population growth is noticeable in both Britain and Ireland as more people move to coastal locations (Devoy, 1992). With this population increase in coastal areas it is logical that there is also a massive increase in the numbers of main and secondary homes near the coast. These are mainly for recreation or retirement purposes. Although increased development related to tourism is beneficial in terms of the economy, this development can have a direct effect on the coastal environment. For example, buildings (either permanent or temporary) encroach onto the upper shoreline in an effort to gain impressive locations with sea views, or through the creation of harbours or marinas for recreational boating e.g. at Bangor marina on the east coast and Ballycastle on the north coast. These buildings, marinas or associated protection structures may disturb general patterns of sediment movement. The main responsibility for controlling development on the coast within Northern Ireland is the Planning Service of the Department of the Environment (DoE). Local authorities do not have a great influence (although they are consultees) and the final decision rests with the planning office.

Fig. 4: Portballintrae with wide sandy beach clearly visible in 1935. (Source: Coastal Studies Research Group, UUC)

Fig. 5: Portballintrae (1987) with narrow gravel beach left after the sand was eroded. (Source: Coastal Studies Research Group, UUC)

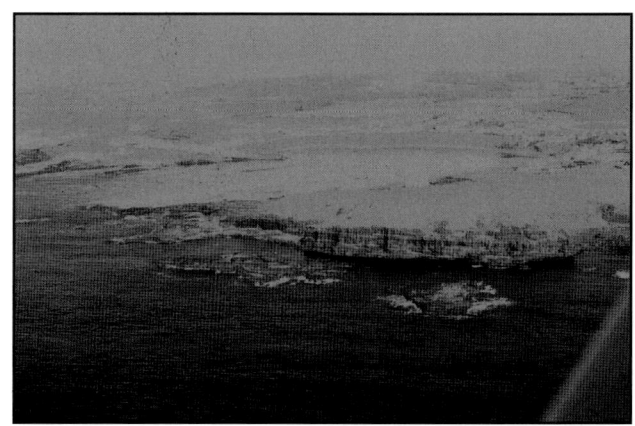

Background

Roads are important lines of communication and are the main medium of transport within Northern Ireland. Many such roads are located on the coast and so are potentially vulnerable to erosion. Figure 6 gives the location of the A-class roads, motorways and dual carriageways that are located within a 100 m buffer of the mean high water mark. In fact the outline of Northern Ireland can be clearly picked out by looking at only these main roads.

The Antrim coast road was built between 1832 and 1842 for £37,000 and was at that time the biggest engineering project in Ireland (McAuley, 1997). It runs from Ballycastle to Larne along the coast and passes through Cushendun, Cushendall, Carnlough and Glenarm. Subsidence problems at Garron Point (approximately 25 miles north of Larne) have caused the implementation of continued coastal repair works to maintain the road. Railways were historically of greater importance in Northern Ireland as many routes have since been abandoned. Ballycastle had a railway link until 1950 and the train from Coleraine to Castlerock once ran along the easterly side of the River Bann, crossing near the Bann mouth training walls to Castlerock on the west bank. However the only main coastal railways that are still operational as important transportation links are those from Belfast to Portrush, Belfast to Bangor and Coleraine to Derry. Infrastructure such as roads and railways along with landuse can greatly influence the management of coastal areas. For example the DoE Roads Service emplaced rock armour to protect the Point Bar road, Magilligan, Co. Derry, while the adjacent farmland is left to erode.

Within Northern Ireland there is no overall governing body to manage the coastal zone and the many different kinds of activities carried out there. The protection of the coastal and marine environment is therefore shared among many government and other non-statutory bodies. This management arrangement can potentially lead to dispute with different departments having conflicting management strategies. Furthermore there is within the UK no legal definition of the coastal zone thus cross-sectoral cooperation is an essential element of the integrated coastal zone management (ICZM) process. Inevitably conflicts arise mainly because different government departments will have differing objectives in terms of their management strategies for the coastal zone. To date the main document on ICZM is a publication from the Environment and Heritage Service entitled *Delivering Coastal Zone Management in Northern Ireland: A Consultation Paper* (EHS, 1995).

Nature and Coastal Conservation in Northern Ireland

The legislative framework currently governing nature conservation in Northern Ireland essentially mirrors that operating in Great Britain. However not only has this legislation been introduced into Northern Ireland very slowly, but the province, despite its small size, has also lagged many years behind Great Britain in the implementation of these provisions. Some of these are given in Appendix 1.

As in Great Britain, habitats and species are protected in Northern Ireland mainly by statute driven largely by the standards set at the European and international level. The two European Directives most influential are Directive 79/409/EEC on the Conservation of Wild Birds (OJ L103, 1979) and Directive 92/43/EEC on the Conservation of Natural Habitats and of Wild Fauna and Flora (OJ L206/7, 1992). These Directives have been given full legal effect in Northern Ireland by

Fig. 6: A-class roads, motorways and dual carriageways within a 100 m buffer of the mean high water mark

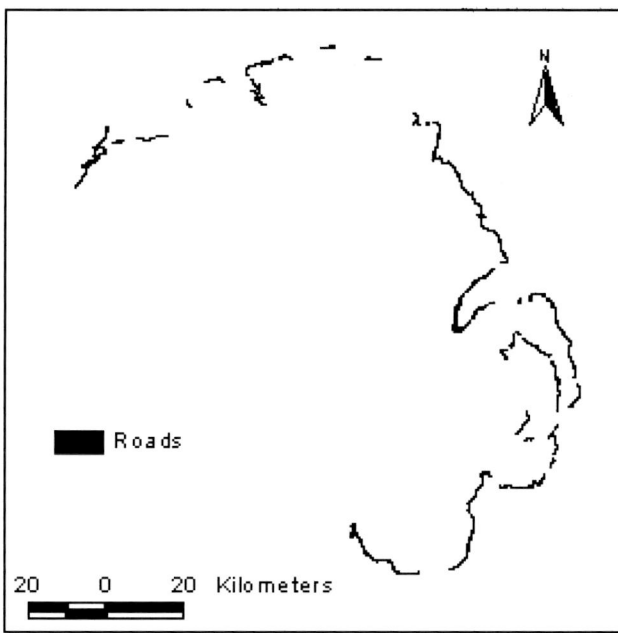

the combined operation of three principle pieces of legislation. The Wildlife (NI) Order 1985, (SI 1985/171) as amended, the Nature Conservation and Amenity Lands (NI) Order 1985, (SI 1985/170) as amended, and the Conservation (Natural Habitats etc.) Regulations (NI) 1995 (SR. No.380). In addition these provisions give effect to the requirements of various international conventions on nature conservation too which the UK is a party, either as a member of the EC or as an individual state.

The planning service also plays an important role in the conservation and management of the countryside and the coastal zone as do agri-environmental policies. In terms of the coast England and Wales have Planning Policy Guideline 20 "Coastal Planning" 1992 and PPG 21 "Tourism" 1992. The equivalent to PPGs in Northern Ireland are Planning Policy Statements (PPS) of which there are currently 11 (25 in England and Wales) there are currently no PPSs which cover the coast or tourism although recreation is covered in broad terms under PPS8 which has been issued for consultation.

The DoE (NI) is the statutory body in Northern Ireland responsible (through its Environment and Heritage Service (EHS) arm) for the formulation, administration, monitoring and enforcement of designated areas.

The assignment of areas with different conservation designations can also greatly influence their management. Within Northern Ireland conservation designations cover an extensive area with almost three quarters of the coastline having some sort of designation.

The main designations that occur in coastal areas (i.e. within 1 km of the high water mark) are shown in Figure 7. The degree of management protection provided by varying designations varies dramatically ranging from virtually none in some of the national designations to strong statutory protection in the European designations of Special Protection Areas and Special Areas of Conservation. Surprisingly however, the prestigious international designations of Ramsar and World Heritage Site bestow no protection per se; one reason why they are designated is that they are already well protected by other designations e.g. SPA in the Ramsar case.

Sites established under National Statute

Areas of Special Scientific Interest (ASSIs)

These are the equivalent to SSSIs in the rest of the UK and the legislation is currently being revised to bring it in line with the rest of the UK. A

Background

Fig. 7: Statutory designations at coastal locations in Northern Ireland

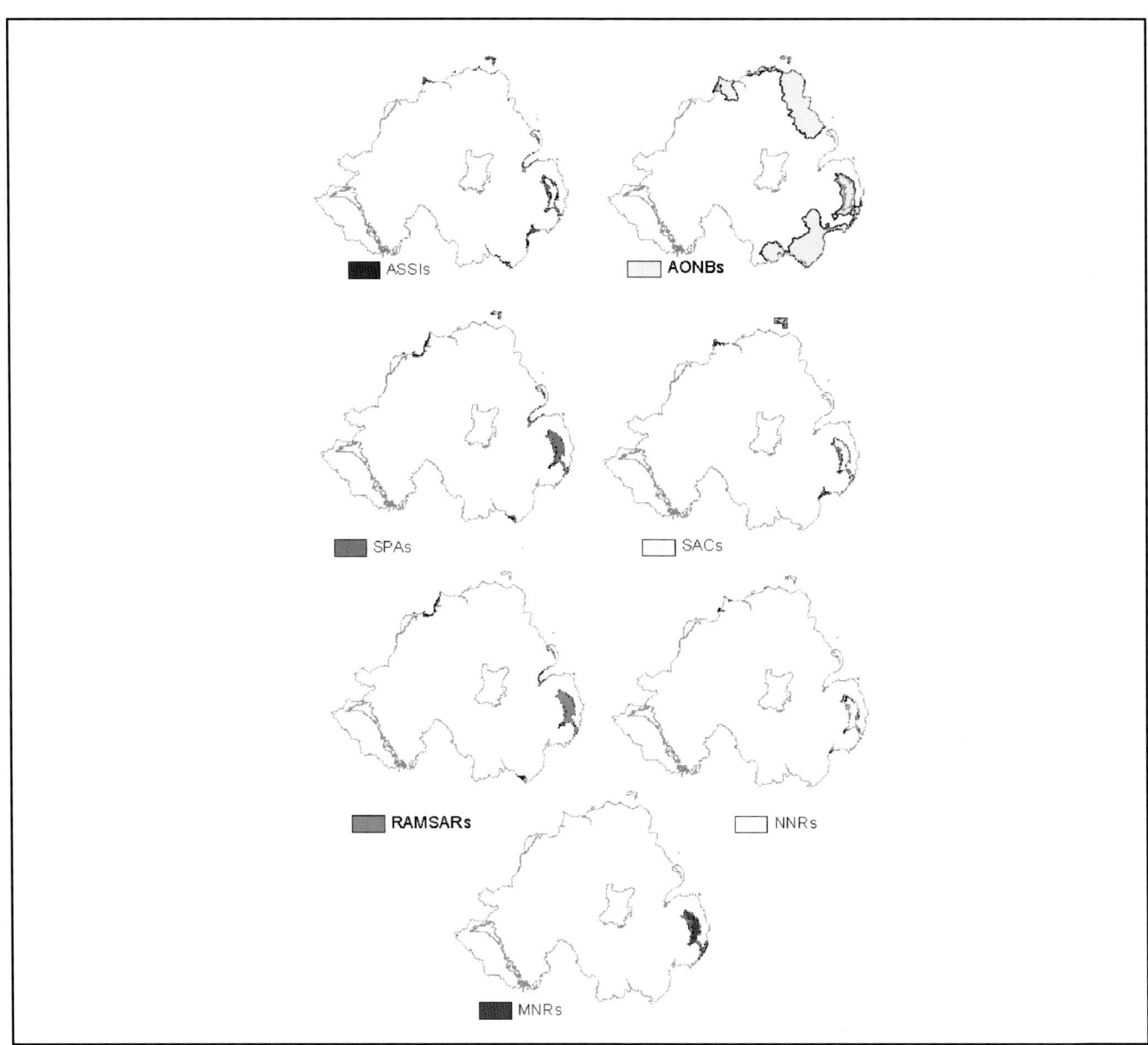

consultative document has recently been published by DoE (NI) (DoE (NI), 2001). ASSIs were introduced by NCALO in 1985. There are currently 181 ASSIs in Northern Ireland of which 40 are coastal. The ASSI designation is the principle tool employed by EHS for the purposes of protecting the most important biological and geological sites in Northern Ireland. An ASSI is declared where EHS is satisfied (after consultation) 'that an area of land is of special scientific interest, by reason of its flora, fauna or geological, physiographical or other features and accordingly needs to be protected' (article 24(1) NCALO 1985). The 1989 amendment imposes a statutory duty on the Department to declare an area of land as an ASSI where it fits the criteria of article 24(1). In practice because until 1989 these were discretionary powers all previous Areas of Scientific Interest (ASIs) are being or have been redesignated

Once declared a list of notifiable operations is drawn up and the landowner informed. These activities or operations are termed 'notifiable operations' because owners and occupiers of land within the ASSI are then required to notify the DoE (NI) of any proposal to carry out any such activity or operation. There is also a provision for management plans to be drawn up and monetary compensation offered to the landowner. In practice very few management agreements have been entered into even though they offer substantial inheritance tax advantages.

Article 30 of the NCALO as amended in 1989 confers general powers on the DoE (NI) or, as the case may be, District Councils to adopt bylaws for land acquired for protection and land that is subject to a management agreement

National Nature Reserves

Nature Reserves (sometimes called National Nature Reserves) contain examples of the most important natural and semi-natural ecosystems and earth science features in Northern Ireland. They are managed and used to conserve their flora, fauna, features of geological, physiographical or other scientific or special interest and or to provide opportunities for the study of and research into their scientific interest. Prior to 1985 they were designated under the Amenity Lands Act (NI) 1965 as Nature Reserves. In practice these sites were generally referred to as National Nature Reserves although the legislation did not provide for National in the title. From April 1985 new sites were designated as National Nature Reserves under NCALO (NI) 1985 as amended in 1989. As there is essentially no difference between the status of these sites they are referred to collectively as NNRs in this publication. There are 18 coastal NNRs out of a total of 63 in Northern Ireland. Figures vary but the coastal NNRs cover approximately 3399 ha (EHS, 2001)

Management agreements can be created for NNRs as can Nature Reserve Covenants i.e. the EHS under article 8 of NCALO 1985 as amended is empowered to accept a covenant from the owner of land restricting the 'use or development' of the land or any part thereof, in any manner. In addition article 19 (1) confers on the DoE (NI) a general power to adopt bylaws for the protection of any Nature Reserve or National Nature Reserve (other than a district council Nature Reserve). There is an extensive list of purposes for which bylaws may be adopted but there are also limitations in connection with the rights of owners and other rights in property which are outside the remit of this publication.

Marine Nature Reserves (MNR)

Articles 20 and 21 of NCALO govern the establishment and management of Marine Nature Reserves. Unlike nature reserves, which are established by the DoE (NI), Marine Nature Reserves are designated by the Secretary of State. This is the only conservation designation that covers the marine environment potentially to the seaward limits of territorial waters. They also have another peculiarity in that most designations in terms of the foreshore are determined by mean high and low water marks, an MNR can include open sea and can extend landwards to the highest astronomical tide. Only one MNR has been declared in Northern Ireland and this will be dealt with in more detail elsewhere in this publication. It is Strangford Lough MNR off the County Down coast and covers an area of approximately 16,500 ha.

Local Authority or District Council Nature Reserves

Article 22(1) of NCALO empowers district councils to 'provide nature reserves on land within their district where the council considers it expedient that the land be managed as a nature reserve'. In providing lands as statutory nature reserves, district councils are required to exercise their functions in consultation with the Council for Nature Conservation and the Countryside (CNCC). These Local Nature Reserves are provided for the same purposes as NNRs, but on account of the local rather than national interest of the site and its wildlife. They generally have a strong emphasis on public access and education. There are three LNRs in Northern Ireland of which one is coastal at Benone in County Londonderry covering approximately 27.5 ha.

Country Parks and Countryside Centres

Environment and Heritage Service manages seven Country Parks and two Countryside Centres of which five are coastal (Portrush, Redburn, Crawfordsburn, Scrabo, and Quoile). In addition to the facilities available at most Country Parks, the Countryside Centres offer exhibitions and audio-visual displays to assist the visitor's understanding of the countryside and of wider environmental issues in general. The Countryside Centres are located within or close to areas which are naturally attractive in terms of scenery and wildlife. There is no legislation providing for the statutory designation of areas as Country Parks, however NCALO does provide for their acquisition and management with the option of passing on the management to other public bodies and the grant aiding of their purchase.

Wildlife Refuges

The statutory provision of an area as a Wildlife Refuge (WR) is a protection mechanism under article 16 of the Wildlife (NI) Order 1985. The provision is tailored to suit the particular interest of each site so protected. It can provide protection from disturbance and destruction, by means of special penalties, for plants and/or animals at any stage of their life cycle. The limitation is that WRs can only be created with the consent of all the owners and occupiers of the area to be protected. The intention was that WRs would replace Bird Sanctuaries established under the Wild Birds Protection Act (NI) 1931 extending its scope to all forms of wildlife. It is the nearest equivalent to an Area of Special Protection (ASP) in the rest of the

UK (Wildlife and Countryside Act, 1981). As yet there are no WRs in Northern Ireland although several Bird Sanctuaries exist under the auspices of the RSPB.

Areas of Outstanding Natural Beauty (AONBs)

Article 14(1) of NCALO empowers the DoE (NI) via the EHS under advice from the CNCC and after consultation with the relevant local authorities to designate an area (not being an area within a National Park) as an area of outstanding natural beauty where the area is of such 'outstanding natural beauty' that it is desirable that it be subject to the provisions of NCALO.

The principal objective of their protection is the conservation of natural beauty. Full regard, however, must still be paid to the economic and social well being of the area. Nature conservation and the provision of recreation are not given explicit reference, although "natural beauty" is defined as including a reference to fauna, flora, geology, etc. Designation is supposed to assist sound planning and development by constituting clear official recognition of the importance of preserving the attractiveness of the areas. They tend to lack extensive areas of open country suitable for recreation and national park status, but are nonetheless of such fine landscape quality that there is a national as well as a local interest in keeping them so. Government assistance is available to assist local authorities in their expenditure in these areas. Assistance leans towards preservation of the beauty of the area rather than public recreation.

At present AONBs cover 20% of Northern Ireland with coastal AONBs covering 14% or 181,870 ha. Over 70% of the coastline falls within AONBs with seven of Northern Ireland's nine AONBs being coastal. It is important to note that the Amenity Lands Act (NI) 1965 provided the original legislative basis for AONBS in Northern Ireland, but this operated simply as an additional form of planning control. NCALO provided for the positive management of designated areas. The role of the AONB designation was considerably enhanced under NCALO, in that, for the first time, provision was made for positive management of designated areas. Four of the seven coastal AONBS remain under the 1965 regulations and as yet have not been redesignated. These are: Lecale coast, Lagan Valley, North Derry, and Strangford. The AONBs designated under NCALO are; Causeway Coast, Antrim Coast and Glens (including Rathlin), and Mourne.

Sites Identified by Statutory Agencies

Nature Conservation Review Sites

NCR sites are non-statutory areas that are the best representative examples of wildlife habitat. NCALO allowed EHS for the first time the legal framework to start a systematic survey of habitats and locate all sites of potential interest for nature conservation. The records of these surveys are held by the EHS and the process is ongoing.

Earth Science Conservation Review Sites

ESRC sites are again non-statutory locations of national and in some cases international importance. They meet qualifying criteria determined by the EHS and CNCC and constitute a suite of potential earth science ASSIs. The selection process identifies single issue sites (SILs) in the context of their geology, palaeontology, minerology or geomorphology. Listing ESRCs provides a small measure of protection in identification terms for any proposed development plan. Listing however confers no right of access. Details are held together

Background

with descriptions at the EHS. Out of approximately 200 ESCR SILS about 50 are coastal. Note that one site may contain more than one SIL.

Non-designated lands

Twelve of Northern Ireland's 26 local authorities have coastal lands within their boundaries. The City, Borough or District Councils concerned manage areas of coastal land for a variety of purposes but largely associated with public open space and amenity. Some sites are however managed for nature conservation (see Local Authority Nature Reserves and Country Parks. There are 37 other coastal sites owned or managed by local authorities. Under this heading it is worth noting that there are Countryside Policy Areas and Green Belts listed in Area Development Plans.

Designations under International Conventions and Directives

World Heritage Sites

The Giants Causeway is the only World Heritage Site in Northern Ireland. The Convention Concerning the Protection of the World's Cultural and National Heritage was adopted in Paris in 1972 and came into force in 1975. Sites selected must have strict continuing legal protection. The Giant's Causeway is owned and managed by the National Trust with a visitors centre jointly operated but owned by Moyle District Council. There is an ongoing controversy concerning development plans for the car park and visitors centre, a possible additional hotel and various other proposals.

RAMSAR sites

These were created under the Convention on the Conservation of Wetlands of International Importance, Especially as Waterfowl Habitat (Ramsar, 1971) There are 15 RAMSAR sites in Northern Ireland of which 5 are coastal.

Special Protection Areas (SPAs)

Established under the 1979 EC Directive on the Conservation of Wild Birds. This requires member states to take conservation measures particularly for certain rare or vulnerable species and for regularly occurring migratory species of birds. In part this achieved by the designation of statutory SPAs. In Northern Ireland all SPAs must first be notified as ASSIs or be designated National Nature Reserves. This has lead to difficulties in establishing SPAs certain species prefer habitats that cannot be designated as ASSIs. There are 11 SPAs in Northern Ireland of which seven are coastal.

Special Areas of Conservation

The Special Area of Conservation (SAC) designation is one of the main mechanisms by which the EU Habitats and Species Directive (1992) is implemented. They are areas considered to be important for habitat and non-avian species of interest in a European context. The protection measures are based around a series of six annexes. Annexes I and II require the designation of SACs for certain habitats and species. Annex lV prohibits the taking of certain species. Annex V requires the taking of certain species to be monitored and annex Vl prohibits some means of capture or killing of mammals and fish. In Northern Ireland this directive is implemented through the Conservation (Natural Habitats etc.) Regulations (NI) 1995 (Statutory Rule No. 380). A guidance note on the Conservation (Natural Habitats etc.) Regulations (NI) 1995 is available from the DoE (NI) and a planning policy statement, PPS2 Planning and Nature Conservation In Northern Ireland there are

43 candidate SACs of which 7 are coastal. As with SPAs SACs must first exist as an ASSI under the regulations. SACs however offer greater protection than ASSIs by imposing more stringent control over the carrying out of potentially damaging operations.

Environmentally Sensitive Areas (ESAs)

European Community authorisation for Environmentally Sensitive Areas is derived from article 19 of Council Regulation (EEC) No.797/85 – National Aid in Environmentally Sensitive Areas. ESAs are statutory areas in which the Government seeks to encourage environmentally sensitive farming practices, prevent damage that might result from certain types of agricultural intensification, and restore traditional landscapes, for which member states are allowed to make payments to farmers. There are 5 ESAs in Northern Ireland of which two are coastal (the Mournes and the Antrim Coast and Glens). To qualify for payments the farmers concerned must enter into a management agreement with the Department of Agriculture and Rural Development. Related to these regulations in Northern Ireland are the Countryside Management Regulations (NI) 1999 which enables payments to be made to farmers for specified management activities on priority habitats whether or not these habitats occur in ESAs.

In addition to the above there are regulations for the protection of archaeological and historical remains both on land and in the marine environment. These are dealt with elsewhere in this guide. There are also protected sites other than those covered above. These include National Trust for example which in Strangford Lough alone owns about 30 islands and 55 separate areas of foreshore as well as on the north coast the Giants Causeway World Heritage Site. Other non-governmental organisations in Northern Ireland who own and manage sites are: Royal Society for the Protection of Birds, Ulster Wildlife Trust, The Wildfowl and Wetlands Trust, and The Woodland Trust.

Finally a government department with a positive management policy towards environmental protection which includes a substantial coastal element (1520 ha at Magilligan and Ballykinder) is the Ministry of Defence.

Whilst there are many organisations and departments in Northern Ireland with ICZM at heart there exists no overall structure to the process as yet. The Coastal Forum concept if and when put in place will rectify this situation and give all involved with coastal management in Northern Ireland and identifiable focus.

Appendix 1: Statutory source material relevant to the Northern Ireland coast

EHS (1995). *Delivering Coastal Zone Management in Northern Ireland – A consultation Paper*, Belfast.

European Union Official Journal L103, 25 April 1979

European Union Official Journal L206/7, 21 May 1992

Statutory Instrument 1985/171

Statutory Instrument 1985 /170

Statutory Regulation No. 380

DoE (NI) (2001). *ASSIs in Northern Ireland. Consultation on Proposals for their future Management and Protection*, Belfast.

Wildlife and Countryside Act 1981

Ramsar (1971) Iran 1971 entered into force 1975. Signed by the UK 1973 and ratified 1976

Low Energy Coasts

Late Devensian glacial events and environmental change around Strangford Lough

Marshall McCabe and Jasper Knight

Introduction

Glacigenic successions around the margins of the Irish Sea Basin (ISB) provide windows into the Quaternary history and ice sheet variability of the wider British Isles (Eyles and McCabe, 1989). The 'Irish Sea Glacier' acted as a major drainage conduit for the last British ice sheet, and as a depositional basin for sediments derived from both landmasses. Ice directional indicators, including drumlins, striae and erratic carriage, generally record centripetal ice flow into the basin, especially in the northern part of the basin (Fig. 8). However, major interpretative problems, including the significance of particular sedimentary successions and landforms, often result because local work often fails to consider the general controls on sedimentation patterns within a basinal context. The area of eastern Co Down is critical to the ongoing debate on the deglaciation of the northern ISB because it shows dating and morphsedimentary evidence for rapid ice advance and retreat, the interaction of native Irish and Irish Sea ice, the interaction of ice and RSL stage, and postglacial RSL change. Landforms and sediments are described from Rough Island, near the head of Strangford Lough, and Killard Point, near its outlet.

The 'Irish Sea Drifts' and the significance of marine microfaunas

The very variable late Pleistocene glacigenic sedimentary successions around the ISB have been termed traditionally 'Irish Sea Drifts' (Wright, 1937). This umbrella term is used to describe muds, muddy diamicts, silts and clays which may contain *in situ* and/or derived marine micro- and macro-fossils. However, the possible significance (in terms of ice sheet dynamics or palaeoclimatic indicators) of the faunal assemblages was not fully appreciated because of a lack of accurate sedimentological descriptions.

Microfaunal species from fine-grained Irish Sea Drifts are varied, including shallow- and deep-water benthic and planktonic, temperate, boreoarctic, cosmopolitan, Pliocene to late Pleistocene foraminifera which vary in abundance from site to site (Haynes *et al.*, 1995). There are various schools of thought on the palaeoenvironmental significance of this species- and age-variability. One group believe that all the microfaunas are derived (Thomas and Kerr, 1987) with a terrestrial ISB glacier flanked by large lakes. A second group assume that the faunas are *in situ* but are dredged onshore by ice advance (Warren, 1985). Others (Haynes *et al.*, 1995) argue that Irish Sea Drifts are complex marine and glaciomarine deposits with both *in situ* and reworked microfaunal components. Ongoing microfaunal studies (see McCabe and Haynes, 1996; McCabe and Clark, 1998) show how this work needs to be supported by detailed facies investigations which can show whether or not fine-grained deposits (which host the microfaunas) are themselves *in situ* or glacially-transported.

Fig. 8: Ice flow and ice limits during Heinrich event 1 in the north Irish Sea basin. Inset, ice flows in Britain during the last glacial maximum

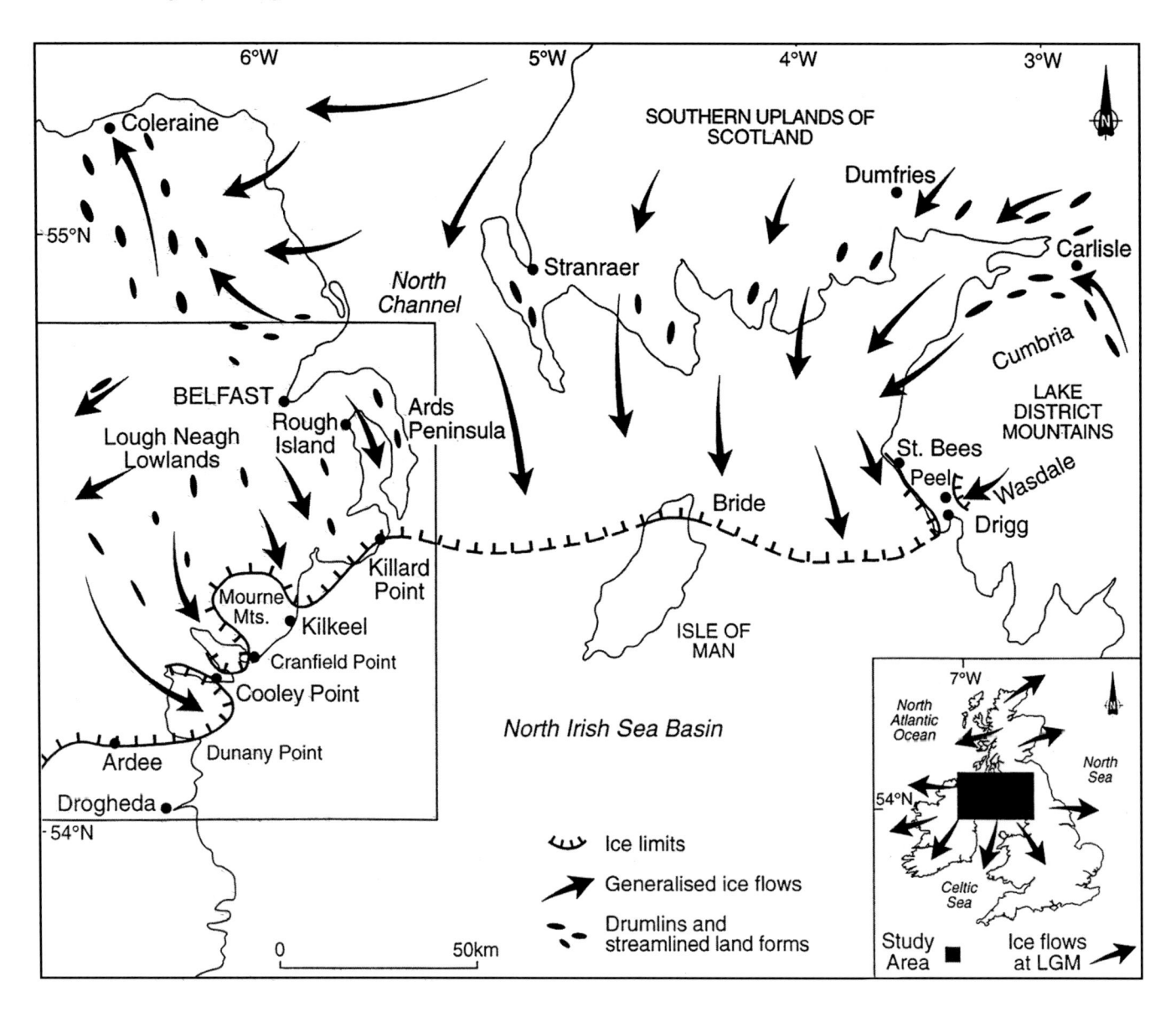

Most useful in this work is the identification of monospecific, Arctic microfaunas which record the first entry of marine waters across a glacioisostically-depressed site immediately following regional deglaciation. After this initial event it is likely that faunas higher up a facies succession will increase in species diversity and widen in provenance because of meltwater pumping and resedimentation from beneath the decaying ice, water current circulation following landward grounding line shifts, and climate amelioration. Therefore one might expect microfaunas to be mixed from a variety of sources (subglacial to marginal and contemporary) by meltwater pulses or jets and show fairly uniform species types and abundance as one goes up a facies succession. This situation has been found across the ISB such as Aberdaron, west Wales (cf. Austin and McCarroll, 1992). A realistic interpretation of well-mixed, diverse microfaunal assemblages may be as a product of post mortem resuspension by meltwater pumping followed by settling through the water column contemporaneously with mud rainout and ice-rafting of larger clasts.

Rough Island, Strangford Lough

Strangford Lough (Fig. 9) trends northwest to southeast across the strike of bedrock which includes Ordovician and Silurian shales and greywackes. This area is structurally and stratigraphically similar to the Southern Uplands of Scotland but shows a much more subdued landscape rising to 150 m OD. Topography in the area of, and flooring, the Lough and the Ards peninsula is dominated by drumlins which show variable thicknesses of glacial diamict masking rock cores. Diamict forms dominate coastward and thicknesses of the glacial diamict carapace decrease inland. There is no good structural or palaeontological evidence from either side of the Lough which provides any clue as to the initial origin of the NW-SE trend of the Lough. In general the long axis of the Lough parallels the local drumlin orientation which may suggest it is glacially overdeepened.

In this part of east-central Ireland Stephens (1958, 1963) suggested that partial dissolution of the late Devensian ice sheet was accompanied by marine transgression across parts of the isostatically-depressed land surface. Morrison and Stephens (1965) described up to 5 m of red marine clay beneath late-glacial solifluction deposits and post-glacial raised beach deposits at Roddan's Port on the outer coast of the Ards peninsula. More recent work shows that similar red clays drape many of the drumlins flanking Strangford Lough, and can be traced upslope as a feather edge to about 16 m OD. Above this level the drumlin flanks have been notched (at 20 m OD) by marine erosion (Stephens and McCabe, 1977). Wave-cut notches are best preserved within Strangford Lough itself rather than on the outer coast around Roddan's Port because of more intensive post-glacial erosion around the exposed the Irish Sea coast (Stephens, 1963).

At the head of Strangford Lough well-defined late- and post-glacial wave-cut terraces occur south and west of Newtownards (Fig. 9). The flat upper terrace surface lies around 20 m OD. Island Hill and Rough Island are erosional remnants of the upper terrace which must have been a much more extensive feature around the head of the Lough during the late-glacial. Some drumlins have been reduced by present marine action to a pile of large clasts known locally as pladdies. Clearly the post-glacial erosion of drumlins has provided sediment

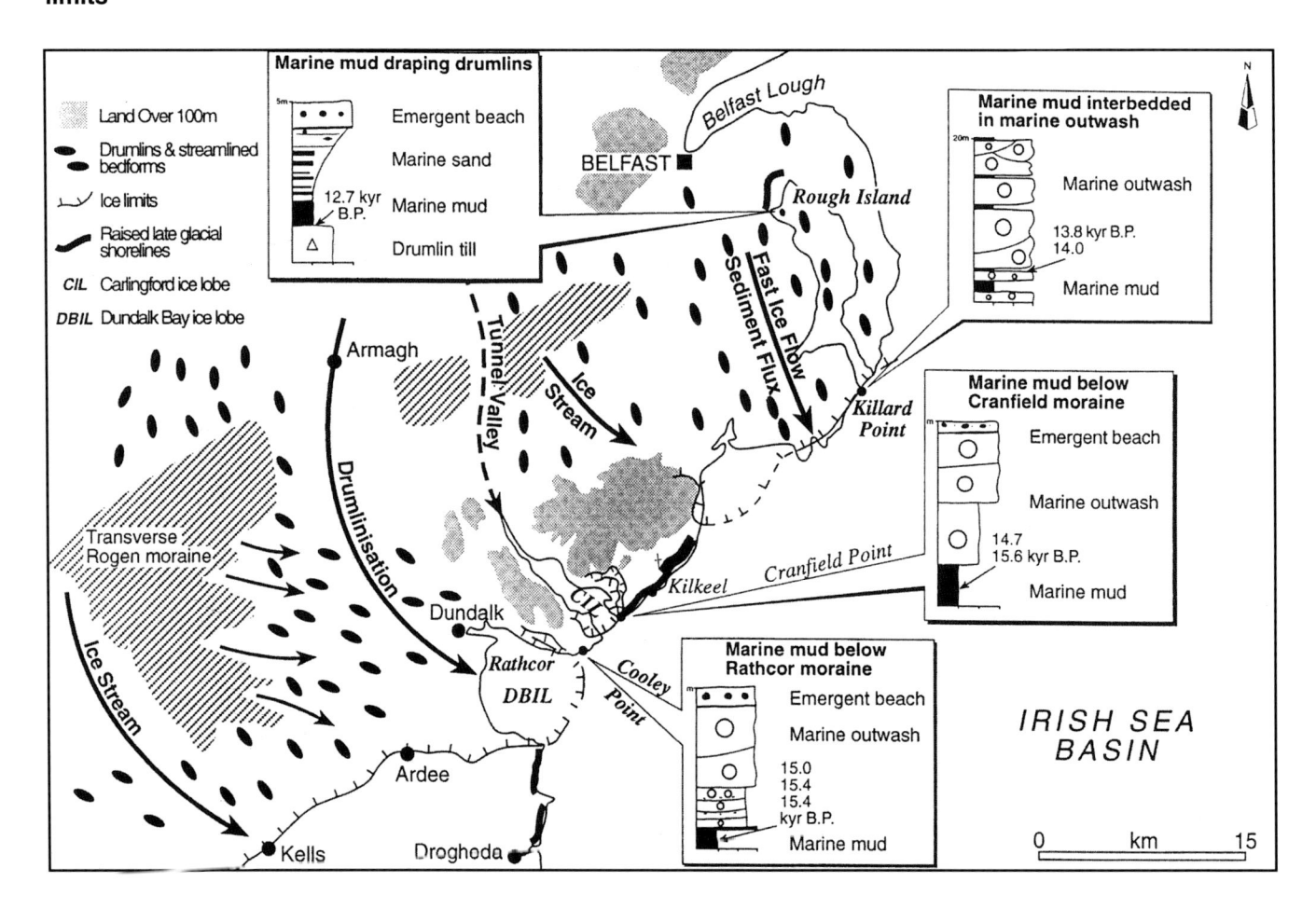

Fig. 9: Ice flows and field evidence related to the Killard Point Stadial in the north-western Irish Sea basin. The stratigraphic position of dated marine mud beds is also shown in relation to Killard Point Stadial ice limits

for redistribution and resedimentation within the post-glacial and current sediment cells of the Lough.

Three sediment facies are exposed in the marine cut cliff on the southwestern side of Rough Island. Immediately above sea level a compact, unweathered diamict (< 1.5 m exposed) is mainly derived from local Triassic sandstones but contains erratics of Cretaceous chalk and flint, Tertiary basalt, red granites and Ailsa Craig microgranite, all of northern provenance. The clasts range from pebbles to boulders and are set in a massive, red sandy-silt matrix. About 40% of the largest clasts show evidence for ice bevelling, shaping and striation. The sedimentary characteristics of similar diamicts found across this region suggests a subglacial origin. Rhythmically-bedded sands and muds directly overlie the unweathered top of the basal diamict at Rough Island. The rythmites are up to 3 m in thickness and show an upward decrease in mud and increase in sand content. At the base, mud beds are massive and up to 20 cm thick. These beds up to 0.5 m above the diamict contain an *in situ* assemblage of marine microfauna dominated by the cold-water marine foraminifera *Elphidium clavatum* (95%) and the cold-water ostracod *Roundstonia globulifera* (< 4%). An AMS ^{14}C date of 12.7 ^{14}C kyr BP has been obtained from this level in the rhythmite succession (Fig. 9). Further up in the rhythmite succession microfaunal tests become weathered with < 50% broken and discoloured, suggesting that resedimentation becomes dominant over *in situ* production. The upward increase in laminated sand beds may suggest an increase in energy during a falling RSL stage. This may possibly reflect marine current activity around the head of the lough during water shallowing. Although the sands are generally thinly-bedded with mud laminae, there are at least two massive sand beds (10-20 cm thick) within the otherwise thinly-bedded succession. The rhythmically-bedded sands and muds are sharply truncated and overlain by poorly-sorted cobble gravel which contains marine shell fragments and archaeological remains. A discontinuous, coarse gravelly lag is present at the base of the gravel which forms the surface deposit of the Rough Island exposure and is part of the regional raised post-glacial beach. Because the sequence coarsens upwards from massive muds to interlaminated sands and muds to beachface gravel it records an overall emergent facies sequence with an hiatus below the shoreface gravels possibly due to wave truncation.

The radiometric date at this site is the only date in the northern ISB to constrain initial deglaciation and the timing of late-glacial marine transgression. Similar deposits in an identical stratigraphic position have been identified from the Solway Firth (Wells, 1997) and indicate a similar sequence of events during the last glacial termination.

The regional distribution of red marine clay which drapes drumlins and feathers upwards towards marine notches and washed limits around 20 m OD shows that glacioisostatic depression was greater that the eustatic sea level fall in the northern ISB. A number of studies in northwest England (Merrit and Auton, 2000) and Wales (Austin and McCarroll, 1992) do not support the model invoking high RSLs during deglaciation of the ISB. This work from the eastern ISB coast does not recognise an emergent glaciomarine/raised beach facies sequence. It may therefore have been the case that a major isostatic hinge-line was present along the axis of the Irish Sea during deglaciation (Stephens, 1963). However, it is difficult to envisage how the large ice dispersion centres in western Scotland and northern England did not result in similar isostatic patterns to that found in the western ISB (cf. Andrews et al., 1973). It is possible that non-recognition of former sea level evidence in the eastern ISB is due to the lack of detailed studies of nearshore sediments which contain the most complete records of sea level fluctuations on glaciated shelves (e.g. Hunter et al., 1996).

Killard Point

A northeast to southwest zone of (~ 1 km wide) of hummocky topography occurs between Killard Point and Ardglass along the coastal fringe of Co Down (Fig. 10). These sediments are at least 20 m thick and overlie an irregular rock base for about 9 km. The surface varies from ridges to kettled topography with a local relief of 10-15 m.

The landform has been termed the Killard Point moraine (McCabe et al., 1984). It is located 1-2 km in front of the drumlin swarms of eastern County Down whose long axes are perpendicular to the moraine line. This close field association shows that both are part of the same integrated glacial system comprising southeasterly ice flow and associated drumlinisation, substrate erosion and sediment transfer to the ice margin around Killard Point. AMS ^{14}C dating of marine microfaunas from muds within the succession at Killard Point place the maximum of this ice advance to ~ 14 ^{14}C kyr BP (McCabe and Clark, 1998). The original extent of the moraine cannot have been more than 1 km offshore because the immediate offshore facies are dominated by muds. The ice oscillation associated with formation of the moraine is termed the Killard Point Stadial and dates, for the first time, the major oscillation of the British ice sheet which preceded the Loch Lomond Stadial.

Three facies associations are present at Killard Point (Fig. 10c). On the glaciated surface the diamict association (4 m thick) consists of stacked, massive and planar beds that are matrix and clast-to-matrix supported, contain a wide range of grain sizes (granules to boulders) and are often separated by stringers of coarse sand or granules. Lithofacies are interbedded and vary from massive to crudely stratified. Many cobbles and small boulders possess a-b planes which lie parallel to bedding planes in the stratified diamict. Some of these larger clasts project above the lower contacts of succeeding beds. Shallow scours (1-2 m across) infilled with interbedded red mud, sand, gravel and diamict beds containing outsized clasts (< 40 cm across) occur within the upper part of the diamict association or are cut into its upper surface. Small-scale fold structures and localised contorted bedding are found within these facies. The degree of interbedding and stratification of the diamict association, and features including soft-sediment mud clasts and slump folds, are in keeping of a mass flow origin following debris release from an ice margin. Textural variability of the mass flows is best explained by varying distances of transport and degree of winnowing, together with more fluid flows associated with channel incision and infill (Lowe, 1982).

A sand facies association infills irregularities and drapes the upper diamict surface for about 150 m. Up to 3 m of parallel laminated and graded sands contain discontinuous mud laminae, water escape structures, isolated cobble clasts, rip-up soft-sediment clasts, small folds and flame structures. Dominant transport mechanisms include sediment gravity flows of low to intermediate viscosity driven by density flows (Middleton and Hampton, 1976).

Fig. 10: Relationships between drumlins and the Killard Point ice limit in Co Down. (A) Location of the Killard Point moraine, (B) lithofacies succession exposed at Benderg Bay, Co Down coast (after McCabe *et al.*, 1984), (C) schematic log of lithofacies succession at Killard Point

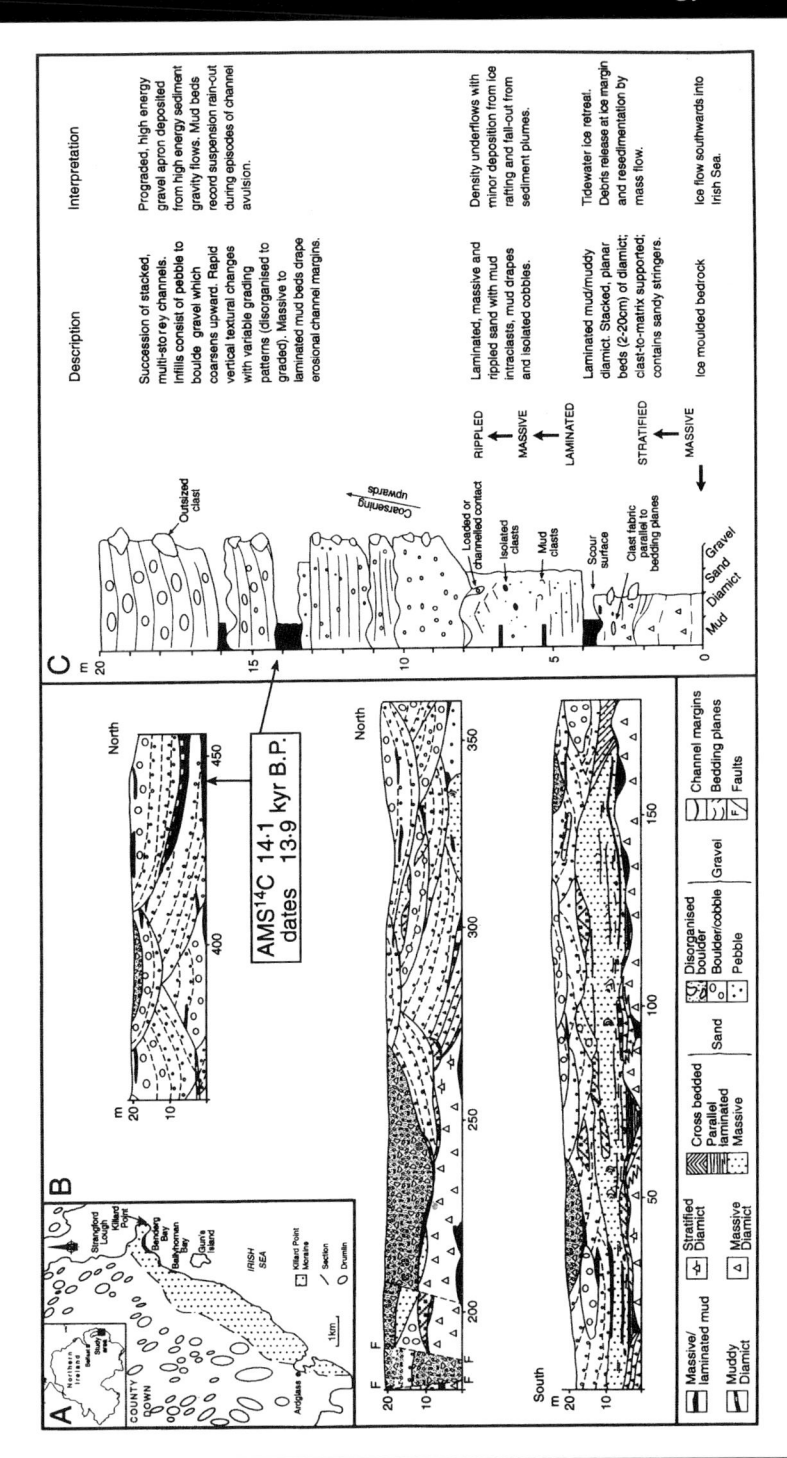

The upper surface of the sand association is channelised and marked locally by soft-sediment gravel dykes. The overlying gravel facies association is a set of fourteen stacked and infilled channels (50-100 m across, 10-15 m deep) identified on the basis of well-defined margins, erosional junctions between adjacent infills and sedimentary contrasts between adjacent infills (Fig. 10c). Channel infills are dominated (80%) by variable boulder gravel facies with subordinate sand and pebbly gravel facies. Gravel infills show a wide range of internal geometries and clast sizes. Individual beds vary greatly in thickness (0.2-1 m) and are mainly massive. Overall the gravel facies coarsen upwards and inferred channel axes indicate southward progradation of the channel system. The nested channels recording repeated cut and fill represent a distributary-type system subject to avulsion and changes in fluid/sediment input. The pulsed nature of the system is suggested by strong erosional channel margins, abrupt bed contacts, abrupt clast size changes and the presence of clay drapes lining erosional channel margins and within channel fills. The variable grading patterns, together with evidence (outsized clasts and boulder clustering) for clast freighting (Postma *et al.*, 1988), suggest deposition by mass flows in which there were strong grain interactions and high dispersive pressures (Hein, 1982). Sediment geometries with disorganised to variably graded beds are very similar to the gravel lithofacies successions described by Walker (1975, 1983) from resedimented, deep-water conglomerates. It is suggested that the gravel lithofacies present are similar to the evolutionary continuum recognised from high density sediment gravity flows.

Red mud beds, laminae and clasts occur throughout the succession. The thickest and most continuous beds occur within the gravel association where laminated and massive mud beds up to 1.5 m in thickness line some channel margins, especially at the northern end of the exposure (Fig. 10b). The presence of mud lining erosive channel floors and margins shows that the phases of cut and fill did not always closely follow one another. Beds of massive red mud at the northern end of the exposure contain well-preserved marine microfaunas dominated by *E. clavatum* (90%) whereas laminated muds present at higher levels in the same channel are abraded and less abundant. Monospecific samples of *E. clavatum* are dated to ~ 14 ^{14}C kyr BP (McCabe and Clark, 1998).

The data from Killard Point are critical to any interpretation of events within the ISB because it is one of the few sites where a zone of terminal outwash (dated from an *in situ* marine microfauna) is the product of subglacial transfer of debris during drumlinisation to a tidewater ice margin (Fig. 11). This integrated glacial system, which is correlated with similar events in the northern ISB and in other sites in the western British Isles, is important within an amphi-North Atlantic context for a variety of reasons. First, it provides a terrestrial record of millennial-scale ice sheet oscillations around 14 ^{14}C kyr BP which is correlated with Heinrich event 1 (McCabe *et al.*, 1998). Second, it allows terrestrial records from a small ice sheet situated in the climatically sensitive northeastern Atlantic to be compared with other hemispheric climate proxies. Third, it is an excellent example of a raised morainal bank which did not evolve into a Gilbert-type delta. Sedimentologically the three facies associations record a prograding system with progressive transfer of coarse sediment by high energy mechanisms along channels into deeper water (Fig. 11). Fourth, the raised morainal bank shows that the ice margin ended at tidewater, therefore that this part of the deglaciation was accompanied by high RSLs. If eustatic sea levels were generally low at this time then at least this sector of the ISB must have been deeply isostatically depressed (McCabe, 1997). This evidence clearly questions the numerical model predictions of Lambeck (1995, 1996) which do not show high RSLs. The current numerical models are based on poorly-constrained and undated field evidence and do not aid palaeoenvironmental reconstructions around the basin.

Fig. 11: Composite model of depositional environment, Killard Point moraine.

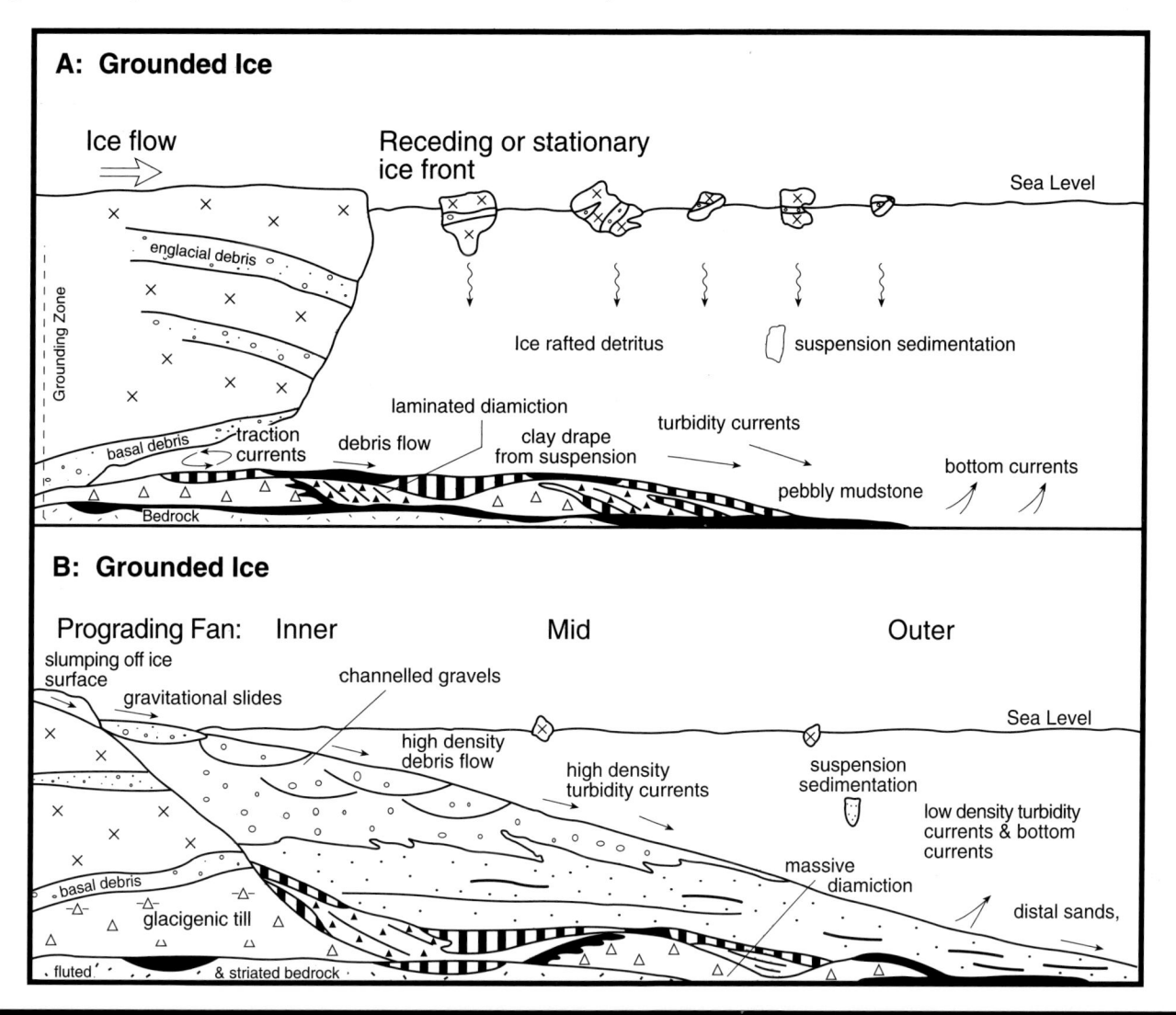

Maritime archaeology in Greyabbey Bay, Strangford Lough

Thomas McErlean, Wes Forsythe and Rosemary McConkey

Introduction

A full archaeological survey of Strangford Lough, Co Down, has uncovered almost 700 coastal and intertidal sites. The survey was commissioned by the Environment and Heritage Service (NI) and carried out by the Centre for Maritime Archaeology at the University of Ulster (McErlean *et al.*, 2002). Greyabbey Bay, located on the north-east shore of the lough (Fig. 12), contains the most representative concentration of archaeological sites reflecting past exploitation of the foreshore by human activities. The bay extends at low water westwards to two large islands, known as Mid and South Islands respectively, which are connected with each other and the mainland by causeways. Both extend south into the lough, forming a sheltered U-shaped bay with the shoreline around Greyabbey. In general the bay is composed of a sand-flat interspersed with pladdies (the local name for submerged eroded drumlins), making access difficult for large vessels of deep draught.

The natural environment

At the end of the late Devensian ice age, sea levels in Strangford Lough were higher than the present day (+20 m OD) forming raised shorelines and draping the glacial material in red marine clay. Sea level then fell rapidly to around −15 to −30 m OD by 9500 BP. After 9000 BP, rapid eustatic rise led to their being at most 20 m below present levels.

The submerged forests of early Mesolithic Strangford were mostly growing at about this period, suggesting that waterlogging was pervasive in coastal areas, particularly around drumlins. Water levels continued to rise during the late Mesolithic, leading to the formation of raised beaches and notches, examples of which can be seen at in the raised terraces around South Island, Chapel Island and elsewhere around the bay's coastline. Geological evidence then suggests a eustatic drop in sea-level concurrent with rise in isostatic uplift in early Neolithic times, which left these beaches on the present dry land. In Strangford Lough, grey estuarine clays were laid down on present dry land at Ringneill between 7345 ± 150 BP and 7450 ± 150 BP.

Evidence for changing conditions is witnessed in the remains of submerged 'forests' encountered along eroding shorelines (Fig. 13). In the past, areas of coastal forest would have been flooded and killed by rising water levels, the remaining stumps and debris eventually becoming exposed in shoreline peats or clays. In Strangford Lough, intertidal forests are represented by the tree stumps, roots and branches recorded at a number of locations, including a notable concentration in Greyabbey Bay. In most cases, these are true organic, freshwater peats as opposed to coastal detrital muds.

Fig. 12: Location of Greyabbey Bay, Strangford Lough

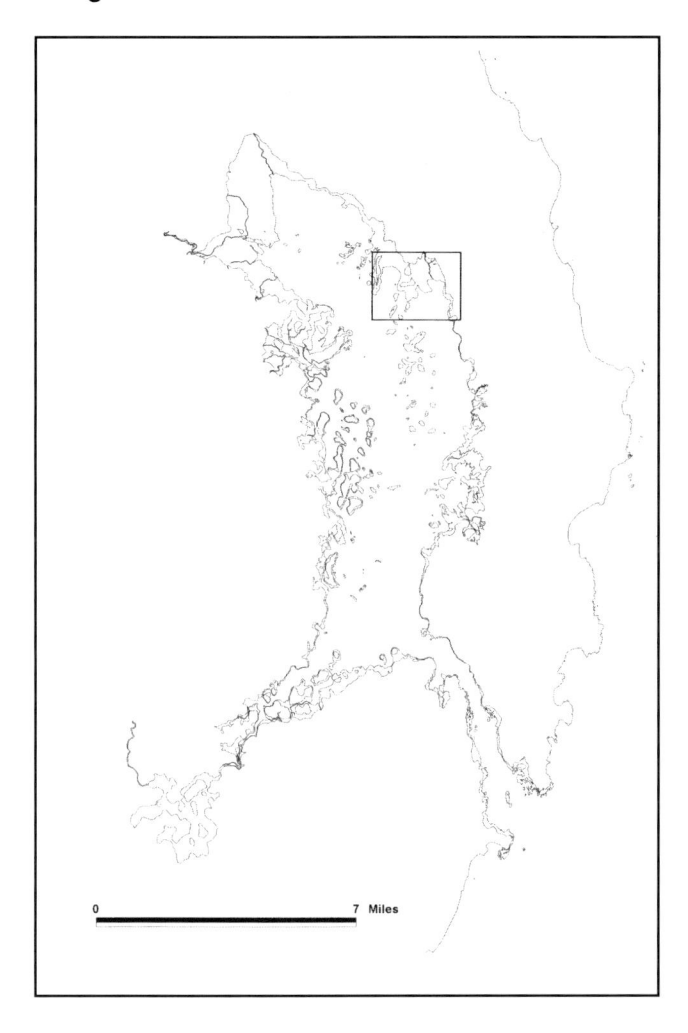

Fig. 13: Tree stumps in the intertidal zone in Greyabbey Bay (McErlean *et al.*, 2002)

Early man

Information on sea-level changes and submerged forests indicates a changing landscape in the early and late Mesolithic periods. As the sea level rose, early sites in low-lying areas within the lough were drowned. Foreshore flint finds from areas such as Bootown and Mount Stewart in the east of the bay attest to this submerged early landscape (Woodman, 1978, p. 299). By the later part of the Mesolithic period the maritime landscape of Strangford Lough, as we know it today, emerged. Hunter-gatherers, and later Neolithic farmers undoubtedly exploited marine resources, as evidenced by 5 oyster middens with associated flintwork located on the Mountstewart and Greyabbey shoreline. Some of the Strangford middens have produced flint evidence ranging from the late Mesolithic period to the Bronze Age. The shellfish resource could be gathered at low water on the extensive intertidal sand- and mud-flats. An analysis of the prehistoric coastal settlement evidence suggests the once

A number of these deposits have been sampled and radiocarbon dated to the Late Mesolithic period (c. 8000 BP).

extensive oyster beds in the lough were an extremely important resource. Neolithic people were also voyaging around the Lough using logboats. An example of an early oak logboat (radiocarbon dated to cal. 3499-3032 BC, 5449-4982 BP) was discovered in the bay near South Island and has been left *in situ* (Fig. 14).

Fig. 14: Neolithic logboat in Greyabbey Bay (McErlean *et al.*, 2002)

Medieval fish traps

Strangford Lough has one of the largest concentrations of medieval fish traps discovered so far in Britain and Ireland and a large number of these are located in Greyabbey Bay. Two late 16th Century maps mark the bay with the designation 'Pascafdry enmomies', a term which may be understood as referring to a 'general fishery' and highlight the former existence of an important medieval foreshore fishery. Surviving archaeological evidence for this is present in the form of a network of fixed fish trapping structures in wood and stone on the foreshore (Fig. 15). The earliest have been dated to the 7th Century, but a later phase was initiated after Affrica de Courcy, the wife of the Anglo-Norman conquer John de Courcy, who founded the Cistercian abbey at Greyabbey in 1193 with monks from the great abbey of Holm Cultram on the Solway Firth in Cumbria (Gwynn and Hadcock, 1988, p. 134). No wooden fish traps have been dated to the 14th, 15th, or 16th Centuries, suggesting that wooden traps were replaced in the13th Century by stone-built ones introduced by the Cistercians (Figs. 16, 17).

The fish species present in the lough include salmon, sea trout, plaice, flounder, mackerel, cod, grey mullet and skate. These species move in and out with the tide and would have provided a steady constituent of the daily catch. It is apparent that medieval communities had a detailed practical knowledge of the local movements of fish, as all of the Strangford Lough fish traps are ebb weirs, intended to catch fish drifting down with the falling tide. The walls and fences that constitute the traps typically converge to a point on the lower foreshore, meaning that every low tide they were exposed for about two to three hours. Large areas of the tidal

Fig. 15: Map of the Medieval wooden and stone fish traps in Greyabbey Bay

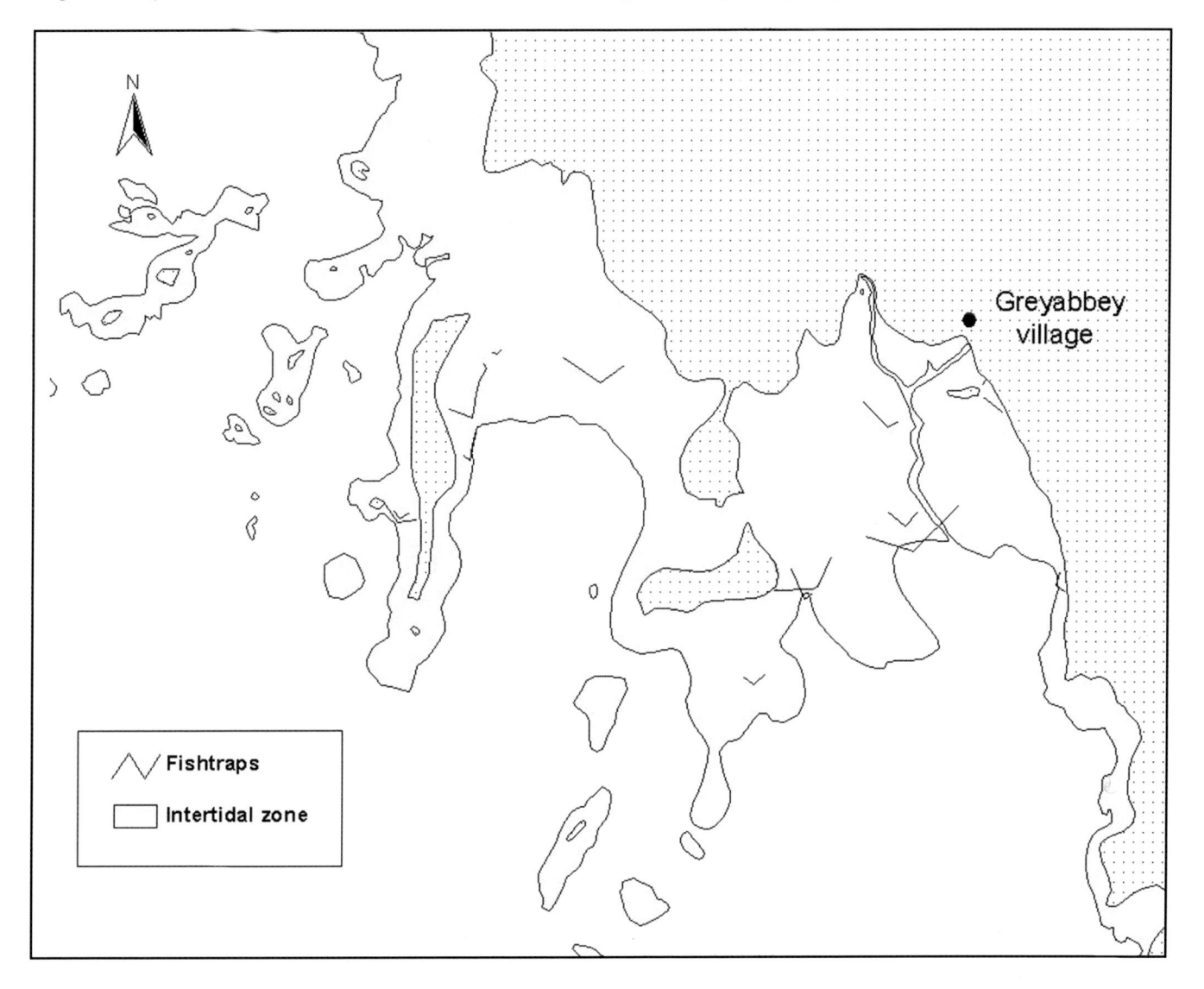

foreshore were enclosed, but there would been sufficient time to remove the catch or repair the structures. The traps are generally located on the tidal channels, some of which have a freshwater component, which would have provided nutrients for feeding fish. Both the wooden and stone fish traps utilise natural features like islands and pladdies in their location and orientation.

In general the traps are V-shaped, the trap mechanism (probably a box or basket) is located at the apex or eye and this is the ultimate destination of the funnelled fish and from where they are collected. Five clear examples of wooden fish traps were found in the Greyabbey Bay area. In their present condition, the wooden traps are represented by the survival of lines of alder or hazel post stumps which would have supported a wattle fence. Tidal erosion and natural decay has reduced the posts down to below ground level in almost all cases, so that only the foundation parts of the structures have survived. Without large-scale excavation, it is not possible to determine accurately the full extent of a trap as many of the stumps may be hidden underneath sediment.

Assessment of the lengths of the leaders (or arms of the traps), based on stump survival in most cases, is likely to be an underestimate but provides a good index of scale which suggests that two types are present. Very large traps have leaders in excess of 200 m and smaller traps have leaders of around 50 m. Two examples of large traps were found in Greyabbey Bay and were obviously designed to trap fish over a very wide area of the tidal flats. In the case of the smallest, that at the Ragheries was positioned to enclose a narrow tidal channel draining a large area of foreshore. This implies strongly that trap size relates directly to its topographical position on the foreshore.

Fig. 16: Post stumps of an earlier medieval wooden fish trap at Chapel Island, Greyabbey Bay (McErlean et al., 2002)

The stone traps are represented by low, double-boulder drystone walls on the foreshore. Few survive to more that one course high. Most take the form of linear, curvilinear or crescentic stone spreads up to 5 m wide within which a well-built core of rubble, on average just over 1 m wide, can be observed. These spreads are likely due to tidal action reducing a wall of greater height to only the basal layer. The stone fish traps are broadly similar to the wooden examples in size and shape, but show some important differences. They range in plan from V-shaped to crescentic. Seven of the Strangford stone traps replicate the simple V shape used in wood trap design. However other variations on the basic V shape are found. One example at Greyabbey Bay is best described as 'tick-shaped'. Here, a very long wall 300 m in length forms a western leader with a small eastern leader only 22 m long. Three are best described as 'curvilinear V' in shape. They consist of a series of straight sections of wall, which meet at slightly different orientations. Perhaps the most interesting of these is Chapel Island East which appears to incorporate two V's, one designed to trap on the ebb current parallel to the shore and one further east to trap a tidal stream.

Kelp industry

Kelp is the commercial name for the burned ashes of seaweed which, in the past, were exploited as the source of an impure form of soda (sodium carbonate) and for iodine. Soda, as an alkali, was in great demand in the 18th Century for a large number of industrial processes, the most important of which were in the manufacture of glass and soap and as an agent in bleaching linen. Kelp-making as a source of

Fig. 17: Air photograph of a stone fish trap in the middle of Greyabbey Bay (McErlean *et al.*, 2002)

Low Energy Coasts

Fig. 18: A kelp grid at Herring Bay to the south of Greyabbey Bay (McErlean *et al.*, 2002)

soda revolutionised the economy of the northern and western seaboards of Ireland and Scotland and provided a cash crop in an otherwise largely subsistence economy. The intertidal zone, previously exploited for wrack and fishing, now assumed a greater economic importance and the possession of a 'kelp shore', as those parts of the coastline supporting suitable growth of seaweed for kelp production were named, was highly valued.

The use of seaweed slag as a source of soda is probably very ancient in origin, but it was not until the 17th Century that documents demonstrate its widespread use. For centuries potash, mainly extracted from wood ashes, had been the main source of alkali and it may have been the growing scarcity of wood may have influenced the shift to seaweed as an important source. Much of the published material on Irish kelp-making is concerned with the 19th and early 20th Century iodine production. In contrast, there is little specific literature on Irish kelp as a source of soda, so only the broad outlines of the history of the industry are known at present. Production for industrial purposes seems well established in Irish coastal areas by the end of the 17th Century as it is recorded as an export item in 1702 (Harper, 1974, p.22) and its origins would seem to lie in developments earlier in that century. During the 17th Century, the exploitation of kelp as a source of soda for glassmaking, especially in England and France, stimulated demand for the product (Godfrey, 1975, p.159). In France, kelp-making for glass manufacture on the coasts of Normandy and Brittany had become a well-regulated industry by the 1690s (Chapman, 1970, p.25). In the early 17th Century, a number of glasshouses were established in Ireland and kelp is mentioned among the stock of one established by the first Earl of Cork at Ballynegeragh in Co Waterford in *c.* 1618 (Westropp, 1920, p.25-30). Another major stimulus appears to have been the Irish linen industry which was well-established, especially in Ulster, by the end of the 17th Century. The industry underwent a rapid period of development in the first decade of the eighteenth century, not least in terms of improved bleaching techniques (Crawford, 1980, p.114-115).

Kelp making consisted of number of well-defined stages: harvesting the seaweed on the foreshore, drying it on shore, burning it in kilns and storing it. Structures relating to all these stages of production have left their archaeological traces on the shore. A superb example illustrating these activities is to be found at Chapel Island, to the west of Greyabbey, where there are kelp kilns and the ruins of a kelp house, while on the foreshore nearby to the east is a large kelp grid artificially extending the seaweed-growing area over a sandy zone near low water (Fig. 18).

The most important impact of kelp making on the coastal archaeology of the lough was the subdivision of the foreshore by low stone walls erected to define seaweed rights and probably to regulate rotational cutting. These intertidal walls normally commence at, or just below, the high water mark and continue down the low water mark or end at the junction of the boulder zone with the mud or sand.

Strangford Lough: Environmental setting and management issues

Gonzalo Malvarez and Fatima Navas

The town of Newtownards and its surrounding area is protected from the tide by sea defences that were originally constructed in 1810 as part of a land reclamation scheme (Fig. 19). The original design, still in use in 1998, was highly reflective to wave energy with a potential erosive effect on the intertidal area. Sea defences were extended in the 1950s followed by further improvements in the 1970s (Fig. 20). In December 1981 the seawall was breached during a storm which resulted in extensive flooding in Newtownards.

After breaching of the sea wall, it was recognised that the existing sea defences were ineffective and that major reconstruction had to be undertaken to (i) enhance coastal protection against tidal floods, (ii) reduce wave reflectiveness and therefore improve durability and reduce potential damage of the sea wall, and (iii) reduce erosive effects that may be introduced by the old design of the wall on the sensitive ecosystem of the intertidal area. This introduces a framework that is topical in the seawall and coastal engineering literature: the concept of sustainable coastal engineering. In this challenging project, coastal managers have to deal with public demands on safety as well as conservation of wildlife and other issues.

Coastal protection is traditionally a controversial issue when private property or highly valuable ecological areas are at risk. Newtownards' tidal flats are one of the latter and as such are designated under many conservation schemes, outlined above.

The necessity for hard engineering solutions to protect the town is particularly sensitive as reclaimed land lies below mean sea level. The intertidal flats immediate to the sea defences are also a delicate ecological setting that requires careful handling because of its rich biological diversity. This potential conflict must then be resolved by serving public demands for protection against flooding and ecological long term damage. A complex scenario is introduced here, where the major reconstruction of a 1.5 km sea wall has to address all this issues without damaging the physical and biological environment of the tidal flat. At the same time, the design of the new sea wall has to embrace the latest advances to reduce wave energy reflectivity (Fig. 21) because of its potential effects on the sedimentation of the tidal flats.

The monitoring programme

An intensive monitoring programme was established to produce baseline data characterising the physical and biological environments (Fig. 22). The physical monitoring programme aimed at defining methods and to collect data that characterises the dynamics of the geomorphology of the tidal flats at Newtownards adjacent to the existing seawall prior to its modification and improvement. The geomorphology of the tidal flats can be analysed carrying out a series of measurement and analytic procedures that can then establish a database. Repeatability of the

Fig. 19: Location of Strangford Lough and Newtownards tidal flats in Co. Down

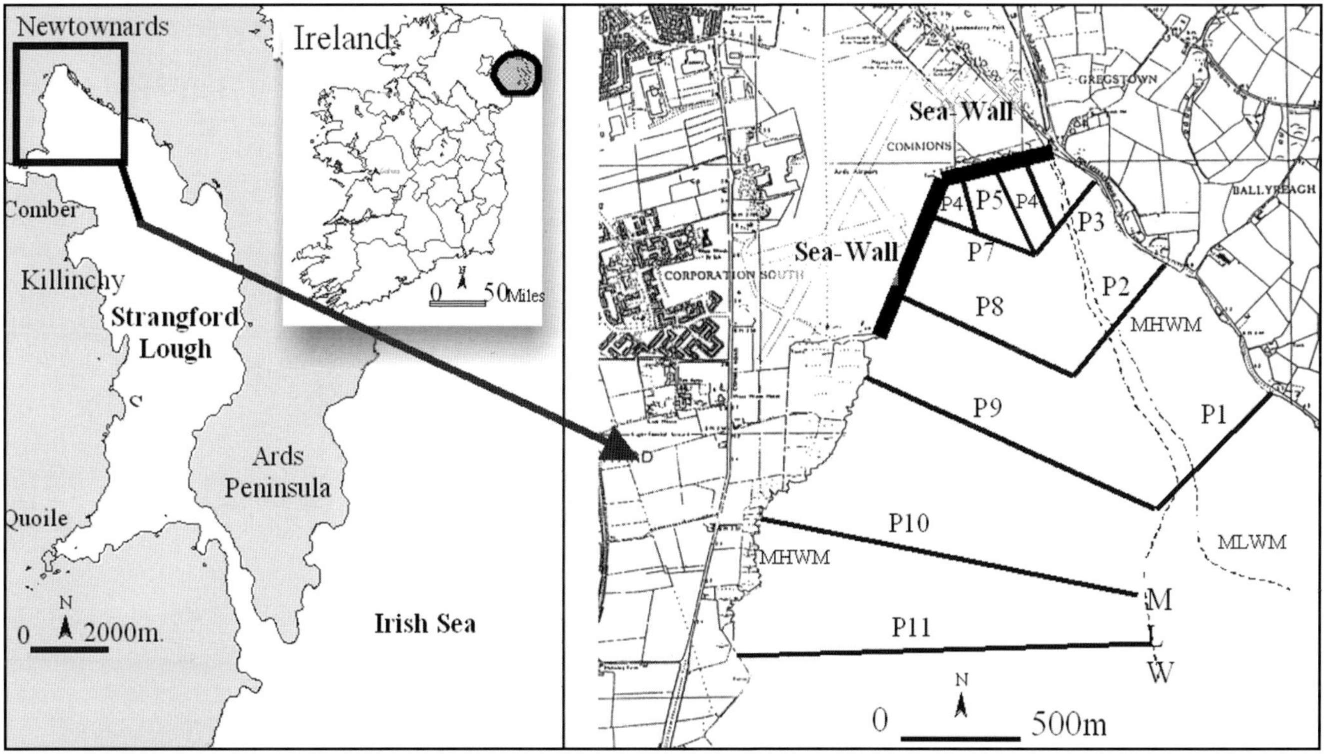

measurements is therefore an essential requirement and high precision equipment is needed to measure topographic profiles, sediments, water levels, climatic variables and wave propagation over the region.

Environmental variables involved in the geomorphological evolution of the sand flats are identified, measured, recorded, organised, analysed and interpreted.

The ultimate objective is the interpretation and discussion of the interaction of the above-mentioned environmental variables to establish the baseline geomorphological condition of the tidal flats at Newtownards prior to seawall improvement works.

Overview of monitoring results (1997-2000)

A number of short-term morphological responses were noted. The maximum elevation change between the highest and lowest points along the 11 transects (Fig. 19) was typically 20-30 cm depending on the location. Transects near the sea wall varied the least. Transects which included reaches further south had more vertical mobility. Reaches of the transects nearest to the mean low water mark showed generally greater mobility. The changes in elevation did not show a consistent seasonality nor appeared to show short term erosion or accretion patterns.

Low Energy Coasts

Fig. 20: Sea defences at Newtownards

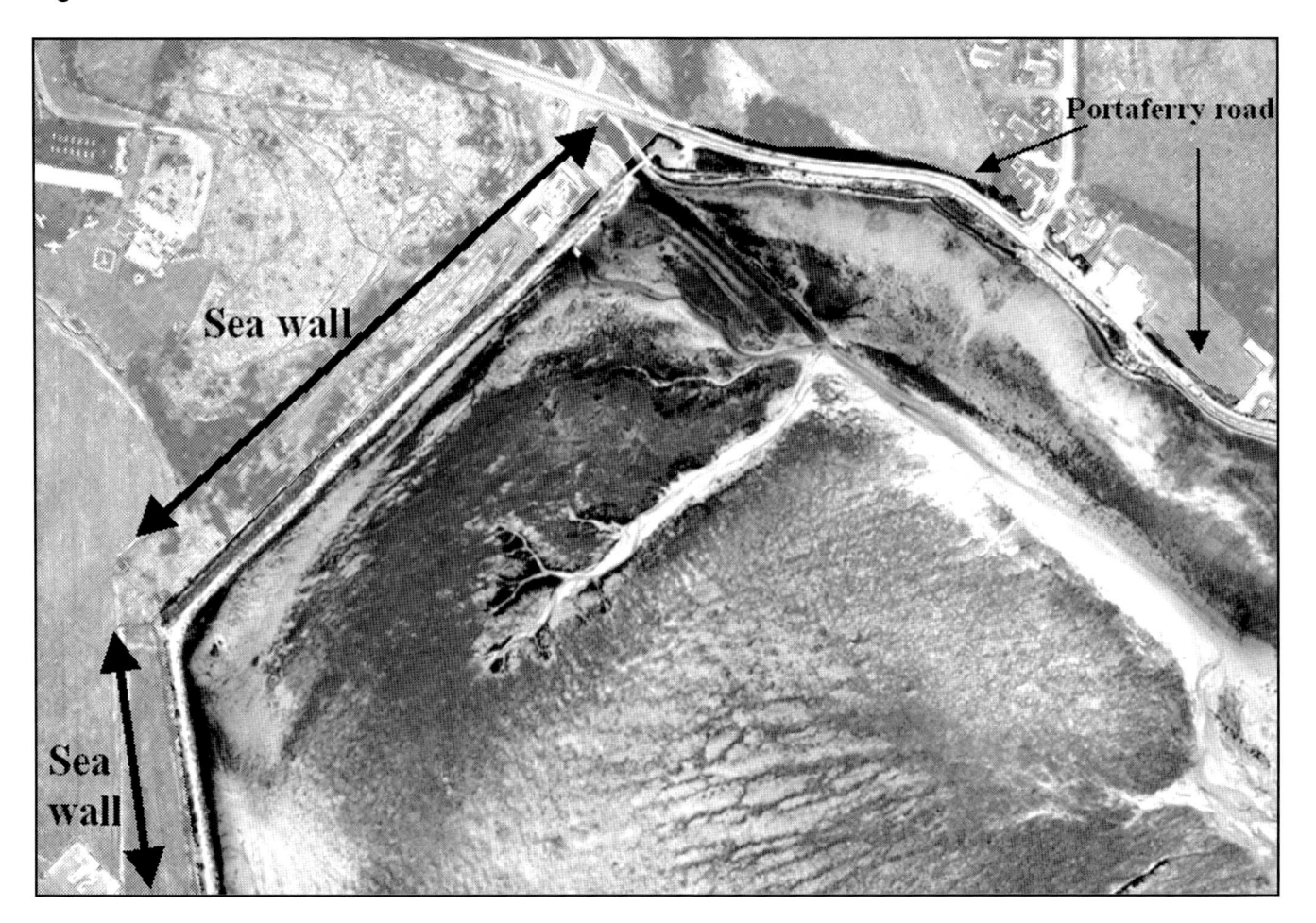

Sediment texture showed little spatial variation over the survey area. The range in sediment sizes was typically 0.12-0.22 mm. Finer particles were found near the sea wall and coarsened towards the low water mark. Grain size in main tidal channels was 0.20 mm. Overall sediment stability was shown by less than 0.05 mm variation in particle size over the surveyed period. The salt marsh shoreline was monitored using a differential GPS. Results here showed no significant erosion or accretion.

The edge of the vegetation of the salt marshes appeared to have an erosive profile but no consistent retreat was recorded.

Computer simulations indicated that the spatial distribution of potential wave activity was higher around the southern reaches of the sea wall. High values were also found along the south-facing shores to the east (along the Portaferry road, Fig. 20) and the southeast of the study area. The flat topography of the western shores leads to a gradual

Fig. 21: Illustration of the old and new seawall profiles at Newtownards

shoaling of waves that may result in sediment resuspension. Under storm conditions, wave heights were low at the northern end of the lough due to shoaling, and highest values were predicted at locations southwest of the sea defences.

A monitoring programme is now in place at the tidal flats at Newtownards to enable quick recognition of short-term anomalies that may be introduced by the transformations carried out during the reconstruction and enhancement of the sea defences.

Fig. 22: Monitoring of the tidal flats at Newtownards

Low Energy Coasts

The ecology of Strangford Lough

Alex Portig

Strangford Lough is a large marine inlet on the east coast of Co Down covering approximately 150 km^2 and some 24 km long and 8 km wide at its broadest part (Brown, 1990). It is virtually land-locked being connected to the Irish sea by a narrow channel, the "narrows", some 8 km long, through which strong currents of up to 7 knots flow. The lough has a semi-diurnal tidal regime with tidal range varying from 3.5 m (spring) to 2.0 m (neaps). The body of the lough is made up from a drowned drumlin field, with numerous islands and "pladdies" (eroded drumlins exposed at low tide), which are more extensive on the western than the eastern shore. There is relatively little freshwater input to the lough, especially when compared to the tidal flow through the "narrows" of some 350 million cubic metres with every tide such that the lough is fully saline except near the Quoile and Comber rivers. The hydrodynamics of the lough are complex but generally there is a reduction of current strength as one moves further north in the lough. As a result of this complexity of wave, tide and geology there are a wide range of habitats in a relatively small area. Exposed rocky shores are found chiefly at the "narrows" to the south and along eastern shores of the lough (Fig. 23). Semi-exposed boulder shores within more sheltered areas of body of the lough, chiefly on the western shore (Fig. 24). Mudflats and sandflats occur in the most sheltered areas and predominate on the western bays and the northern areas (Fig. 25).

As a result of this diversity of habitats the biological diversity is high; 72% of all sub littoral species found in Northern Ireland are found in Strangford Lough and, of these, 28% are only found in Strangford Lough. The intertidal sandflats at the northern end of Strangford Lough are characterised by an infaunal community that is dominated by the Cockle (*Cerastoderma edule*) and polychaete species such as the Lugworm (*Arenicola marina*). Beds of Dwarf eelgrass (*Zostera noltii*) and Eelgrass (*Zostera marina*) also grow on these sandflats (Fig. 26). These marine angiosperms form an important ecological function and thus are of conservation importance as they are extremely productive, stabilise sediments as well as being an important

Fig. 23: Exposed Bedrock Shore – Strangford Lough

Fig. 24: Boulder Shore – Strangford Lough

Fig. 25: Sandflat – Strangford Lough

Fig. 26: *Zostera marina* – Strangford Lough

Fig. 27: *Laminaria digitata* – Strangford Lough

food resource for overwintering wildfowl. The boulder and rocky shores support extensive growths of brown and red algae such as the Knotted rack (*Ascophyllum nodosum*) and kelps such as *Laminaria digitata* (Fig. 27). These seaweeds coupled with the physical environment create a diverse habitat, which supports a wide range of other species.

The islands of the lough also support breeding populations of birds. Terns are perhaps the most notable, e.g. Sandwich (*Sterna sandvicensis*) and Arctic (*Sterna paradisaea*) terns, while other breeding birds include Cormorant (*Phalacrocorax carbo*), Guillemott (*Uria aalge*), Red breasted Merganser (*Mergus serrator*), Oystercatcher (*Haematopus ostralegus*), Ringed Plover (*Charadrius hiaticula*) and, increasingly, Eider duck (*Somateria mollissima*). The lough also supports Grey (*Halichoerus grypus*) and Common (*Phoca vitulina*) seals with the latter being more common. Otters (*Luttra luttra*) are resident within the lough.

The overwintering bird species of the lough are numerous with over 20,000 birds utilising the lough at any one time. Pale bellied Brent Goose (*Branta bernicla hrota*) which breeds in Greenland and arctic Canada, overwinters almost exclusively in Ireland, with some two-thirds of the total population occurring on Strangford Lough in the early winter months (Fig. 28). Redshank (*Tringa totanus*) and Knot (*Calidris canutus*) also occur in numbers that are of international importance (1% or more of the total flyaway population) as well as many other species that occur in numbers of Irish and UK importance.

The lough in common with most other coastal estuaries in the UK has been much influenced by man. There has been reclamation of land e.g. the northern saltmarshes during the 19th century for agricultural use. Construction of causeways and fords to islands has also occurred altering tidal flows and sedimentation patterns e.g. to Island Reagh and Mahee Island. There has also been construction of sea defences most extensively in the northern end of the lough. The lough itself is used for a wide range of recreational and enterprise purposes. Recreational pastimes include wildfowling, dog-walking, sailing and general leisure activities while commercial activities include fishing, dredging, shellfish farming, shellfish gathering and bait digging. Waste disposal

Fig. 28: Brent Geese – Strangford Lough

with sewage outfalls of varying degrees of treatment are present at Ballydrain, Ballyrickard, Greyabbey, Killyleagh, Downpatrick (Quoile), Kirkubbin, Strangford and Portaferry (Davison, 1991). All these activities have greater or lesser impacts on the biology and status of the lough. Strangford Lough has seen an increase in the resident human population particularly since the 1960s and there has been a rise in recreational activities and commercial enterprise.

All these changing influences also have an impact on the ecology of the lough and discriminating natural and anthropogenic change in a highly variable environment is problematic. For example, seagrass beds that develop in intertidal and shallow subtidal areas on sands and muds are characterised by a high incidence of natural and anthropogenic disturbances. Eelgrasses are considered to be plants of low nutrient environments and show efficient recycling of nutrients and require requiring good light conditions (Fig. 29). Sediment stability is considered important where the amplitude and frequency of disturbance is a factor. Stable conditions create a continuous bed of eelgrass; with increasing disturbance, a patchy

Fig. 29: Eelgrass bed – Strangford Lough

bed is created, until a threshold of disturbance is reached when the seagrass becomes extinct. However, seagrasses themselves have a stabilising effect on the sediments through binding effects of their roots and rhizomes, so their loss from an area may create a situation that where lost conditions are subsequently unstable for recolonisation, or it may be very slow.

Historically on Strangford Lough a perennial species *Zostera marina* was the dominant species both in the intertidal and subtidally but a "wasting" disease in the 1930s, an epidemic that was widespread in Europe and North America, caused a wide spread decline and mudbanks that this species grew on were eroded. Currently, the dominant form of eelgrass on Strangford Lough is the smaller species *Zostera noltii* though *Z. marina* still occurs in the subtidal and is represented now by an annual form in the intertidal zone (Fig. 29).

Strangford Lough management

Eric Bann

Strangford Lough on the east coast of Northern Ireland is an outstanding example of a large, enclosed fjardic sea lough. Sea water enters the lough through a narrow entrance, expanding into a broad, mostly shallow basin that has a central deep channel (30-60 m deep), which carries rapid currents and causes great turbulence in some parts, particularly the Narrows. With a wide range of tidal stream strengths and depths, there is a remarkable marine fauna within Strangford Lough and it is one of the most diverse sea loughs in the UK. The communities present range from very rich high-energy communities near the mouth, which depend on rapid tidal currents, to communities in extreme shelter where fine muds support burrowing brittlestars, the Dublin Bay prawn *Nephrops norvegicus* and a rich community associated with horse mussels *Modiolus modiolus*.

In 1999 the Strangford Lough Management Committee (SLMC; an advisory committee appointed by Government) initiated a communication project to make information on science, management, tourism and recreation in relation to Strangford Lough, more accessible and better integrated. The committee commissioned research, which identified the specific information needs of the general public and specialists. No single organisation could address all these needs and so an information network was formed. The network is coordinated by the Strangford Lough Office and apart from advice from the Department of Agriculture and Rural Development (DARD), the Environment and Heritage Service (EHS) and the two Universities in Northern Ireland, the member organisations of SLMC are:

- Ards Borough Council
- Association of Strangford Lough Yacht Clubs
- Council for Nature Conservation and the Countryside
- Down District Council
- Joint Council of Wildfowling Associations for Strangford Lough
- Minister's Nominees
- National Trust
- Northern Ireland Agricultural Producers' Association
- Northern Ireland Environment Link
- Northern Ireland Federation of Sub-Aqua Clubs
- Northern Ireland Fish producers Organisation Ltd.
- Royal Society for the Protection of Birds
- Royal Yachting Association
- Shellfish Association of GB
- Sports Council for Northern Ireland

- Strangford Lough Fisherman's Association
- Strangford Lough Nature Conservation Association
- Ulster Farmers Union
- Ulster Wildlife Trust

The Strangford Lough Management Scheme was formally launched on 8th October 2001. Much legislation already in place has had to be incorporated in the management scheme, a summary of which is covered below.

In Northern Ireland, the requirements of the Habitats and Birds Directives have been transposed into domestic legislation by the Conservation (Natural Habitats etc) Regulations (NI) 1995, usually referred to as the Habitats Regulations. These Regulations introduce specific measures for the management of marine areas; notably, the provision to develop management schemes for European marine sites. The recognition of Strangford Lough as a European site comes on top of several other statutory nature conservation designations (see elsewhere in this guide for definitions and descriptions). The foreshore plus some islands have been declared as Areas of Special Scientific Interest (ASSIs). The Marine Nature Reserve (MNR) includes all the waters, seabed and shores up to mean tide high water mark and an area around the mouth of the lough. The area involved is 150 km^2 of the lough including 50 km^2 of foreshore and 40 km^2 seaward of the entrance. Parts of the lough are National Nature Reserves (NNRs) under the management of Environment and Heritage Service or the National Trust. Strangford Lough is also a Ramsar site under the Convention on Wetlands of International Importance.

This SLMC management scheme is intended to safeguard the conservation status of those features for which Strangford Lough has been selected as a candidate Special Area of Conservation (SAC) and classified as a Special Protection Area (SPA). The Scheme sets the framework through which activities will be managed, either voluntarily or through regulation, so as to achieve the conservation objectives of the European marine site. Management of the conservation interests will work to accommodate, and may in some cases encourage, appropriate human activities. The management scheme attempts to establish a benchmark of environmental sustainability, which should underpin other plans and strategies.

Because of the wide diversity of activities (40 at 119 sites – EHS Human Use Survey 1997) other statutory legislation is particularly relevant at Strangford. Fisheries Regulation is an important aspect of the management of the Lough. Under the Fisheries Act (NI) 1966, the Department of Agriculture and Rural Development is responsible for the management and regulation of fisheries and for fostering the development of fisheries.

Commercial fishing in Strangford Lough has made a significant contribution to the local economy. The main fishing activities today target scallops, queen scallops, lobster, crab, Buckie whelks and Dublin Bay prawns. Hand collection of periwinkles and cockles also takes place. In 1991 the fishing industry, responding to concern, volunteered to forego a number of the potentially damaging fishing practices and agreed to zoning in the use of mobile gear. In response to this initiative and following consultation with the industry and the wider interests, the Department of Agriculture introduced new regulations in 1993, which included measures specific to Strangford Lough. This legislation, The Inshore Fishing (Prohibiting of Fishing and Fishing Methods) Regulations (NI) 1993, is primarily aimed at protecting the fisheries of the lough while maximising the scope of the existing fisheries legislative base to reconcile fishing and conservation. The measures in the Regulations specific to Strangford Lough (in which "scallops" refer to King Scallops (*Pecten maximus*) only) are:

- the banning of suction dredging, beam trawling, the use of tickler chains on trawl nets, the use of a dredge to capture sea fish other than scallops and fishing for horse mussels;
- a closed season for taking scallops between May 1 and October 31;
- the zoning of fishing/diving for scallops to the southern part of the open Lough and of trawling to the northern part, and a size restriction on fishing vessels to 15.24 metres maximum.

An amendment to the 1966 Act, currently being progressed, will give DARD powers to both regulate commercial fishing in the intertidal zone and sea fisheries for environmental purposes. This amendment may have partly arisen as a result of a High Court case involving the National Trust (*Adair v National Trust for Places of Historic Interest and Natural Beauty* – Chancery Division, High Court of Northern Ireland, Times NI Law Report, 19 December 1997) The case arose out of a disputed claim by a local fisherman to collect shellfish from the foreshore of the lough established under common law principles. The court conclude that common law rights pay little regard to environmental concerns (which must be addressed through legal reform) and thus upheld the fisherman's rights to collect shellfish irrespective of any subsequent environmental harm. The whole issue of rights is a complex one and extremely relevant in the context of the management of the lough. Extensive areas of foreshore and some of seabed are, however, owned or leased by the National Trust and other conservation organisations including EHS. District Councils also lease foreshore as do some commercial shellfish growers. The National Trust holds the sporting rights to most of the intertidal area. Many of the islands, and most of the land surrounding the lough is in private ownership.

Many people with land holdings around or close to Strangford Lough claim rights to take seaweed, and/or gravel. These are generally written into title deeds. The Crown Estate Commissioners own most mineral rights in the SAC/SPA. Other mineral rights are, in some areas, associated with foreshore, which was formerly part of large estates. Common law rights have been established for the collection of wild shellfish and for digging bait for fishing.

The Crown, as "Government", holds inalienable rights in trust for the public in relation to foreshore, seabed and inshore water. These include rights of free navigation (to sail, anchor and move goods and passengers) and rights to take commercial fish species including shellfish and bait but excepting farmed stock, oysters and mussels in beds, and to spread nets out to dry on the shore). There is, surprisingly, no actual right of the public to be on Crown foreshore except for the purposes of exercising rights of navigating and fishing. However, the Crown Estate Commissioners normally place no restriction on access for amenity and recreational purposes over their tidal lands. This does not extend to right of access over private foreshore or over private land to reach Crown foreshore. However, there is a perceived right of access over the foreshore owned by the Crown, which it is unlikely to withhold.

The Fisheries Division of the Department of Agriculture and Rural Development (DARD) licenses marine aquaculture. It is the Department's aim to stimulate the development of aquaculture in Northern Ireland in ways, which are not harmful to the environment. Regulation is achieved through fish culture licenses and shellfish fishery licenses. Various interested parties (including SLMC) are routinely consulted on shellfish license applications and permits for scientific research within Strangford Lough.

The EU Shellfish Directive is also relevant with regard to Strangford. The EC Directive on the quality required of shellfish waters requires Member States to designate coastal and brackish waters which need protection or improvement so as to support shellfish life and growth. In 1983, a 5.41 km^2 area in Ardmillan Bay and Ringneill was designated as a shellfish water. In addition, two further designations at Skate Rock and Marlfield Bay were made in 1999. A water quality-monitoring programme has been initiated for the new sites. Shellfish flesh is monitored at all sites under a combined shellfish-monitoring programme between the Food Standards Agency, EHS and DARD.

Water quality is obviously an important issue within Strangford Lough and comes under the management remit. Since its enactment, the Water Act (NI) 1972 has resulted in routine monitoring for water quality in the Strangford Lough catchment and the improvement of industrial and sewage discharges. More recently EC Directives and other legislative measures have further contributed to this improvement and will continue to do so.

The Urban Waste Water Treatment Directive sets minimum standards for sewerage and sewage treatment and some industrial discharges across Member States. A timetable has been set, targeting larger discharges in the first instance, for improved discharge standards.

Deposits in the sea are controlled under Part II of the Food and Environment Protection Act (1985). This refers to the disposal of dredged material at sea and construction below mean high water spring tide. There are no licensed disposal sites within Strangford Lough. However, any construction works are subject to a full consultation process under the Act. The licensing authority is the Water Quality Unit, Environment and Heritage Service.

Voluntary initiatives are also encouraged and included in the Management Plan.

Leaders of organised activities have been encouraged to introduce voluntary codes for participants and club members. In many cases the Strangford Lough Management Committee has been involved in the establishment of these codes working closely with clubs such as the Association of Strangford Lough Yacht Clubs and the Northern Ireland Federation of Sub-Aqua Clubs. The latter organisation has in fact, since Underwater Conservation Year in 1977, subscribed to a system of three underwater reserves in the Strangford Narrows, an area around Bird Island (off Kircubbin) and another north east of Killyleagh. Inside these three areas divers belonging to clubs in NIFed voluntarily agree not to remove live specimens.

Murlough dunes

Julian Orford and Joanne Murdy

Introduction

The development of Murlough as a mid- to late-Holocene prograded dune field resting on a gravel-dominated beach ridge system offers some problems as to how regressive beach-dune building occurred and what processes and timescales control the actual beach – dune exchanges.

Murlough dunes

Murlough dunes, Dundrum Bay, Co Down, is the largest dune site in eastern Ireland (Curtis, 1991). Murdy (2000) has reviewed the dune site's geomorphology and stratigraphy, identifying a mid- to late-Holocene emplacement by ^{14}C and luminescence dating determinations. The dune field is essentially linear in form, stretching southwest to northeast for c. 10 km, with a limited inland extent that is about 1 km at its maximum (Fig. 30B). The contemporary prevailing wind is southwest or west and flows essentially offshore or sub-parallel to the overall dune field, posing the question as to how the dunefield developed on a shoreline with a prevailing offshore wind. However, there is the limited presence of southeasterly, onshore gale/storm force winds during the autumn, set up by westerly Atlantic depressions driving against blocking continental high pressure systems that persist across southern Britain, which have the onshore potential for dune building. It is likely that the limited inland dune extent is a reflection of the prevailing westerly offshore and south-west alongshore winds that

Fig. 30: (A) Oblique air-photograph of Murlough dunes in 1954 looking north. Note the lack of vegetation, the northeasterly parabolic dune reworking and the basement gravel-dominated beach ridges exposed in blowouts. (B) Vertical air-photograph of Murlough in 1994 showing the strong vegetation cover reintroduced after nearly three decades of prohibited public access.

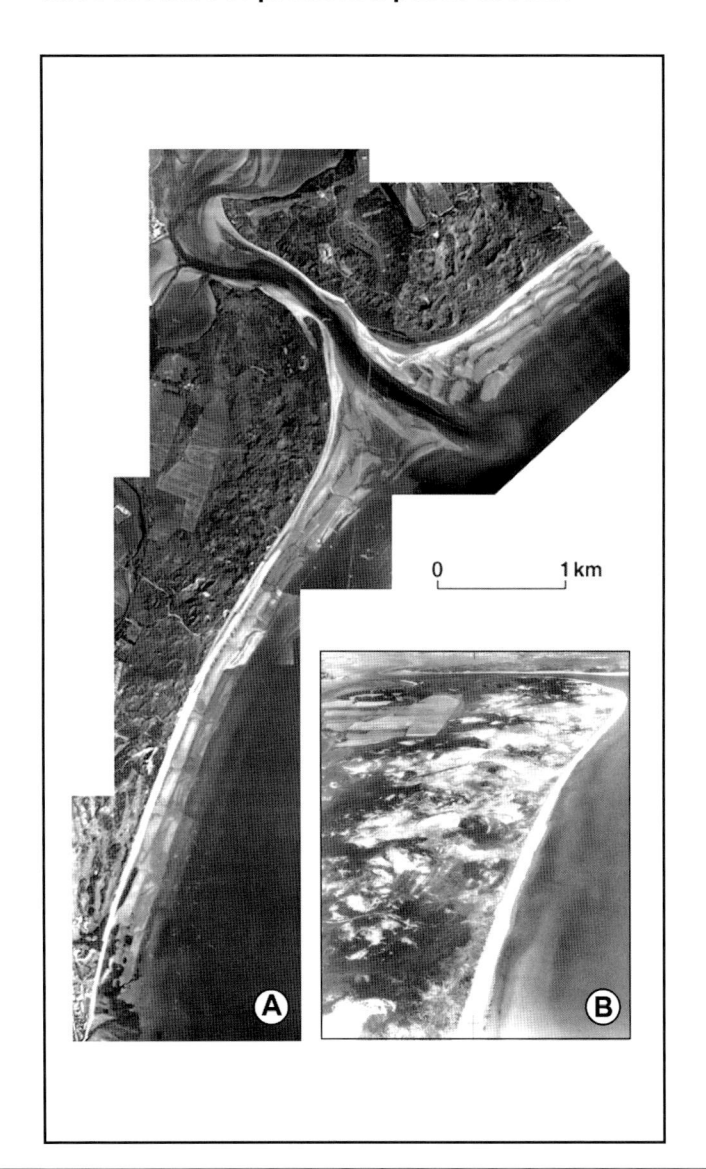

reworked and limited the dunefield's westward progression. The contemporary dune surface has substantial blowouts generally associated with northeast orientated parabolic dunes (elevation up to 30 m OD), which lifted the present surface ('New Dunes' – a terminology commonly used) considerably above the initial dune elevation ('Old Dunes').

The dunes are fronted by a wide dissipative macro-tidal beach (5 m range at high springs, mean Hs: < 1 m: Orford, 1989). The beach exhibits multiple stationary longshore inter-tidal bars (ridge and runnel) that are prominent during non-storm conditions (Short, 1991). There is an absence of any foredunes, the last were eroded in 1977, with the current dune/beach boundary shown as an eroding cliff-edge to the dune, emphasising the lack of any major transfers between beach and dune. Fronting this dune-cliff is a gravel beach that shows well-developed cross-beach shape-size gravel sorting as an indication of textural maturity and stability (Forbes et al., 1995). The surrounding (and presumed underlying) terrestrial basement has a variable heterogeneous glacigenic cover including remnants of Tertiary (Mourne Mountains) igneous intrusives (granites) and lower Palaeozoic mudstones and greywackes (North Down).

Murdy (2000) has identified the lithofacies stratigraphy of the dunes and the sub-dune sediments using trenches, auguring and ground penetrating radar. At the dry base of dune blowouts is an undulating gravel surface that has been identified as the top of a subsurface gravel ridge sequence (Mitchell and Stephens, 1974). Figure 30A shows an oblique air-photograph of Murlough (1954) in which beach ridge sets can be identified in several major blowouts. The genesis of the gravel ridges has been based principally on minimal surface morphology as exposed at the base of dune blowouts, while the "gravel" nomenclature relates generally only to the surface gravel, since access to the internal structure and composition of the gravel basement has been hitherto lacking. These older beach ridges trend parallel to sub-parallel with the modern beach orientation and show a lack of bifurcation and cross-ridge termination normally associated with a longshore drift-dominated supply. Orford (1986) has argued that the ridges reflect a swash-alignment that is bay-scaled (Dundrum Bay), and hypothesised that these features were essentially built synchronously around the bay under swash refraction control (plan-view), i.e. their sediment source was emerging from a reworking of the beach face stretching out into Dundrum Bay. Mitchell and Stephens (1974) identified, using a resistivity survey, the cross-shore profile of these basement beach ridges and showed the overall seaward declination in their heights. The landward ridge is c. 8 m OD while their penultimate seaward ridge is c. 4 m OD, approximately the same as the present-day gravel ridge. Mitchell and Stephens (1974) are the only investigators who invoke a higher-than-present Holocene sea level (+2 to 3 m) to establish the origin of a coastal gravel ridge basement underlying a major coastal dune field (Murlough Dunes, Dundrum Bay). However without in situ dating this perspective was regarded by Carter (1982) as suspect, as Mitchell and Stephens had no dating control, no sea-level index points, and could only use the seaward declining height of the beach ridges to infer a past higher sea-level position. The beach ridges rest on a surface that was presumed to be of glacial origin. Orford (1986) observed from borehole analysis that there were units of interbedded gravel, sands and silts of supposed fluvial origin, lying under the gravel ridges and presumed to be overlying a glacially modified surface. This middle sequence was related to fluvial reworking of glacial debris associated with the late-glacial regression (prior to the mid-Holocene highstand). This reworking and redistribution of sediments would have reached out into Dundrum Bay given the fall of mean sea level to approximately –10 m OD as indicated by Carter (1982). It is also suggested by Orford (1986) that this unit was the principal source for the beach ridges and dunes at Murlough, being reworked by the mid-Holocene transgressive RSL.

A number of organic-rich surfaces have been observed in the sidewalls of blow outs in the dune cover, which have been dated. Smith *et al.* (1971) and Cruickshank (1980) undertook ^{14}C dating of charcoal from several dune horizons and interpreted the original landscape level as undulatory but not as extreme as the present day surface. Murdy (2000) interpreted the original dune emplacement as essentially diachronous, pre-dating the oldest dune hiatus dated at 4778 ± 140 years BP (UB412), and extending with progradational development to at least 2065 ± 85 years BP (UB669), and potentially recent (historical time) given optically stimulated luminescence (OSL) dating determinations. OSL dating by Murdy (2000) of dune sand underlying the oldest organic rich dune layers, determined ages of 5300 ± 400 cal. years BP (M5.Risø no. 990401) and 5900 ± 600 cal. years BP (M2/1, Risø no. 990403). These are the earliest date determinations of dune activity phases post the mid-Holocene transgression in eastern Ulster. Although it is difficult to identify the age(s) of major blowout activity *per se*, whose effects dominate the contemporary dunescape through parabolic dune reworking (Fig 30a), interpretation of associated archaeological artefacts (Norman 12th Century AD) and OSL dates (Murdy, 2000) suggests that this major reworking is probably as recent as the Little Ice Age (16th - 18th Century AD). This last major disturbance may be related to the intersection of climatic shift (stronger and more persistent westerly wind (?) superimposed on vegetation stress caused by the introduction of rabbits to Murlough by the Normans. Murlough dunefield has been part of a National Nature Trust Reserve since 1967 and as a consequence of strict public access control, the non-vegetated surfaces shown in Fig. 30A have now been re-occupied by grass, heather and shrub vegetation (bracken and gorse) and now presents a stabilised surface (Fig. 30B). The National Nature Reserve has gained protected conservation status under EU Habitats Directive legislation as well as having NI designated status for its heath land vegetation. This means that access is still strictly controlled and that the field trip will have to be conducted via board walk and designated paths.

Beach ridge and dune emplacement

Murlough deposition has to be viewed in the light of the continuing debate (Carter, 1982; Lambeck, 1996, Lambeck and Purcell, 2001) about the elevation and location of a mid-Holocene peak in RSL: 2 –3 m above present day OD at *c*. 6.8 kyr BP on the north coast and *c*. 5.5 kyr BP on the east coast, and its likely influence on coastal deposition. The debate centres on the timing and elevation of the peak and the persistence of any regressive tendency in the decline to present day sea level. There are around the coast of the north of Ireland, a number of coastal dune fields that overlie basements composed of multiple gravel-dominated beach ridges. These dune/gravel assemblages have been ascribed to the mid-Holocene deceleration in relative sea level (Orford and Carter, 1988), although the exact mechanism for this superimposed sequence has not been readily understood. Both the timing and cause of sediment partition or decoupling by which the superimposition was formed have to be considered. Two extreme scenarios are proposed;

Sequential Sediment-Sourcing (SSS): the complete gravel ridge sequence was first deposited, subsequently buried by an aeolian cover, i.e. subsequent aeolian deposition as a function of sediment source changes, and/or forcing changes. This is called sequential, as only one macro switch in sediment source would have occurred.

Alternating Sediment-Decoupling (ASD): A form of synchronous deposition where the ridges and dune cover are sequentially built as composite units in some prograded context whereby sand-domination and gravel-domination alternated. This requires a shift from a reflective beach state during which gravel based ridges are deposited, to a dissipative beach state in which aeolian deposition would be dominant.

The appropriate model selection depends on the relative dating of both the gravel ridges and the superimposed dunes.

Gravel-dominated beach ridges

Three trenches (< 5 m deep maximum and a cumulative length of *c.* 100 m) in the gravel surface exposed in blowouts (Fig. 31) were excavated in December 1996. The trenches were strike-directed and crossed 11 ridges forming two sets: ridges 1-4 and ridges 5-11 with dune cover of *c.* 100 m separating ridges numbered 4 and 5. The trench side-wall stratigraphy is shown in Fig. 32. Ridge 1 is nearest to the sea and is presumed to be the youngest. Infrared stimulated luminescence (IRSL) ages, using the signal from 180-212 μm potassium-rich feldspar grains (Wintle *et al.*, 1998), were obtained for six samples selected from inter-bedded sand units in the gravel under ridge crests (Fig. 32: R1, R4, R5, R10 and R11). IRSL dating was undertaken at the Geography Dept, University College, Aberystwyth, Wales.

The terminology of gravel-based ridges needs to be adjusted to that of gravel-dominated ridges as all ridges show a substantial volume of sand. All sedimentary units exhibited a general overall seaward dip. Sand-unit boundaries are often sharp and unconformable, reflecting reworking or truncation surfaces. These are well-defined under crest ridge positions. The majority of sand units show parallel stratification associated with swash-backwash activity, though there is some evidence of massive bedding associated with rapid-deposition. Ridge crests are based on sand units that outcrop at the surface and form the rear landward dipping surfaces (Fig. 32: R1, R3, R4, R8 and R11). These sand units usually show a truncated seaward edge that starts steeply under the ridge crest and declines in angle to seawards, until it is sub-parallel to the inter-ridge surface slope. Usually the gravel unit, unconformably bedded against this truncation surface, defines the upper seaward surface to the crest. In general the gravel and sand dominated units are cleanly interbedded across the width of the section. Upper boundaries of coarse units tend to show an irregular transition into sand, in contrast to their sharper lower distinctive boundaries.

The six IRSL dates vary between 2000 and 3400 years (excluding error terms), when the error term is included, ages vary between 1800 and 3800 years. The ridge dates are spatially consistent except for ridge 10 compared to ridge 11. The two samples taken from the same unit in R10 to establish within-ridge variability, have 50% overlap with reference

Low Energy Coasts

Fig. 31: Location of excavated trenches in the sub-dune gravel-domimated beach ridges at Murlough. The site is located in the southwest section (bottom left hand corner) of Murlough in Fig. 30A.

Table 3: Murlough gravel-dominated beach ridge age and development rate characteristics

BEACH RIDGE AGE DETERMINATION — IRSL AGE DETERMINATION (years BP)

	Ridge No	Distance (m)	Mean Age	Oldest Age	Youngest Age
Set 1-4	1	0	1950	2150	1750
	2	6			
	3	15			
	4	27	2450	2700	2200
Set 5-10	5	120	3050	3250	2850
	6	129			
	7	142			
	8	151			
	9	164			
	10	170	3350	3750	2950

BEACH RIDGE BUILDING OCCURRENCE (1 ridge per X years)

	Mean Age	Oldest Age	Youngest Age
Set 1-4	125	238	13
Set 5-10	50	150	17
Overall	80	185	15

BEACH RIDGE PROGRADATION RATE (m yr^{-1})

	Mean Age	Oldest Age	Youngest Age
Set 1-4	0.05	0.03	0.55
Set 5-10	0.17	0.06	0.50
Overall	0.15	0.09	0.62

to their error term range and are considered to be effectively contemporaneous. Sample R11 has been left out of subsequent calculations due to its unconformity in time. All calculations of ridge building rates (Table 3) have been undertaken using both the shortest time periods (determined age - error term), determined age time period and the longest time period (determined age + error). Exclusion of R11 means that the analysis tends towards a longer time period for ridge development.

There is a mean inter-ridge spacing of 11.9 m (s: 6.8 m) when all 11 ridges are considered. If the extreme distance between R10/11 is excluded, mean ridge spacing drops to 9.8 m while variability is radically reduced (s: 2.7 m). There is a non-significant reduction in ridge spacing between Set 1-4 and Set 5-10 (9.2 m >x> 10.2 m). The offset in distance between R5 and R4 (100 m) allows the two subsets to be compared for changes over time. The range and consistency of dates indicate a strong progradational beach phase between 3500 and 2000 cal. years BP. It is uncertain as to whether a normal or forced regression (Posamentier *et al.*, 1992) is the cause of the progradation, though the slight seaward fall in beach ridge height reported here (as part of the trend observed by Mitchell and Stephens, 1974) is more likely to be associated with a forced regression. There is a shift in mean progradation rate from 0.17 m yr^{-1} between 3750 and 2850 cal. years BP for Set 2, to 0.05 m yr^{-1} between 1750 and 2700 cal. years BP for Set 1. This progradation rate reduction is likely to be due to a reduction in the nearshore sediment availability, as the rate of RSL fall decreased as it approached contemporary sea level. Such a shift in progradation rate might also be the result in a fall in sediment input to the beach. However any beach face volume reduction would normally be associated with a rise in the elevation of the gravel beach ridge crests as bigger breakers are allowed closer to the shoreline, which is not observed at Murlough. The overall consistency in the coarse/fine ratio of sediments in the ridges also suggests no long-term reduction of gravel supply to the Murlough beachface.

The presence of substantial beach sand interbedded with the gravel indicates that the transitions between morphodynamic regimes are more common than supposed for the SSS model to be considered viable. It is possible that morphodynamic domain threshold conditions for sand or gravel sedimentation are more readily achieved than otherwise supposed. The strong lenticularity of beach units suggests that the beach face is dominated by alternating sets of morphodynamic conditions. This again suggests that the SSS model is not that likely because the morphodynamic regime shift is operating at time scales substantially less than 1000 years given the observed dating range for these ridges. The SSS model is also less likely than the ASD model given the age range of dune hiatus surfaces (3936 cal. years BP: UB352 and 2012 cal. years BP: UB669) overlying older gravel-based ridges landward of the observed beach ridges (built between 3000-2000 cal. years BP). These date ranges indicate that aeolian deposition was approximately contemporary with seaward prograding beach ridge building, although the two morpho-sedimentary environments are not necessarily in phase, i.e. the ASD model is applicable. The dunes are likely to be prograded foredunes, anchored to older beach ridges as dune decoration and unable to show major onshore growth due to the lack of a prevailing onshore wind. As the beach basement prograded, the depositional focus of the dunes also moved seaward, consistently landward of beach ridge deposition.

Mesoscale beach ridge building

The back slope of beach ridges are generally formed from sand units onto which capping gravels (defining the beach ridge crest) are deposited upon seaward directed erosion surfaces cut into the underlying sand wedges (Fig. 32). The gravel emplacement at high water positions is likely due to south-east storm wave activity in the Irish Sea. The actual deposition model for the underlying sand base is not that strategic to the analysis, other than it reflects an occurrence interval associated with the ridge formation. Both upper beach swash bar building by constructive swells (Komar, 1976) or by extreme storms (Aagaard *et al.*, 1998) is going to occur on an inter-annual, if not a sub-decade, basis and hence provide a sizeable and consistent dune sand source landward of high tide water activity.

Ridge building can take between 15 and 250 years based on the IRSL chronology. The observed ridge periodicities could be considered as a function of joint occurrence probability of two independent processes: sand ridge presence/preservation and gravel ridge building. Any sand ridge preservation potential would be a joint function of the initial high-water sand ridge volume, the deflation rate of ridge sediment to landward dunes, the storminess activity rate that would dictate the seaward ridge face erosion rate and the rate of seaward movement of high water position as the beach system prograded. It should not be assumed that these sand ridge remnants reflect the only sand ridges that occurred between 2000-3000 cal. years BP, in that ridges may have been built that had been totally eroded by deflation and storm activity.

If it can be assumed that these high-water sand ridges are the major sediment sources for landward foredune building, then it is unlikely that the ridge remnants defined in the trench sections could be the only source of observed dune sediment given the substantial budgetary volume of the dunes and the low mesoscale probability of mixed ridge occurrence (*c.* 1 in 50-130 years). More sand based ridges are required to deliver this sediment, which is a problem in that sand ridges, though more likely to occur at periods substantially less than 1 in 50 years, do not appear in the beach ridge record per se. The requirement for more sand could be met by the presence of further sand ridges that were totally removed but added volume to the foredunes. As the coastal system prograded, forced by a falling RSL, the occasional persistent sand ridge remnant, though storm eroded and deflated, could have been sealed by gravel-based storm activity. This sand-ridge remnant was effectively preserved and then locked into a prograding beach face as well as being sealed above by later aeolian deposition from younger seaward beach sources.

The development of *surviving* ridges changes over time with a mean ridge periodicity of 1 in 50 years for ridge set 5-10 and 1 in 130 years for ridge set 1-4 (Table 3) and again might reflect the deceleration on the falling RSL from the highstand. It might also reflect an associated reduction in beach face sediment volume, i.e. it takes longer to achieve the critical prograded distance by which ridge survival can be ensured, given less input volume. This differential timing but consistency of ridge spacing identifies a well-regulated ridge building system whose forcing is more a volume problem rather than one of process change.

Although the emplacement of sand and gravel can be explained in terms of relative environmental

Low Energy Coasts

Fig. 32: Stratigraphy of section trench walls. R1-11 are location of beach ridge crests as used in the analysis.

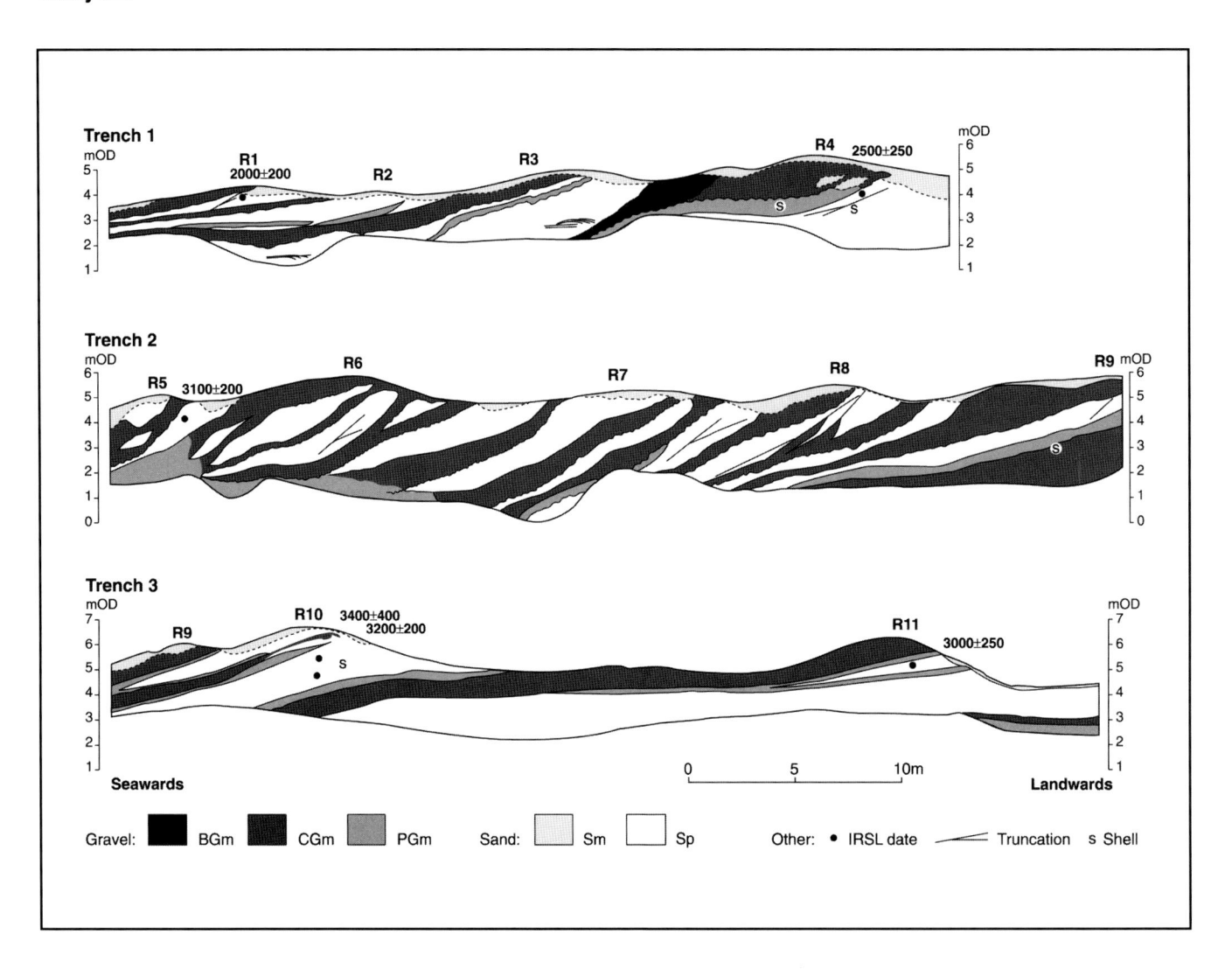

synchronicity, there is still a remaining problem as to how the morphodynamics of two contrasting modal sediment situations came to be achieved. The occurrence of gravel as the dominant facies during storm capping of sand ridges must indicate reflective morphodynamics, occurring during periods when beach face sand volumes are low, rather than when the gravel volume input to the beach face increased. Gravel could only be mobilised once the beach sediment body was reduced by successive beach ridge building and deflationary exchange to the dunes. Such a leakage of sand from the beach face appears to have taken around 50 to 130 years (i.e. century-scale mechanism). The variable time base to the multiple ridge and dune sequence identifies a fluctuating repetition of this overall sediment forcing and is likely to be due to a fluctuation in the overall falling RSL rate during the late–Holocene regressive phase. In support of this perspective, it is worth noting the state of contemporary sand exchange between beach and dune at Murlough at a time of relative stationary sea level (Taylor et al., 1986). There has been virtually no exchange in the last twenty years and no foredune development, indicating a deficit sand component in the contemporary beach. The result of this deficit is seen in the development of a reflective inner-beach surface cover of gravel at the contemporary high-water position – a possible precursor for the latest gravel-dominated beach ridge in the Murlough system and a modern analogue for the late phase of the ASD model.

Dundrum Bay: Coastal processes and modelling

Fatima Navas and Gonzalo Malvarez

Dundrum Bay is located on the south-eastern coast of Northern Ireland (Fig. 33). The bay system is bounded to the southwest by rocky headlands south of the town of Newcastle, and by the Craighalea rocks to the northeast. The bay system comprises (1) Dundrum inner bay, a back-barrier environment with extensive tidal mud and sand flats that develop landward of (2) an extensive Holocene dune system that includes the Murlough and Ballykinler complexes divided by a channel that connects Dundrum inner bay with the open sea; and (3) Dundrum outer bay, which includes the beaches, intertidal and offshore areas of Newcastle, Murlough and Ballykinler, as well as an extensive ebb-tidal delta associated with the mouth of the inner Dundrum Bay inlet channel.

The coastline experiences low to moderate wave energy conditions as a result of the restricted fetch

Fig. 33: Location of Dundrum Bay, County Down, Northern Ireland.

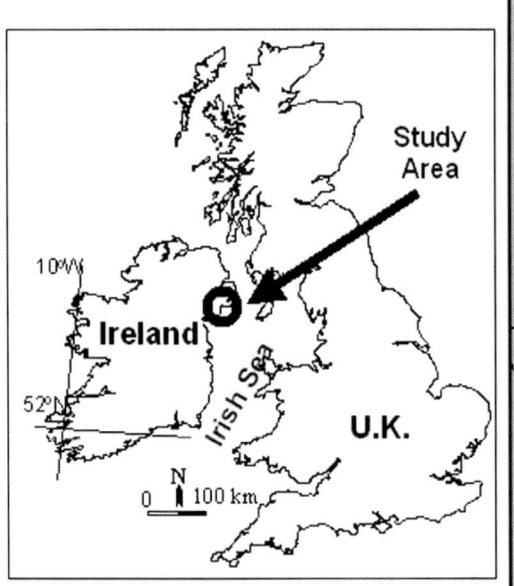

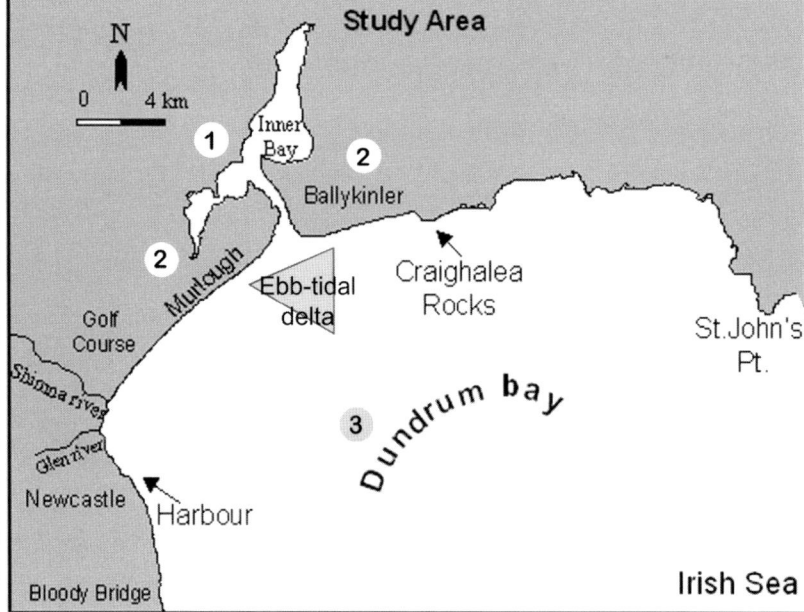

of the Irish Sea (< 200 km). Wave climate is dominated by locally generated wind waves. Wind action in the area is strong and dominated by south westerly to southerly modal winds, while most storm winds are from the south-eastern quadrant. The area is macrotidal with a tidal range of > 5m spring tide.

During low tide it is possible to recognise up to five wide littoral sand bars lying parallel to the shore in the intertidal zone, plus a further subtidal one (Fig. 34). The bars are aligned parallel or sub-parallel to the shore, increasing in spacing but decreasing in amplitude seaward. The morphology and dynamics of these features are characteristic of a *ridge* and *runnel* system. The ridge and runnel system in Dundrum Bay could be described as semi-permanent, on the basis that the ridge topography is flattened following storms.

Fig. 34: Aerial photograph of the intertidal area of Murlough Beach, Dundrum Bay.

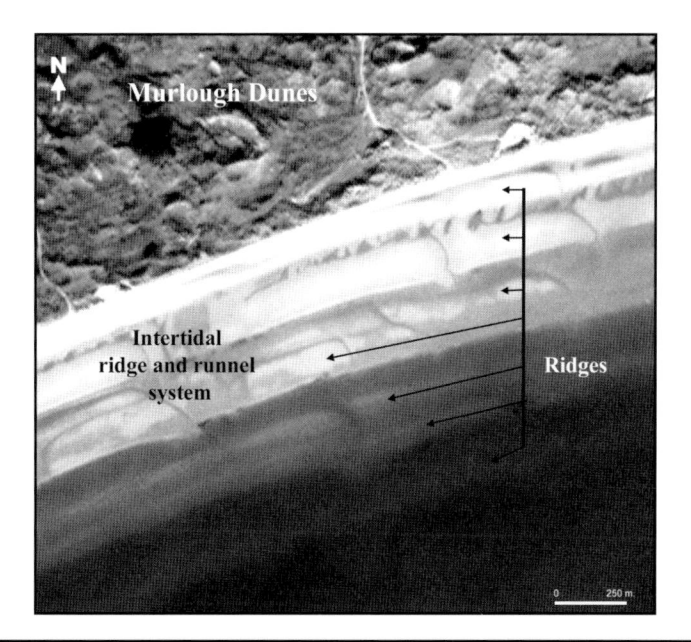

Although the average beach/nearshore slope profile (tan $\alpha=0.0118$) defines the area as a dissipative environment (slope <0.017=dissipative), the upper beach or high tide beach is characterised by a steeper slope (0.0846) and composed generally of coarse material (pebbles and gravel). The lower beach, which is composed of sand (mean grain size 0.37 mm) has a gentle slope (average 0.0078). Sediment grain size on the beach varies from 0.116-0.643 mm which fines seaward. The intertidal zone ranges from 400 m to 900 m in width (measured at low tide). The average width of the surf zone is greater than 1 km under modal wave conditions. The surf-scaling parameter for Dundrum Bay varies between 20 and 200, corresponding to purely dissipative environments.

During the last 150 years a series of events, geomorphological and socio-economic, have coincided in space and time in Dundrum Bay. One of the most marked changes in the system since the mid nineteenth century, has been the accumulation of sediments in the subtidal zone of Dundrum Bay (Fig. 35) which has itself led to changes in wave propagation patterns that in turn have affected the distribution of sediments and associated geomorphology.

An analysis of wave propagation, modelled over mid nineteenth century bathymetric data, has permitted the interpretation of wave-induced circulation (Fig. 36). The analysis showed that the main trend of the wave-induced stress gradients were onshore and towards the southwest. This may imply accumulation of sediment offshore of Newcastle's beach during storms. High energy events are therefore likely to have been the main mechanism for the initialisation of onshore-directed transport on this scale. The initially gentle slope portrayed in the early bathymetric contours (mid

Low Energy Coasts

Fig. 35: 2-D representation of volumetric changes between the 1860's and the 1960's bathymetries in Dundrum Bay, Northern Ireland.

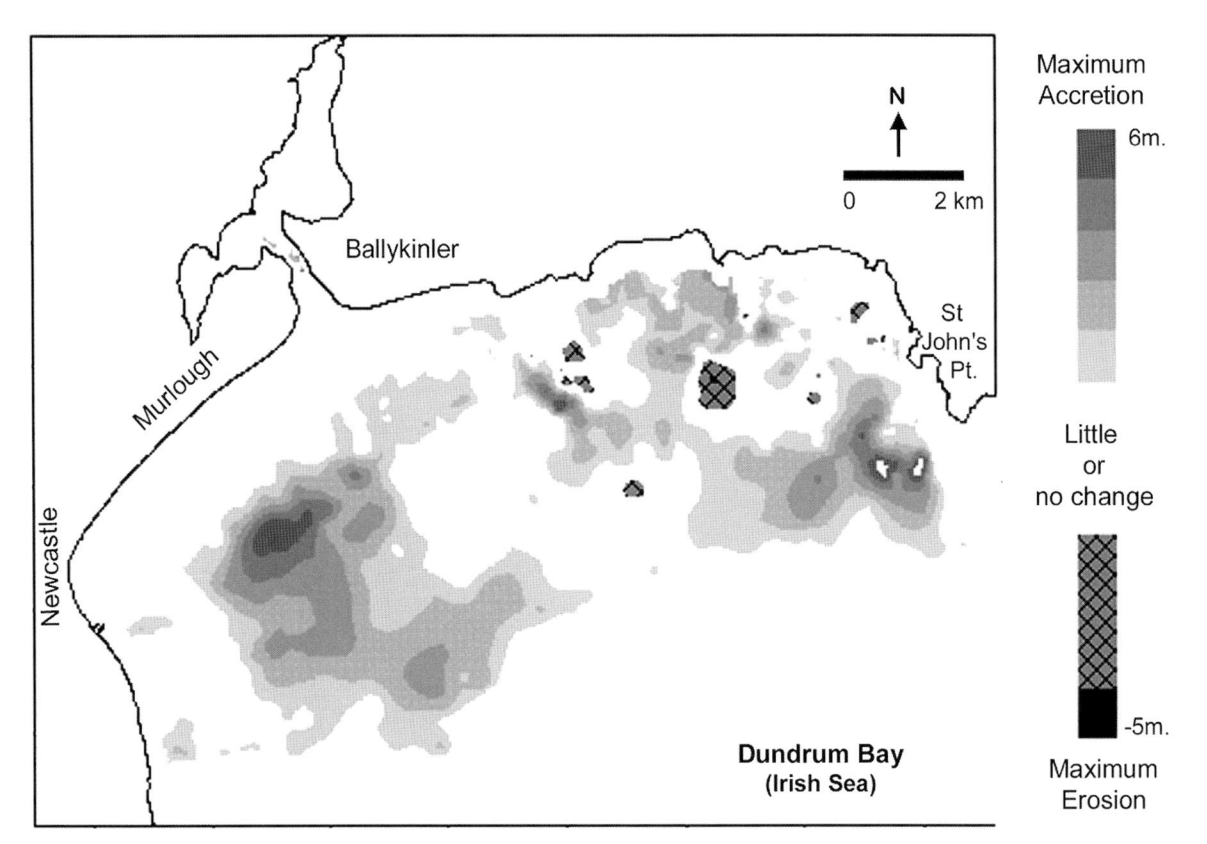

nineteenth century) adjusted storm waves to release energy gradually, thus generating positive gradients and a net southwesterly circulation. This tendency may have influenced changes in the seabed morphology that introduced considerable variations in the patterns of wave refraction in the bay. Simulations of wave propagation over a seabed morphology, generated with later bathymetric data, suggest there may have been a consequent change in direction of the flows of radiation stress which by the end 1960's have assumed a northeasterly direction. This pronounced shift in the directional component of wave forces led to more acute dissipation of energy upon the ebb-tidal delta after the end of the 1800's.

The historical development of Newcastle as a resort commenced around 1830. It should be noted that the above-mentioned bathymetric changes in sea bed topography of the bay occurred after the town of Newcastle was beginning to grow (Fig. 37).

It thus appears that onshore sediment transport processes have dominated deposition in the bay and that this may even have provided the basis for the establishment of the tourist resort at Newcastle which is based mainly on beach use. Approaching the turn of the 19th century, the shift in sediment

Fig. 36: Schematic interpretation of main fluxes of modelled wave-induced stress over 1860s and 1960s bathymetries in Dundrum Bay. Storm waves from southeast.

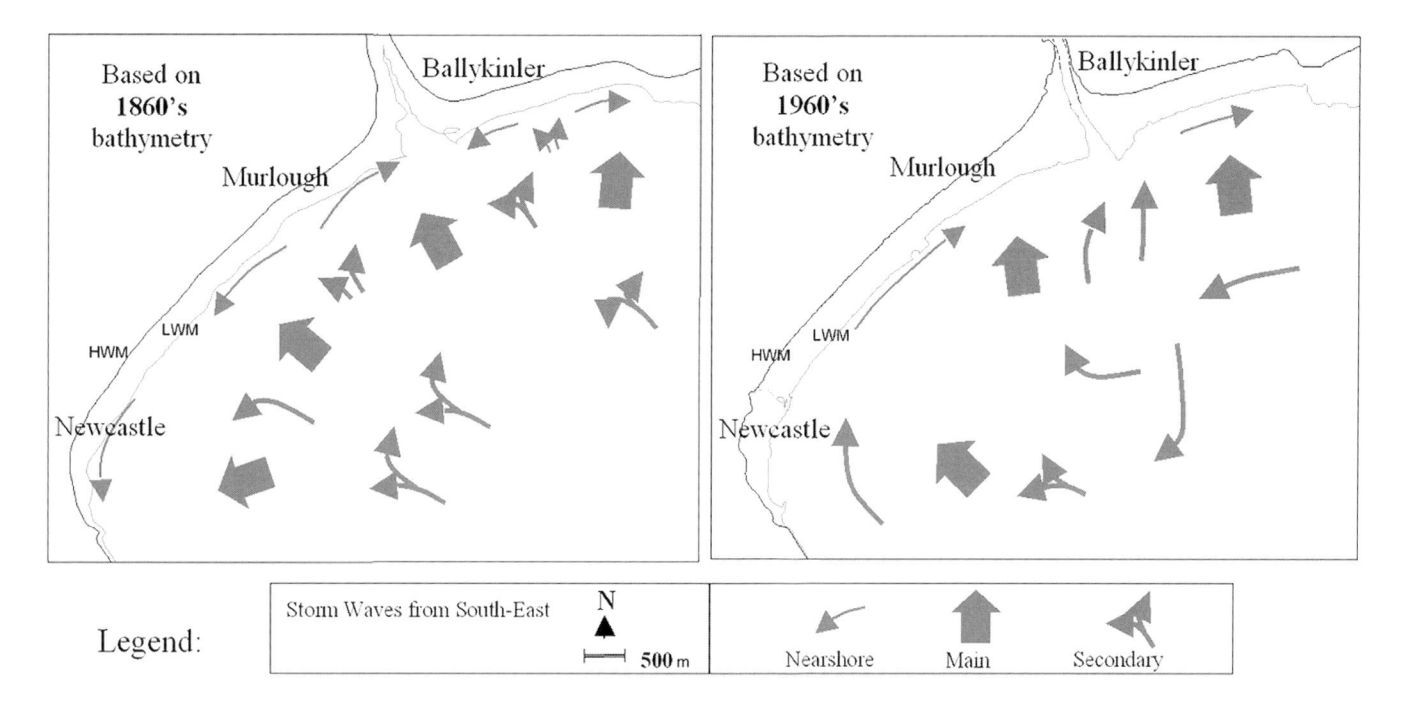

transport patterns to the northwest (as highlighted above in response to changing bathymetry) can be traced by the development of a number of morphological features. Sand transport towards the northeast resulted in the formation of a spit, whose northerly growth started at the Murlough side of the tidal inlet around 1900 (Fig. 38). At the same time, the ebb-tidal delta also migrated towards the northeast, and the Ballykinler side of the inlet grew larger, suggesting sediment transfer from southwest to northeast. This may have been enabled by channel switching such that sediment is transferred from one side of the channel to the other.

During this period of ebb-tidal delta growth, spit formation and changing wave-induced sediment

Fig. 37: The promenade at Newcastle has always been enjoyed by visitors, as shown by this postcard of the 1930s.

Low Energy Coasts

Fig. 38: Shoreline comparison and spit growth

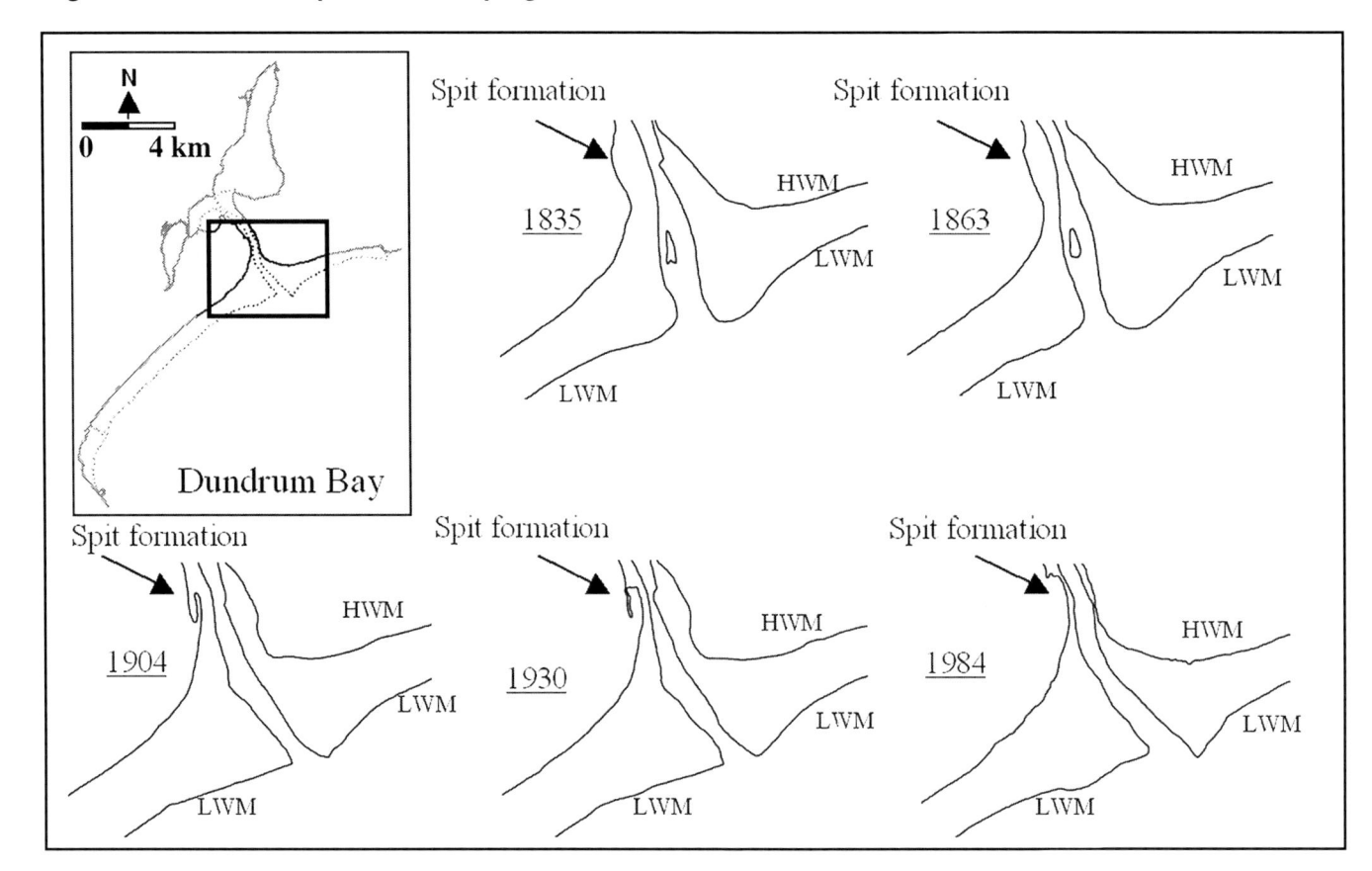

transport patterns, Newcastle continued developing as a tourist resort and it was in the early 1900's when the first losses of sand were noticed and the first shore-protection measures were implemented.

Since the 1930s longshore sediment transport to the northeast continued. Shoreline comparison studies suggest that during this time the spit in the channel at Murlough continued its development. Substantial accretion was also experienced at the shoreline of the Ballykinler area. This may be related to the continued shift of the main tidal channel and associated submerged delta that may be acting to bypass sediments drifting from the southwest areas of the bay, following the general northeasterly longshore drift.

During the 1930s the socio-economic development of Newcastle continued and shore-protection measures were extended, indicating a shortage of sediment at the Newcastle's end of the Bay.

In the 1980s, beach growth continued at Ballykinler, suggesting that northeasterly trend in longshore sediment transport during this time and bypassing of the main tidal channel was well established. This is also shown by the fresh growth of embryo dunes as well as beach and foredune progradation. However, localised erosion occurred at the dunes of the Murlough side of the channel, probably due to reworking of sediments around the submerged delta and lateral movement of the channel. This localised erosion was also manifested at Newcastle, where starvation of sediment appears to have continued to affect the resort during its development.

It appears that during the latter part of the century, and especially after the 1980s, a series of factors contributed to an accentuated erosive sequence of the intertidal beach at Newcastle. The continued development of the sea front promenade and progressive construction of infrastructure and housing seaward culminated with the construction of the Newcastle Centre (Fig. 39). The recreational building was set onto the back-beach and had to be protected with rock armouring. Meteorological data show that the occurrence of storms had been above average of the previous 40 years for the period 1990-1996. The increased wave action that may have accompanied this stormy period appears to have had an impact in the recent evolution of the intertidal beach of Newcastle as hard engineering structures have been constructed.

Although the development of Newcastle as a resort posed problems of erosion in this part of the bay, this should be regarded as a temporal and spatially constrained problem of erosion in a system where sediment has been accumulating overall, both in time and space.

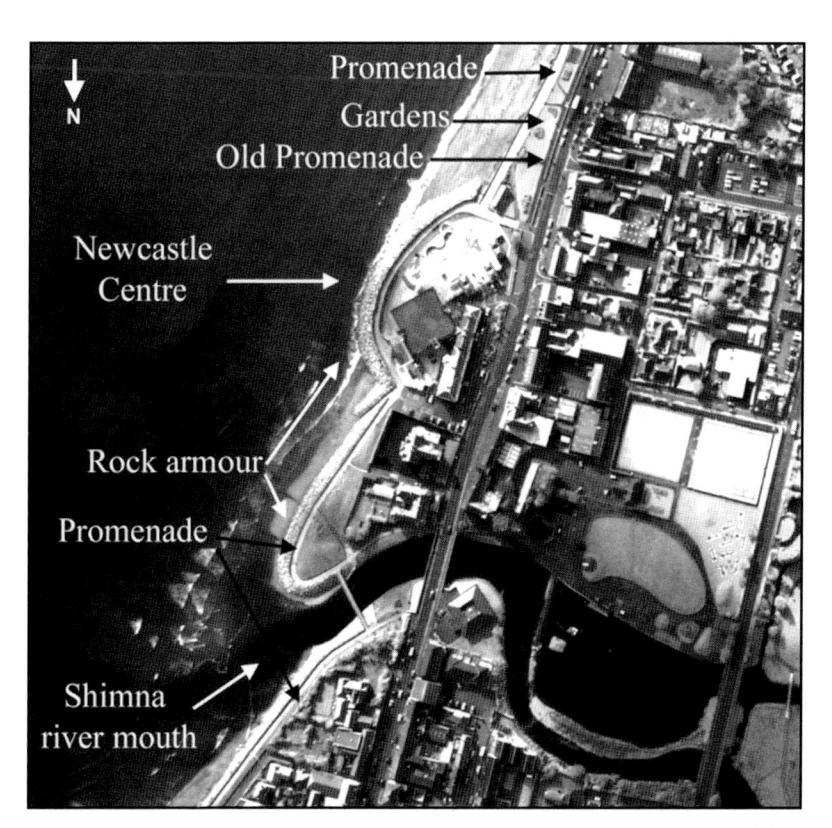

Fig. 39: Aerial photograph of the shorefront of Newcastle, Co. Down.

Coastal zone management at Newcastle, County Down

Joanne Hanna

Introduction

Coastal lands are richly endowed with ecological, conservation, cultural and recreational attributes. Due to their copious qualities it is imperative that they are effectively managed, not only for this generation but also so future generations will experience the same remarkable assemblage of coastal sites as there are today.

In the past, coasts have been taken for granted, ignoring the fact that they have a finite capacity to cope with human activities, to absorb human waste and to offer a sustainable habitat for wildlife. At Newcastle tourism has been the dominant man-induced factor exerting pressure on the coast. Its relatively unplanned nature along the coast has led to inevitable degradation in both the physical and biological environment.

Coastal management to date at Newcastle has lacked co-ordination and sufficient support from a sound scientific background. Too many piecemeal attempts at coastal zone management (CZM) have been employed. A new policy of integration is required, with concerted action at all levels. Within this the local population, the regional and national government and socio-economic factors all have a role to play.

This study is an attempt to orchestrate the requirements for an integrated CZM plan for the Newcastle area. Efficient management should be directed around a strategy based on balanced development which is compatible with the environment. In conjunction with criteria for effective management and with findings from research, recommendations have been made to maintain sustainable levels of use at the coast, while simultaneously improving the state of the coastal environment. The effective management of the coast at Newcastle is of benefit to all its inhabitants, whether the coast provides a place to live, the means of providing a livelihood or a venue for recreation.

Evolving tourism patterns at Newcastle

Over the past century Newcastle has been one of Northern Ireland's most famous seaside resorts. It is situated at the heart of Co. Down in Dundrum Bay. The five mile stretch of beach, although somewhat changed, is still the essence of the resort, and is visited each summer by tourists.

As early as 1837 Newcastle had expanded into a bathing resort, nearly a mile in length, containing several large and handsome dwelling houses, with numerous comfortable and respectable lodging houses (Evans, 1967). The Victorian era brought with it a new-found prosperity, and some called Newcastle the "*Brighton of the North*". By 1869 the establishment of the railway suddenly meant the town was within an hour's journey from Belfast, and very soon people were taking advantage of the cheap trips to the seaside. At the start of the twentieth century concrete promenades were constructed, local facilities were improved and the number of boarding houses in the town rapidly increased. During this period Newcastle enjoyed a boom in tourism, with thousands flocking to its shores each summer. Even in 1983 the shores were packed, with a record amount of people at the beach.

Unfortunately as time has progressed Newcastle has had to adapt to survive the changing trends in tourism, most notably the growth of cheap package holidays to foreign destinations. Emphasis is now being put on other assets the area has to offer, with less attention being focused on the beach. Despite advocating Newcastle as a popular tourist resort, little concerted effort has been made to improve the coastal scene. The town resembles a holiday resort similar to that found in the 1960s. Management now needs to bring Newcastle up-to-date, comparable with a resort of the twenty-first century.

Problems at the coast

Undoubtedly the coast is an intensively used resource. At Newcastle pressures predominantly stem from tourism, and its unplanned characteristics. Over the years new problems have been created and existing ones have snowballed. Before management can be implemented, it is paramount that these current conflicts and incompatibilities within the coastal zone are identified, in order to tailor a management plan to the specific needs of the area.

Areas of perceived conflict at the Newcastle coast include:

- **Uncontrolled development** - Development from tourism has overburdened the natural carrying capacity of the coastal zone, polluting and degrading natural resources, destroying the landscape and reducing the quality of life for locals in the area. Urbanisation directly adjacent to the coast has imposed a fixed structure between the land and sea, creating instability of the coast. Inappropriate development at the coast has undoubtedly increased problems, important habitats have been lost, along with the coast's ability to function properly.

- **Lack of management co-ordination** - In years past there has been a lack of co-ordination between the various authorities involved in management at the coast. Each has operated in isolation of the other, while community participation has been an after-thought. Despite the recognition and the overwhelming importance of co-operation, institutional arrangements have too often been poorly articulated, ineffective and inefficient. Action has been predominantly piecemeal and too thinly spread.

- **Coastal erosion** - Coastal erosion has appeared to be the predominant process operating at the Newcastle coast, and is perceived to be the factor which has transformed the characteristics of the beach, most notably the disappearance of sand. "Solutions" which have attempted to fight the forces of nature have compounded problems while wasting scarce financial resources.

- **Congestion** - Although only a town of 7000 inhabitants during the winter months, these figures are swelled by about 15,000 during the summer. These strong seasonal variations in tourist activity further complicate the management of the coast and introduce the question of feasibility of management for a few months. During these periods of tourist influx local resources can not cope with the increased demand on resources. Roads are congested, traffic is almost brought to a standstill and the town centre and parking facilities adjacent to the coast are inadequate.

- **Coastal degradation** - Despite large crowds visiting the town, the coastal scene is not what it used to be. Facilities are limited, while activities available are minimal. The overall quality of the beach environment is poor, reflecting inadequate maintenance and insufficient upkeep of the coast. Bathing water quality does not reach the same high standards as neighbouring beaches Murlough and Tyrella.

As these problems and conflicts at Newcastle are recognised, appropriate measures must now be identified to improve the situation. Clearly further research will be needed to discover the true extent of these problems and to formulate the best practices which might be employed to prevent such problems escalating.

Coastal defence

There have been numerous attempts of *"hard"* engineering within the bay at Newcastle – none of which have appeared to improve the area, but yet are still being planned for the future. Although protecting the land behind, these measures disrupt the natural functioning of the coastal system and impose an artificial fixed line on a dynamic coast. The old Urban Council was responsible for the original groynes, along with the old section of the promenade and sea wall. Later the Down District Council added various measures to this. They erected more goynes and a 3-phase scheme involving rock armouring, the building of the Newcastle Centre and an extension to the promenade. This took place in the early 1980s, but it quickly made changes to the coast. The rock armouring was a means of sea defence, to dissipate wave energy, protecting the newly built Newcastle Centre. Meanwhile, groynes were installed to trap sand. Rock armouring was also carried out at the harbour to prevent further destruction of the harbour walls.

Coastal protection works of whatever kind can confer only local benefits, and will most likely be harmful to the neighbouring coastline. This is especially the case with groynes; they retain sediment that would have otherwise passed leeward, but instead this area is deprived of sediment and erosion is accelerated. According to Carter (1988) their development is still more of an art than a science. The promenade which doubles as a seawall at Newcastle has saved the land behind from the sea. However, as Williams (1960) stated, *"the construction of a seawall on a sand or shingle foreshore is in itself calculated to bring about the denudation of the beach, and the whole wall may become before long the agent of its own destruction"*. Seawalls introduce a major reflective element into the nearshore zone during storms, which causes sediment to be moved seaward. The seawall provides a static feature, conflicting with the dynamic changes, impeding land-sea sediment exchanges. The rock armouring has had a similar effect around the Newcastle Centre, creating a fixed boundary to the coast and disrupting the natural curve of the shoreline, dividing the bay and altering processes.

The Royal County Down Golf Club situated at the western end of the Murlough dune complex has been responsible for a significant proportion of hard engineering works. In order to protect the golf course timber groynes and a row of protective railway sleepers were installed in the 1930s. Following severe erosion during 1961, a further 3000 sleepers were installed with the aim of absorbing wave energy and trapping shingle along the beach. After significant erosion in February 1990 and January 1991, planning permission was granted to protect three further sections of the dune frontage with rock armouring. This was installed in 1992 and 1993 (Ferguson and McIlveen, 1997).

Following further erosion during the autumn and winter of 1995/1996 the club decided to consider possible courses of further action. Further armouring was proposed, plans were passed, and despite Murlough being an Area of Special Scientific Interest and part of a proposed Special Area of Conservation designated under the EU Habitats Directive, work commenced in 1997.

Erosion is a natural ongoing process and is just one manifestation of shoreline adjustment. Control or regulation of one part of the coastal system may easily lead to negative effects elsewhere on the coast. This is not only difficult to control, but it may fall outside typical human perceptions and outside legislative boundaries of control. According to Carter and Bartlett (1990) CZM should be based on the understanding of coastal processes and not derive from subjective assessments related to the needs of political expediency. The conclusion is that in the long run man can do little to prevent erosion, the forces of nature are too great. Temporary palliatives are possible, but their benefits are short-lived.

Public opinion

A beach perception study, carried out at Newcastle with the intention of deriving management suggestions, assessed preferences and priorities of beach users. A study such as this is useful as it discovers those changes which would be advisable to increase user satisfaction within the beach environment, while still maintaining the quality of the natural features of the coast. For effective beach management, managers should be aware of perceptions of beach users. Unfortunately it is often the case that little information regarding the desires of beach users percolates through the system without effect.

The beach perception study indicated how the public felt the coastal scene had improved very little over the years. There was a general consensus that the beach quality had deteriorated, less sand, more stones, green algae, litter, lower bathing water quality etc. The lack of sand on Newcastle beach was an issue of much concern for beach users. Facilities and activities improved little over the years, despite the importance placed upon them by beach users. Overall findings suggest management schemes need to enhance the attractive qualities of the area to ensure its survival, and to check the unacceptable problems before further deterioration occurs.

A questionnaire which was sent to local people influenced by tourism in Newcastle (e.g. those within the accommodation sector, recreational facilities, restaurants, members of the *Newcastle 2000* committee), also reiterated a lot of what was observed in the beach perception study. There was widespread opinion that tourism had degraded over the years. While facilities and activities remained relatively unchanged over the years the beach quality degraded. There was a general consensus that the upkeep of the coastal zone had been poor. It was felt future management was essential regarding bathing water quality, pollution on the beach and safety provisions. Sentiment was particularly high concerning the diminishing amount of sand, with much uncertainty regarding the implementation of future coastal protection. Proposals for future development at the coast were safe swimming and play areas, designated watersport areas, upgrading of facilities etc. It was felt efforts should be made to clean the beach, and to ensure that sand and water quality is maintained at a high standard. Although all recommendations could not possibly be enforced, there are many suggestions which could be taken on board.

Recommendations for management at Newcastle

On the basis of evidence observed a management plan is required to begin the process of Integrated CZM at Newcastle. Management is imperative to improve the coast, increase tourist appeal and generally enhance the natural quality of the Newcastle coastal area. The need for management arises from the significance of the coast's ecology and the use made of the site by people for recreation and amenity.

Careful and effective planning is required in order to achieve a sustainable and productive management strategy. Natural resources need to be maintained, physical processes disrupted as little as possible, while human uses should be managed in the most sustainable ways. Management should aim to balance policies for conservation and those for development to a point where one does not hinder the other. Throughout the management process all parties with an interest in the coast should have the responsibility, through successful and innovative partnership, to care for and manage the coast's assets for future generations.

In order for management to be effective, it must follow the principles of good CZM, as outlined by the EU (1999):

- Take a wide-ranging perspective
- Build on an understanding of specific conditions in the area of interest
- Work with the natural processes of the area
- Ensure that decisions taken today do not foreclose options for the future
- Use participatory planning to develop consensus
- Ensure the support and involvement of all relevant bodies
- Use a combination of instruments

It is recommended that integration will be the key to effective management. Co-operation and participation of all the relevant stakeholders will be required for this. It appears that there is presently a limited amount of consultation and co-operation among the various authorities involved, which has led to the development of piecemeal attempts of coastal management along the coast. It is suggested that all levels of government, private parties and the public must get involved in the decision-making process, all aiming for the same goals in a concerted programme of action.

Unlike management in the past, future decisions will need to take account of the physical processes which operate at the coast. The coast is a very dynamic system and previous attempts of hard engineering at the coast do not appear to have recognised this. Consequently changes have been imposed on the coast and new problems have been created. Natural controls such as the hydrodynamic regime and the sediment circulation system will in the future be integrated into management decisions. What is required of the coastal managers is *"the ability to integrate planning of the physical aspects of coastal change with those human aspects... that define and drive the need for coastal management"* (Orford, 1992).

Proposed management strategies include:
- **Recreational zoning plan:** Increased activities for beach users, zoning of water-borne activities safe play areas etc.

- **Facility improvement plan:** Beach safety provisions, litter facilities increased, basic amenities upgraded and better kept.

- **Beach improvement scheme:** Improved cleanliness, sustained programme to spruce up Newcastle's coastal image, sand replenishment, higher standards of water quality.

- **Conservation initiatives:** Maintain the physical system in as natural a state as possible, maintain and enhance the natural beauty of the coast, seek environmentally sensitive and resilient solutions, make conservation objectives clear to the public.

It is advised that future management of the coast at Newcastle be centred on achieving sustainability. To accomplish this the quality of the natural environment must to maintained and enhanced, while simultaneously allowing a sustainable amount of economic development. The coastal resource is finite in physical and spatial terms, decisions taken by managers now must not foreclose options for the future, but rather ensure that a high quality natural environment will be present for future generations to enjoy.

Conclusions

Over the years man has added to the long-term changes of the coast at Newcastle. He has acted against the forces of nature, which would otherwise have operated towards dynamic equilibrium of the coast. Most frequently these changes have been inflicted by imposing inflexible structures within the coastal zone, which have exerted a fixed line on a dynamic system. Planning of the coastal zone has been inappropriately designed in the past, with little consideration given to the natural functioning of the system. Due to increased rates of erosion and degradation of the general coastal environment, tourism has suffered and the once thriving holiday destination is gradually losing its tourist appeal.

At present management along the coast is fragmented with landowners/managers including Local Authorities, the National Trust and the Royal County Down Golf Club. This limited amount of consultation and co-operation is hastening the speed of degradation at the coast. All the relevant stakeholders now need to come together and develop policies consistent with effective integrated CZM. Management must balance development and human use, within the limits set by the natural dynamics and carrying capacity of the coastal system. The coastal zone at Newcastle does have immense potential, and through effective management this can be achieved. It is anticipated that coastal managers will eliminate current conflicts and incompatibilities, and will redevelop a coast which works with the natural processes, reinstating a coast which is enjoyed by its users, all within the limits of sustainable utilisation.

High Energy Coasts

Quaternary events and history on the northern coastal fringes of Ireland

Marshall McCabe

Introduction

The Quaternary record along the north coast of Ireland is dominated by glacial deposits mostly dating from the last (Devensian) ice sheet termination. However records of pre-Devensian glaciations are fragmentary and based on erratic distributions and diamicts identified from drill or well-cores. In some cases multiple glaciations are based on lithofacies evidence alone (e.g. Colhoun, 1971). Stratigraphic data from lowlands in central and southern Ulster show early and middle Devensian deposits which record an early glaciation separated from the late Devensian glaciation by shallow-water detrital organic deposits (Colhoun *et al.*, 1972) (Figs. 40, 41). At Aghnadarragh near Lough Neagh geochronological data suggest that part of this climatic amelioration occurred during oxygen substage 5 (Bowen, 1999).

Understanding the history of the last ice sheet in the British Isles at the last glacial maximum (LGM) and during its termination has been advanced by new approaches, in particular, by cosmogenic nuclide surface-exposure dating, aminostratigraphy of shelly glacial deposits, and AMS radiocarbon dating (Bowen *et al.*, 2002). Many believed that the British Isles was mainly ice free between oxygen isotope substage 5e and the late Devensian when the LGM occurred. As such the British ice sheet was out of phase with marine and ice core records and other large ice sheets in western Europe. Recent cosmogenic and AMS dates now show that the British ice sheet was sensitive to changes in the North Atlantic with a pattern of pulses followed by extensive deglaciations from neighbouring continental shelves (Bowen *et al.*, 2002). Contrary to current opinions it seems as if the British ice sheet existed and was mobile throughout the Devensian period.

In the north of Ireland radiometric dates from Co Donegal suggest that the last ice sheet withdrew from the continental shelf around 22 kyr BP. Marine muds exposed at the head of Trawbreaga Bay record this ice-free interval along this coastal segment earlier than 17 kyr BP, which agrees precisely with the evidence for extensive early deglaciation of the continental shelf first identified by McCabe *et al.* (1986). This interstadial is termed the Cooley Point interstadial (McCabe and Haynes, 1996) and is recorded by dated sediments from widely separated sectors of the last ice sheet in the west, north and most especially on the margins of the Irish Sea Basin (McCabe and Clark, 1998). Importantly, the Irish Sea basin was a major drainage conduit for ice draining southwards from neighbouring land masses (Eyles and McCabe 1989). The interstadial is also dated by cosmogenic surface exposure dating around Rasharkin near Coleraine to 15 kyr BP (Bowen *et al.*, 2002). Subsequent ice sheet advance is recorded by ice overriding and deformation of marine muds at Corvish in Trawbreaga Bay sometime between 15 and 14 kyr BP. Again this

Fig. 40: (A) Possible correlations of litho-and bio-stratigraphic units of Midlandian age in Ulster. Dots indicate known unconformities (after McCabe, 1987). **(B)** An outline curve to indicate general temperature oscillations and major events during the Midlandian cold stage (modified from Mitchell, 1976).

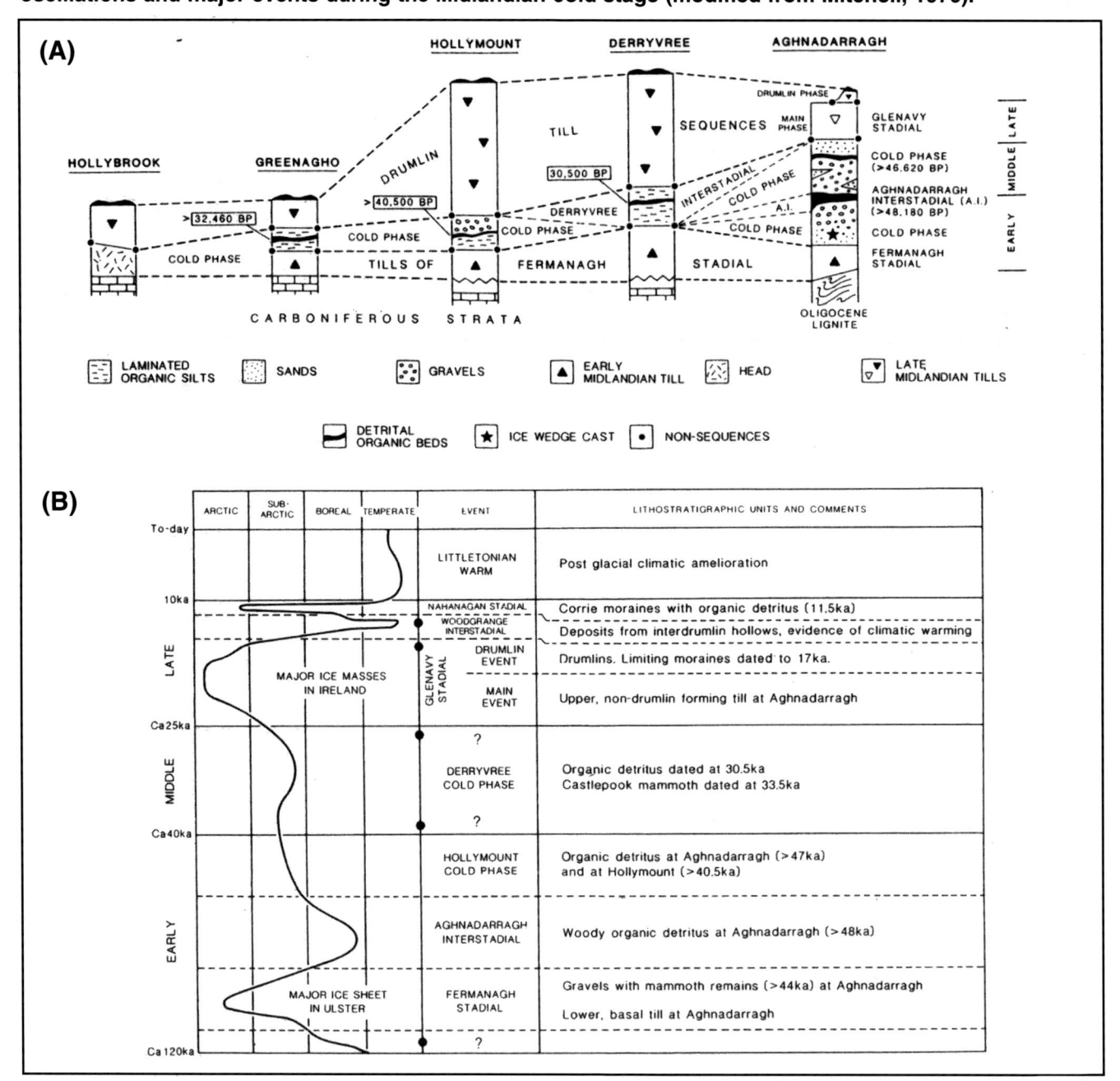

event can be identified from all of the marginal sectors of the ice sheet in Ireland and in the Irish Sea basin where ice readvance peaked around 14 kyr BP. McCabe and Clark (1998) and McCabe *et al.* (1998) for the first time have shown that last British ice sheet participated in the Heinrich event 1 iceberg discharge episode, and suggested links within the atmosphere-ocean-ice system of the amphi-North Atlantic. This millennial time-scale variability allows correlations to be made in a North Atlantic context, but further dating programmes are necessary to better constrain the emerging chronology. The main glacigenic sediment formations preserved in the north of Ireland can now be placed tentatively and discussed within the above chronological framework.

Previous work

Investigations on the glacial history of the north coast began with the publications of Dwerryhouse (1923) and later by Charlesworth (1939). These workers evaluated earlier mapping work by the Geological Survey and related the distribution of glacigenic landforms in terms of ice sheet advances followed by deglacial chronologies based on ice dammed lakes. More recent studies summarized by Stephens *et al.* (1975) question the extent of Scottish ice in Co Antrim and relate lithofacies in the Carey valley (near Ballycastle) to varying strengths of southern and North Channel/Scottish ice. They and others (e.g. Hill and Prior, 1968; Prior, 1970) recognised the former presence of a discrete ice cap on the Antrim hills and valley glaciers in Glendunn and Glenaan, though they did not explain the temporal relationship to the regional ice masses. They did not recognise the Antrim Coast readvance ice limits drawn by Dwerryhouse (1923) and Charlesworth (1939, 1963, 1973). However this criticism may be premature because we now know that the last termination was punctuated by ice sheet oscillations and there is firm stratigraphic evidence from Ballyrudder on the east coast of Antrim that a phase of non-glacial conditions was followed by deposition of a till sheet on the flanks of the large rotational slumps at Ballygalley (Praeger, 1895; McCabe, 1999). It is also certain that the last incursion of Scottish ice onto the north coastal lowlands which reached Armoy and Ballymoney (Stephens *et al.*, 1975) must also have had a related component moving south along the east coast of Antrim (Fig. 41). This pattern, driven from the large centres of ice sheet dispersion in western Scotland and comprising a westward movement across north Antrim and a southward one in east Antrim, is a more probable ice sheet geometry than the current notion of an exclusive movement to the Armoy line (cf. McCabe *et al.*, 1999). If this is the case the North Channel would be filled with ice and parts of Ayrshire may provide records of this event.

Main events and glacial stratigraphy

1. Bovevagh Formation (Irish Grid Reference C668140). The stratotype comes from Bovevagh Old Church which is located south of Limavady about 12 km inland at 60 m OD. Sediments here were recognised by Portlock (1843) and considered by Colhoun (1971) to represent marine deposits reworked and transported by ice from Scottish sources. The exposed part of the formation consists of very poorly-sorted beds of cobble, and pebble gravel which are interbedded with fossiliferous marine muds (Fig. 42). Contacts between the rapidly changing lithofacies are conformable but there is not enough of the exposure available to decide whether or not the succession is in situ or transported. Elsewhere on the lowlands bordering

Fig. 41: General ice sheet movements in Ulster during the Midlandian Cold Stage and location of sub-till organic beds (after McCabe, 1987).

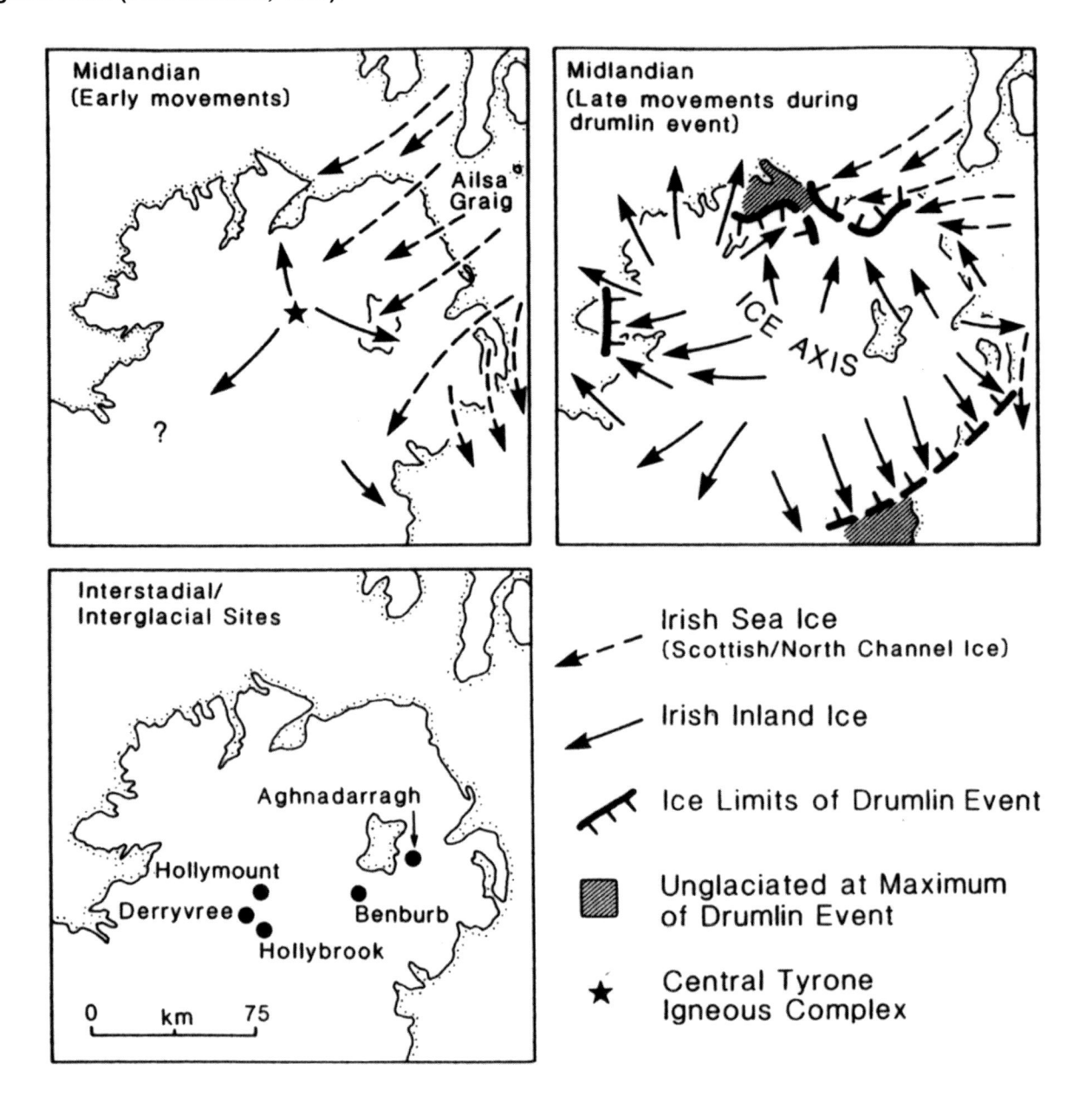

Lough Foyle there is a buried stratigraphy with a wide range of muddy to sandy diamicts which contain marine shell fragments and variable microfaunal assemblages. The age of these lithofacies is poorly constrained but are generally thought to be older than the last glaciation (McCarron, 2001). A ^{14}C date of 45,262 (SSR 4781) was obtained from whole valves of *Turritella communis* collected from Bovevagh Old Church (McCabe, 1999). However it is possible that much of the shelly lithofacies which underlie the late Devensian stratigraphy in the Dungiven Basin has been tectonically influenced by the last ice sheet to variable extents. As outlined above the restricted nature of most exposures does not permit accurate assessments to be made of the sediment geometry. A general conclusion suggests that the shelly facies around Dungiven represent the effects of a major incursion of Scottish ice onto northern coastal fringes with deep isostatic depression. The resulting marine and glaciomarine facies were subsequently overrun by late Devensian ice.

2. Late Midlandian at its maximum. Ice flows at this time are based on the alignments of drumlins, streamlined rock-ridges, striations and erratic/till carriage. In most accounts ice flows originate in centres of ice dispersion to the south in the Omagh basin and in the Lough Neagh basin (Colhoun, 1970). In the Dungiven area Colhoun (1970) recognised that the Gelvin Till was deposited by this ice flow. Generally the ice flows at this phase were northward and ended on the continental shelf. Striae and small-scale roches moutonnées on the foreshore at Portballintrae record this ice flow onto the shelf (McCabe *et al.*, 1994). However it is difficult to separate some of these basalt-rich tills from similar facies deposited during later ice sheet activity.

3. Ice sheet activity during Heinrich Event 1. The distribution of drumlins and location of prominent lines of terminal outwash/moraines in north Counties Antrim and Londonderry are thought to represent complex ice sheet movements from both Irish and Scottish centres of ice dispersion towards the end of the last glacial termination (Fig. 43). It is

Fig. 42: Temporary exposure at Bovevagh Old Church, Co Londonderry (A.M. McCabe, unpublished).

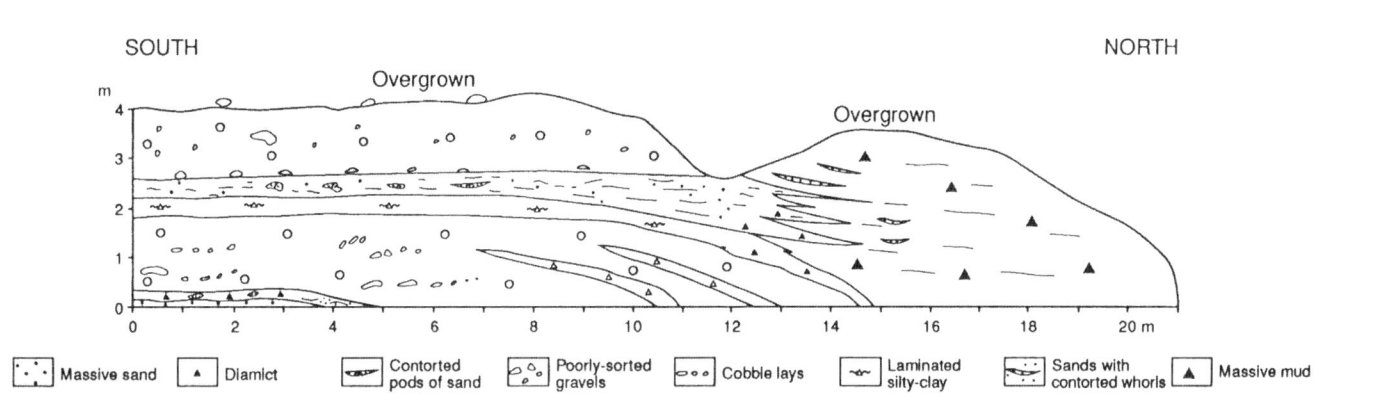

Fig. 43: Relationships between subglacial bedforms and the Armoy moraine, north Co Antrim. Note that the subglacial streamlined landforms maintain a similar orientation on both sides of the moraine (McCabe et al., 1998).

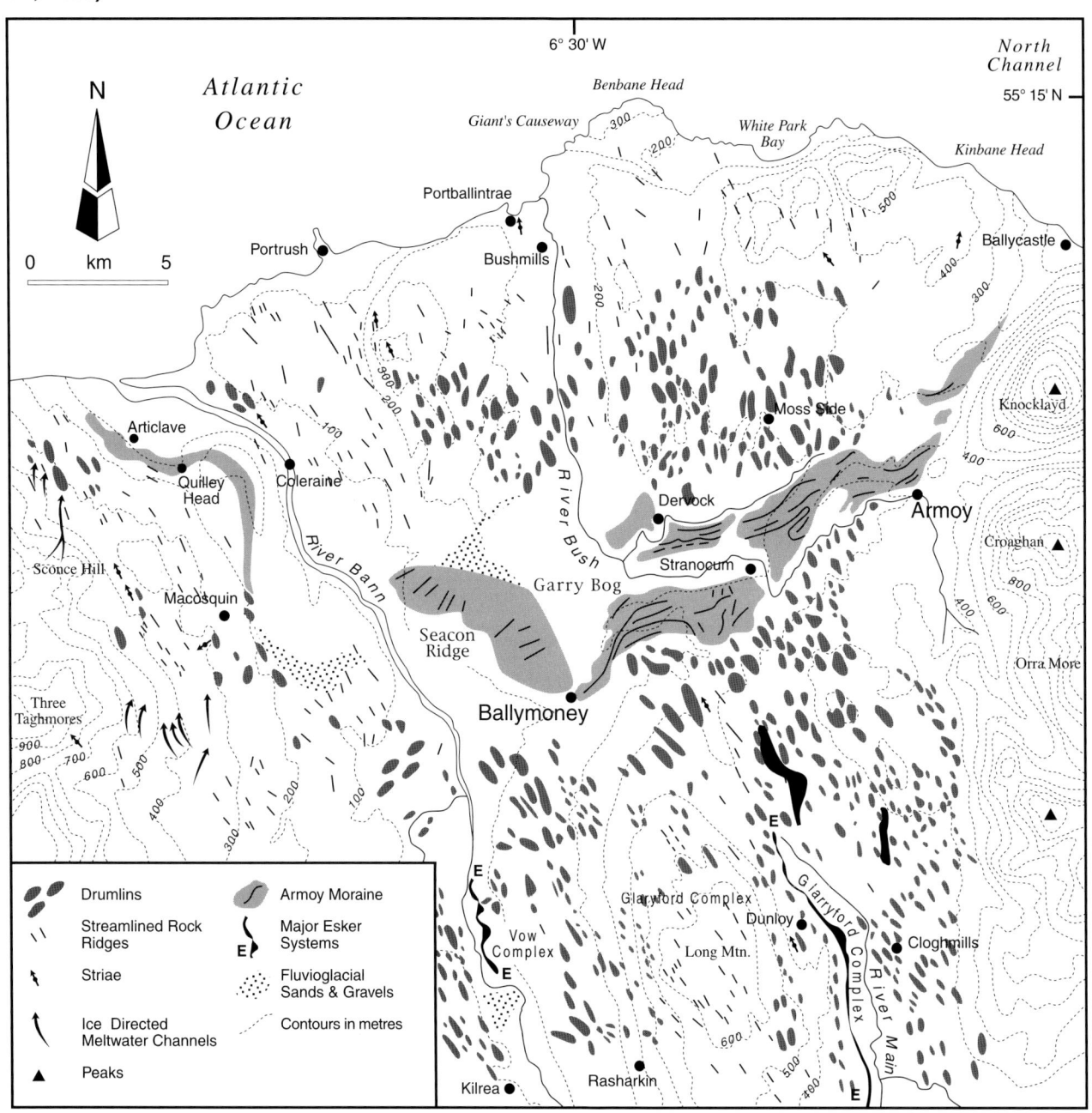

argued that these events occurred around 14 kyr BP because they represent the only regional ice sheet advance following the LGM and immediately preceding the Loch Lomond Stadial (Younger Dryas) which is documented from the western Highlands (Sissons, 1979) (Fig. 44). In the Inishowen Peninsula, 50 km west of Coleraine, marine muds at Corvish record a major deglaciation of the continental shelf prior to 17 kyr BP followed by an ice advance from the mountains into the fjords of north Donegal, followed by deglaciation after 14 kyr BP (McCabe, unpublished data). Similar patterns and events are dated in the Irish Sea area and in the west of Ireland (McCabe et al., 1998) (Fig. 45).

Field evidence from detailed mapping shows similar regional patterns in the Dungiven basin and in the north Antrim area. These basins are separated by the western part of the Tertiary basalt uplands which form steep scarps facing into both basins and facing north at Binevenagh (373 m OD) (Fig. 46). These uplands trend north/south and clearly influenced the ice sheet marginal configuration especially where the ice was thin.

Dungiven Basin. Terminal outwash ridges and spreads of sand and gravel are present around Ballykelly and on the northern slopes of Keady Mountain and Springwell Forest (Fig. 46). These deposits are thought to represent a series of ice marginal settings including deltaic, subglacial tunnel venting and tectonic deformation with sectional shortening. The westward slope of the feature from 240 m OD at Dunbeg (near Springwell Forest) to around 60 m OD at The Moys shows that the ice sheet source was from the east. This inference is also supported by erratic carriage in till associated with this ice advance beneath the gravel ridges at Sistrakeel (Fig. 47). McCarron (2001) has also documented extensive deformation of the Triassic bedrock which floors the Curly river near Lady O'Cahan's Bridge. The deformed rock directly underlies the morainic gravels at Dunbeg and is interpreted as ice marginal thrusting when the ridges formed along the northern slopes of Keady Mountain. Deep river sections at Sistrakeel and Ballyrisk provide farther evidence of ice sheet thrusting, deformation and erratic carriage from the northeast (Figs. 47, 48). The progressive upward deformation of proglacial sediments at Ballyrisk clearly records ice overriding proglacial successions with eventual homogenisation and till deposition. The Sistrakeel sediments contain evidence for the carriage of slices of the former sea bed muds (derived from the Malin Sea) which contain macrofaunas older than 45 kyr BP. Because this fauna is mixed, amino acid ratios suggest that the youngest faunal elements are late Devensian in age (Bowen et al., 2002). In addition, these sediments seem to have been emplaced against an old cliff line immediately downstream from Sistrakeel Bridge (Fig. 47). The presence of erratics of Tertiary basalt in the thick basal till immediately above the transported marine muds confirms ice transport from the east. The nearest basalt outcrop occurs on the slopes of Binevenagh, 11 km to the east. It is also evident that erosion of the basalt scarp at this time by westward moving ice destabilised the basalt slopes by undercutting resulting in large, rotational landslips. It is therefore suggested that the hummock and ridge topography from Keady Mountain south-westwards to Ballykelly represents the limit of ice which originated in western Scotland and moved over the bed of the Malin Sea into the Lough Foyle lowlands. The tills, transported marine muds and bedrock deformation below the morainic

Fig. 44: Generalised ice flows and ice limits during the Heinrich event 1 readvance in northern Britain (~ 14 ^{14}C kyr BP). The extent of ice during the later Loch Lomond Stadial (Benn, 1997) and other ice limits on the continental shelf at the last glacial maximum are also shown. H1 ice limits in Scotland are poorly constrained. It is likely that ice advanced into the North Sea during the H1 event and that ice limits on land represent the decay and stabilisation/re-equilibriation of various ice lobes especially along the firths of eastern Scotland (modified from McCabe et al., 1998).

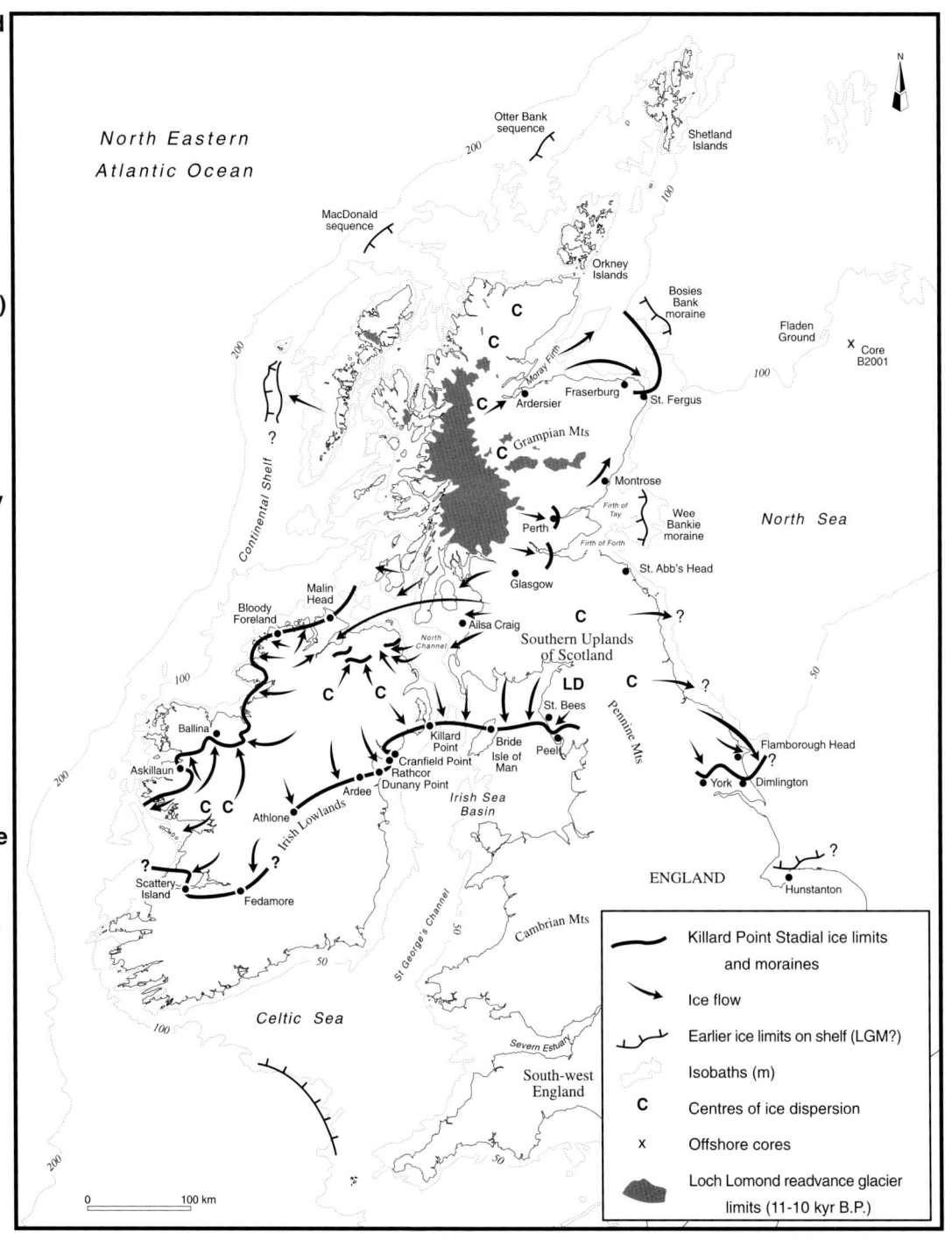

Fig. 45: Cartoon of the glacigenic system operating during the Killard Point Stadial in the northern Irish Sea Basin showing the relationships between subglacial bedforms, dated marine muds, lithostratigraphy, relative sea-level and terminal outwash (from McCabe et al., 1998).

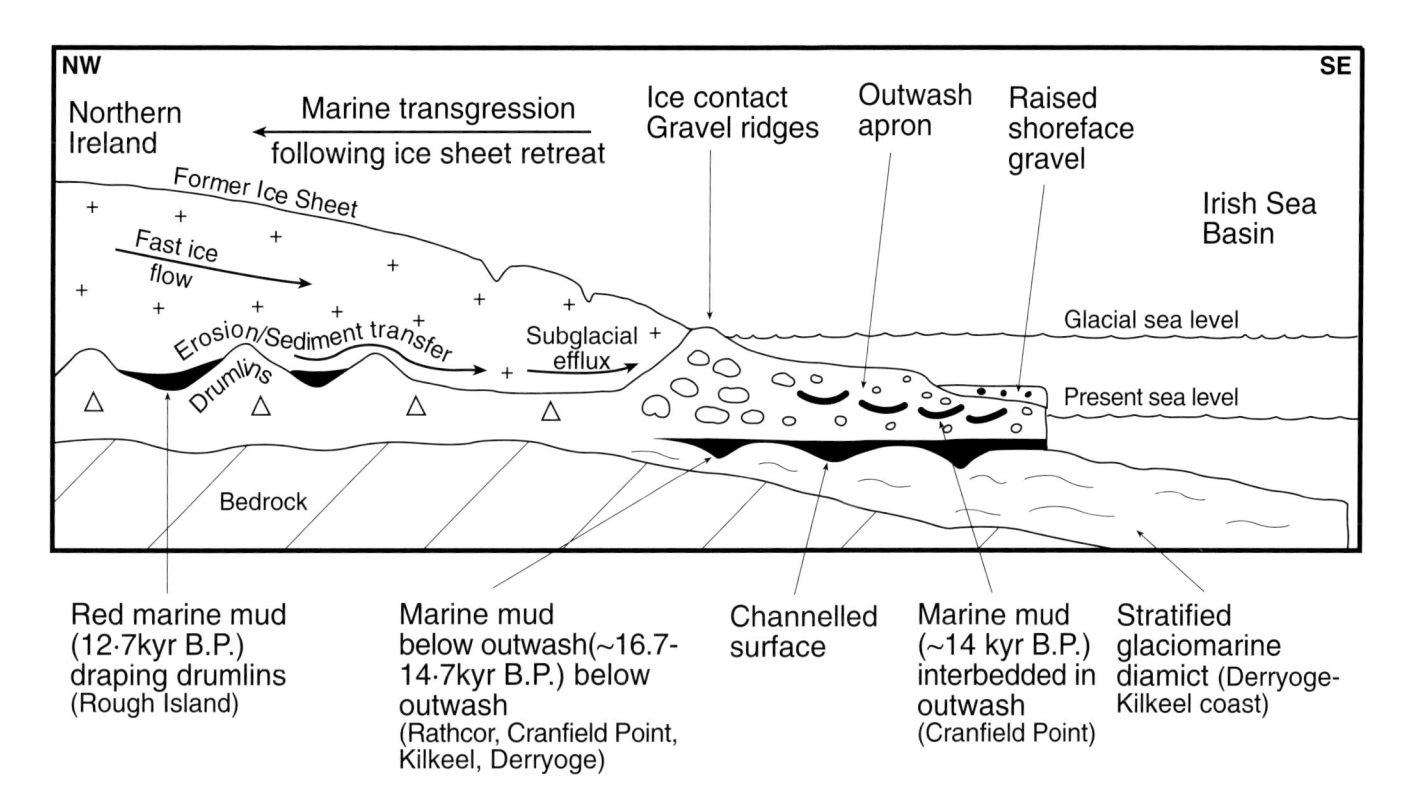

deposits are the subglacial component of this ice sheet readvance.

The phasing relations between this readvance from Scotland and ice from Irish sources can be constrained from morphological evidence in the southern part of the Dungiven depression (Fig. 46). Ice contact and extraglacial deltas up to 240 m OD in the upper Roe and Faughan valleys record the presence of a major ice dammed lake in these valleys. Directional indicators associated with these deltas show that ice originated on the lowlands to the south of the Sperrin Mountains and was only strong enough to feed through the cols along the southern rim of the Dungiven depression (Fig. 49). Because the Dungiven depression opens northwards into Lough Foyle, the only recorded ice sheet which could have blocked this meltwater outlet was the one which formed the Ballykelly moraine (Fig. 46). This close field relationship of ice marginal positions, lake bodies in the northward facing valleys and delta distribution shows contemporaneity between maximum positions of Scottish and Irish ice advances in this area. A critical inference is that separate centres of ice sheet

Fig. 46: Glacial landforms and evidence for Killard Point Stadial ice limits around Lough Foyle. (A) Generalised ice flows in the areas bordering Lough Foyle during the H1 event. (B) Glacigenic landforms on the Foyle lowlands and Dungiven depression. Contemporaneous ice sheet limits are recorded at Ballykelly (Scottish ice) and along the northern margins of the Sperrin Mountains (Irish ice).

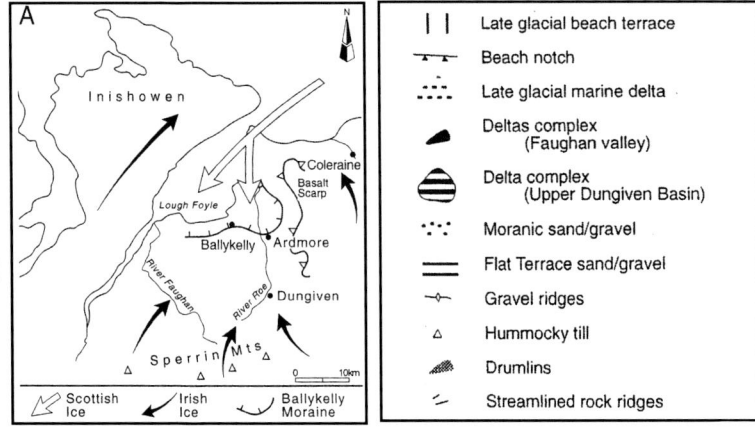

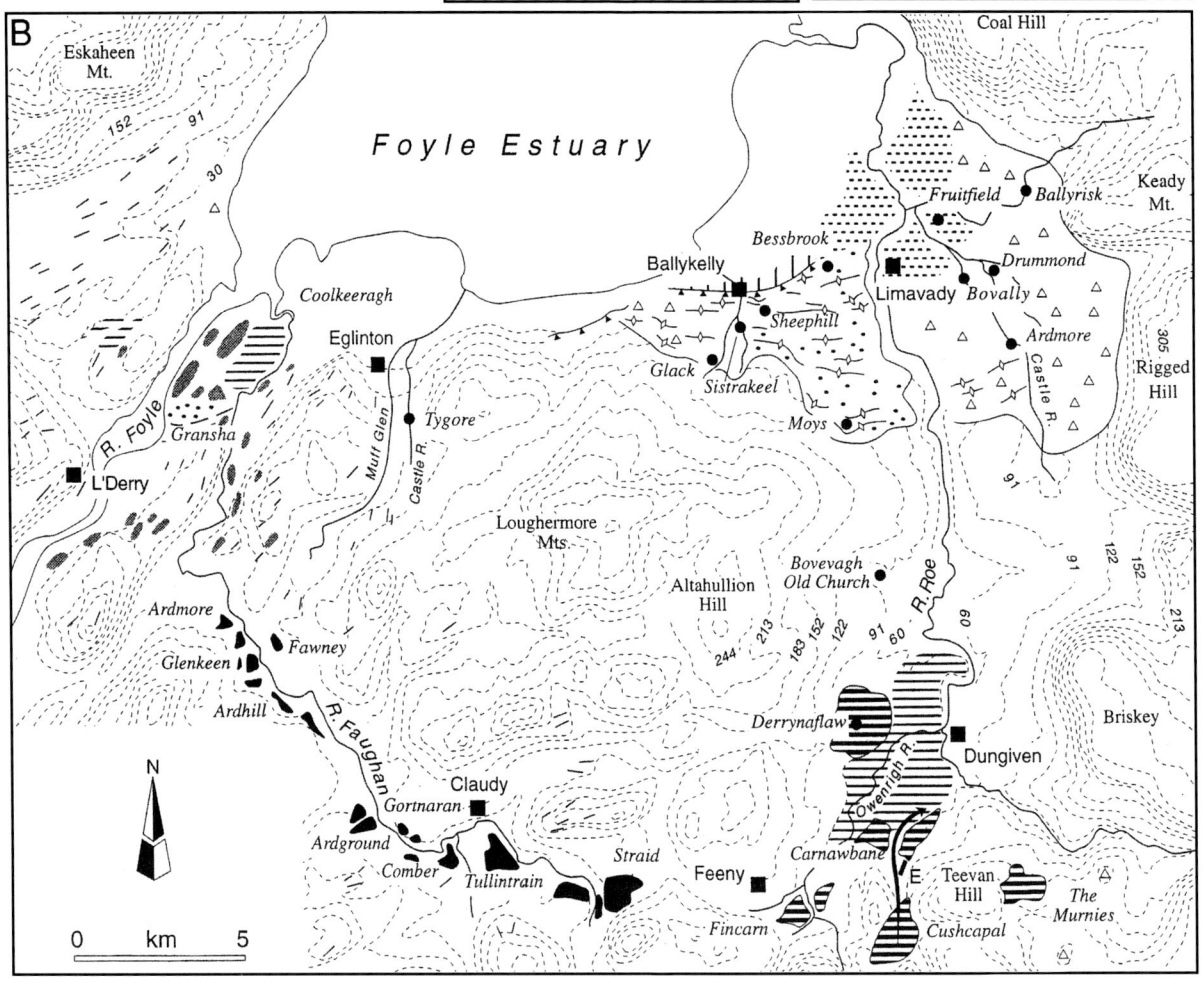

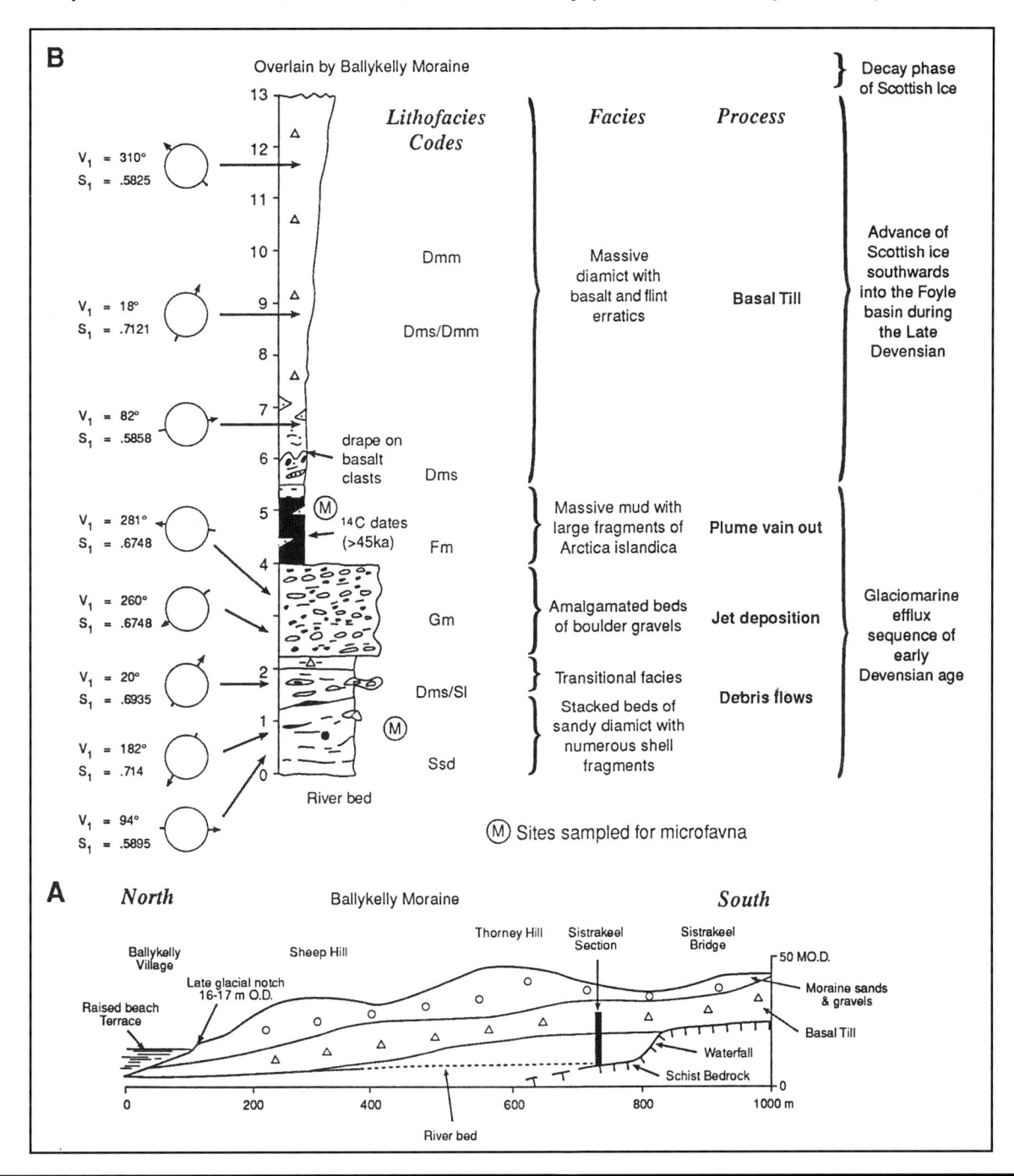

Fig. 47: Exposure in river bank, Sistrakeel, Co Londonderry (A.M. McCabe, unpublished).

Fig. 48: Exposure in river bank, Ballyrisk, Co Londondery (A.M. McCabe, unpublished).

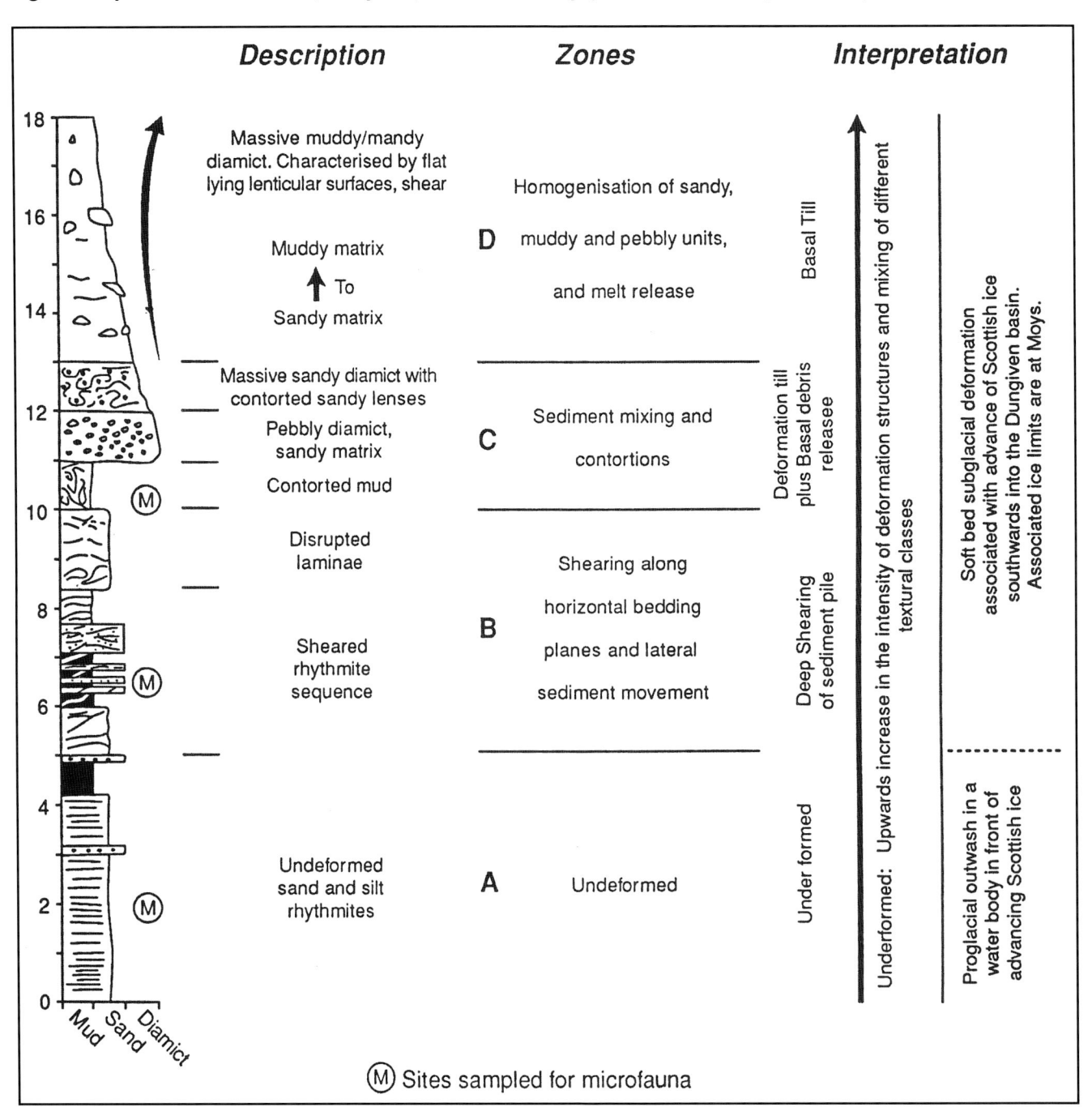

Description	Zones	Interpretation
Massive muddy/sandy diamict. Characterised by flat lying lenticular surfaces, shear. Muddy matrix ↑ To Sandy matrix	D — Homogenisation of sandy, muddy and pebbly units, and melt release	Basal Till
Massive sandy diamict with contorted sandy lenses. Pebbly diamict, sandy matrix. Contorted mud	C — Sediment mixing and contortions	Deformation till plus Basal debris release
Disrupted laminae. Sheared rhythmite sequence	B — Shearing along horizontal bedding planes and lateral sediment movement	Deep Shearing of sediment pile
Undeformed sand and silt rhythmites	A — Undeformed	Under formed

Underformed: Upwards increase in the intensity of deformation structures and mixing of different textural classes

Soft bed subglacial deformation associated with advance of Scottish ice southwards into the Dungiven basin. Associated ice limits are at Moys.

Proglacial outwash in a water body in front of advancing Scottish ice

Ⓜ Sites sampled for microfauna

Fig. 49: Extraglacial deltas and glacial landforms in the upper Dungiven Basin (after McCarron, 2001).

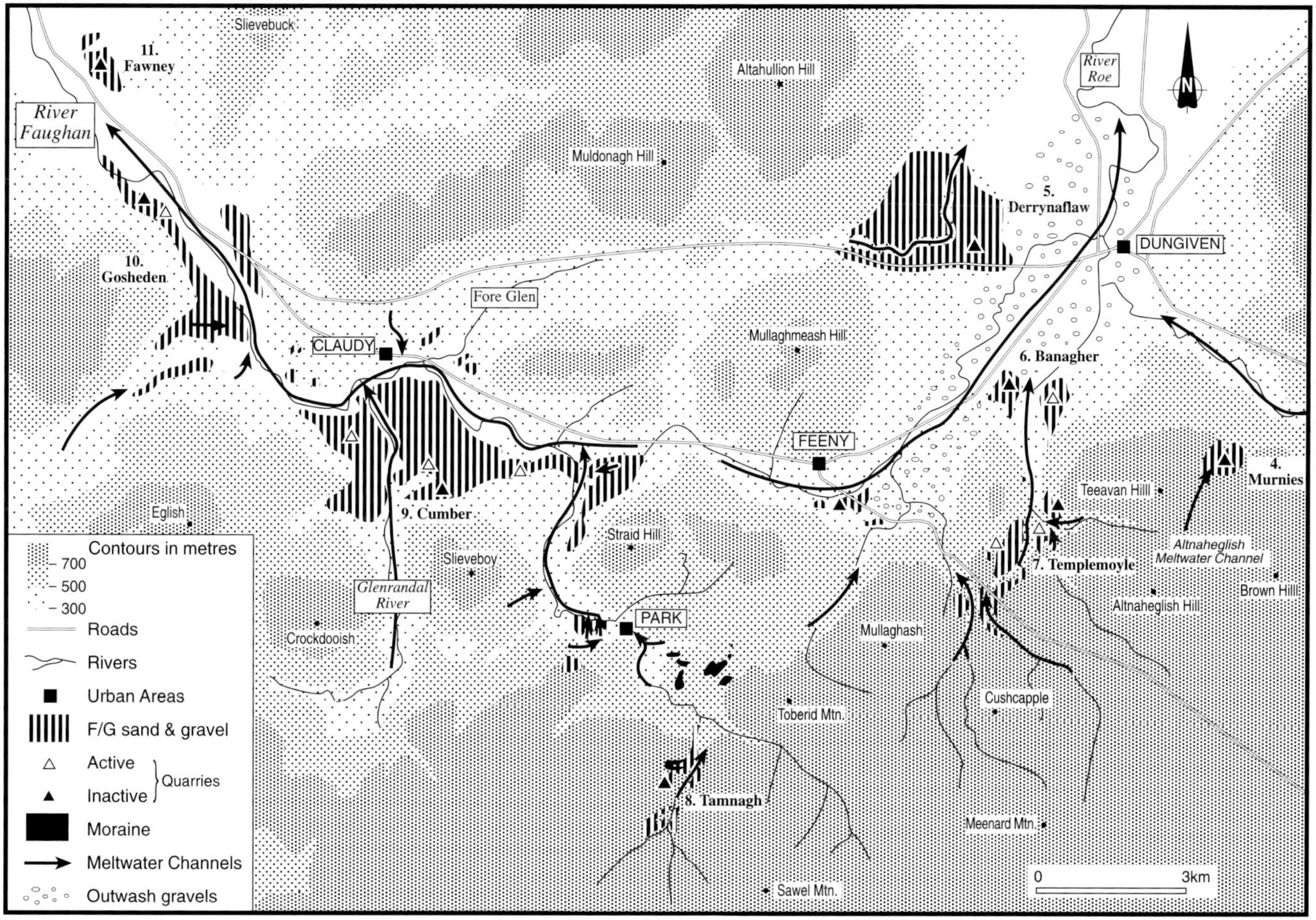

dispersion in western Scotland and in the lowlands of north central Ireland reacted to the same climate signal during Heinrich event 1 (Fig. 44).

These two penecontemporaneous phases of ice sheet activity undoubtedly followed the extensive deglaciation of the northwestern European continental shelf which dates to before 17 kyr BP (McCabe *et al.*, 1986). An interesting corollary to the phasing relationships and renewed growth of ice in the lowlands of north central Ulster is the extent of deglaciation on the lowlands at 17 kyr BP. The fact that the latest ice sheet advance northwards across the Sperrin Mountains could only reach the margins of the Dungiven depression suggests a very extensive deglaciation (Cooley Point Interstadial), possibly leaving a series of ice domes at the original centres of ice dispersion. Detailed mapping supported by AMS ^{14}C dates show that the ice could only reach the coastal margins in eastern, northern and western ice sheet sectors (McCabe et al., 1998) (Fig. 44).

North Co Antrim/Bann Valley. In north Co Antrim another line of morainic ridges occurs from Armoy southwestwards to Ballymoney and then northwards on the western side of the Bann river to Quilley, a distance of about 50 km (McCarron, 2001). The Armoy moraine consists of several (maximum of 6) subparallel ridges individually up to 70 m high which trend parallel to the overall convex form of the complex (Figs. 50, 51). Records (Shaw and Carter, 1980) suggest that large-scale glaciotectonic structures/shears control the orientation of the ridge crests (Fig. 52). The large depression on the ice proximal (northern) side of the moraine at Garry Bog defines the outline of subglacial imprint of the former ice lobe. Lithologically the moraine consists of ice-pushed sediments which are mainly fine-grained and represent deposition in a former lake basin sited along the Tow valley depression. The large-scale structures record intense sectional shortening with duplication of stratigraphy and ice pressure from the north. Small gravel pits contain abundant foreign igneous erratics probably from western Scotland. Ridge orientation also controls the present course and direction or the river Bush.

The presence of lake sediments in the Tow valley and adjacent areas along the Bann shows that at the time of maximum ice extent in northeast Antrim a large lake was created by the presence of Scottish ice on the lowlands (Fig. 43). Irish ice advancing from the Lough Neagh basin to the south was sited immediately south of Ballymoney and acted as the southern margin of the lake. Around Glenlough, 3 km south of Ballymoney, flat topped spreads of outwash record deposition from the Irish ice margin.

Along the Bann valley at Vow an esker ridge consisting of subglacial fan efflux deposits were deposited into the lake as the Irish ice retreated southwards. This site is of special sedimentological interest because the coarse, disorganised boulder and cobble gravels are interbedded with thick rhythmically-bedded silts and clays deposited from suspension in the turbid lake (Fig. 43). Ice-contact deltas at Kilrea also record slightly longer episodes of sedimentation when subaqueous fans had time to evolve into ice-contact deltas.

When the ice lobe which deposited the Armoy moraine wasted, good examples of deglacial topography were formed along the lower Bann valley around Castleroe with extensive kettling of the outwash. It is noted that the outwash at Castleroe contains abundant erratics from Scottish sources but the palaeocurrent indicators record unidirectional flow northwards as ice located in the upper Bann valley melted.

In 1939 Charlesworth created a major problem in the literature when he argued that the drumlins and other bedforms in north Antrim terminated south of the Armoy moraine thus creating the hypothesis that because the Armoy moraine post dates the drumlin field the drumlin field to the north of the moraine was destroyed by ice advance from Scotland (Fig. 43). The apparent absence of bedforms to the north of the moraine has been perpetuated in the literature and in maps of bedform distribution (e.g. Davies and Stephens, 1978; Stephens et al., 1975; Hoare, 1991) which leads to flawed ice sheet models. However more detailed mapping shows clearly that drumlin swarms occur on both sides of the moraine and consistently show similar trends on both sides of the moraine (Fig. 43). Undoubtedly they record fast ice flow from the lowlands of central Ulster northwards onto the continental shelf. This ice

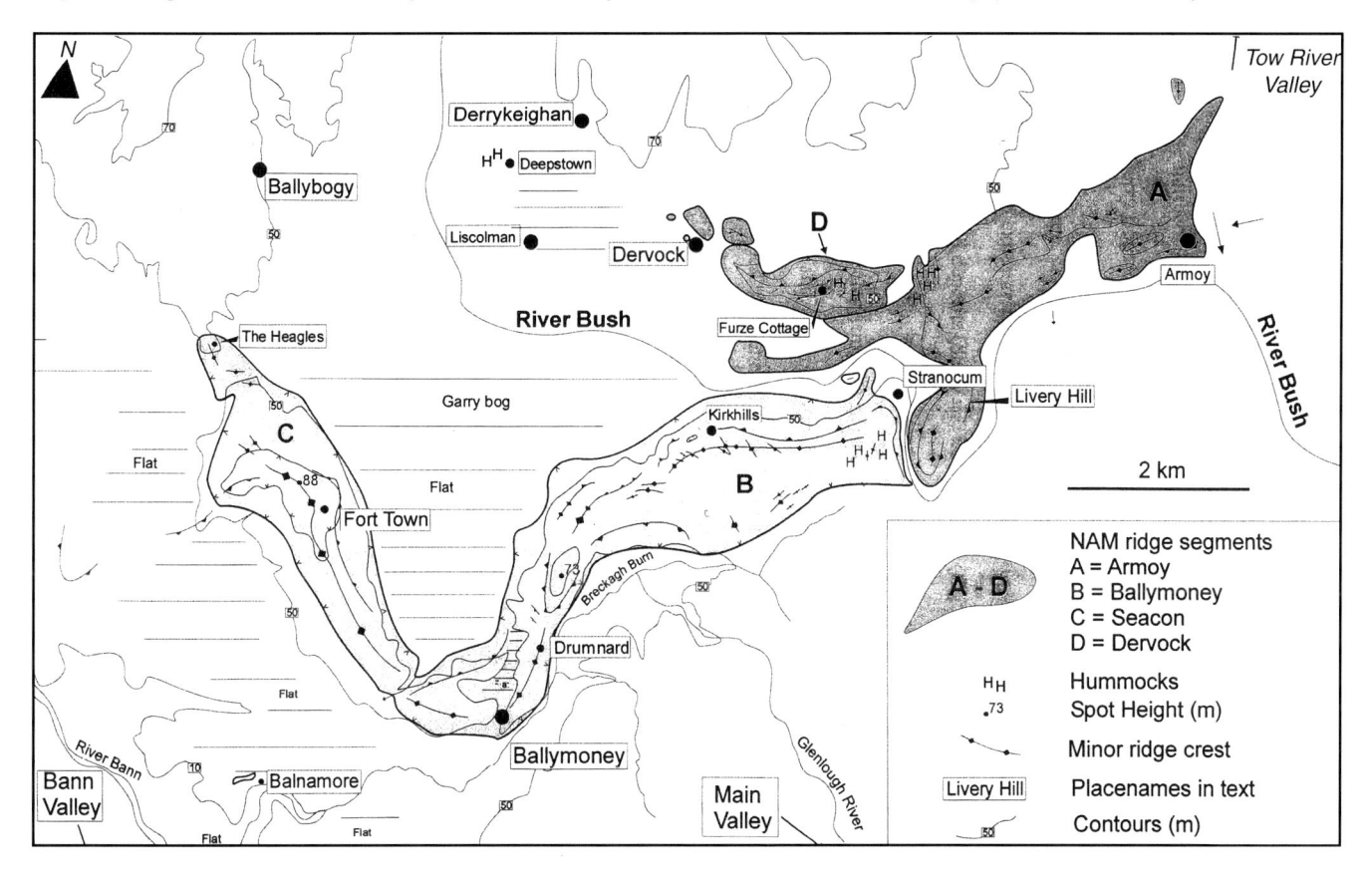

Fig. 50: Segments of the Armoy moraine (NAM) to the east of the Bann valley (McCarron, 2001).

High Energy Coasts

Fig. 51: Segments of the Armoy moraine (NAM) to the west of the Bann valley (McCarron, 2001).

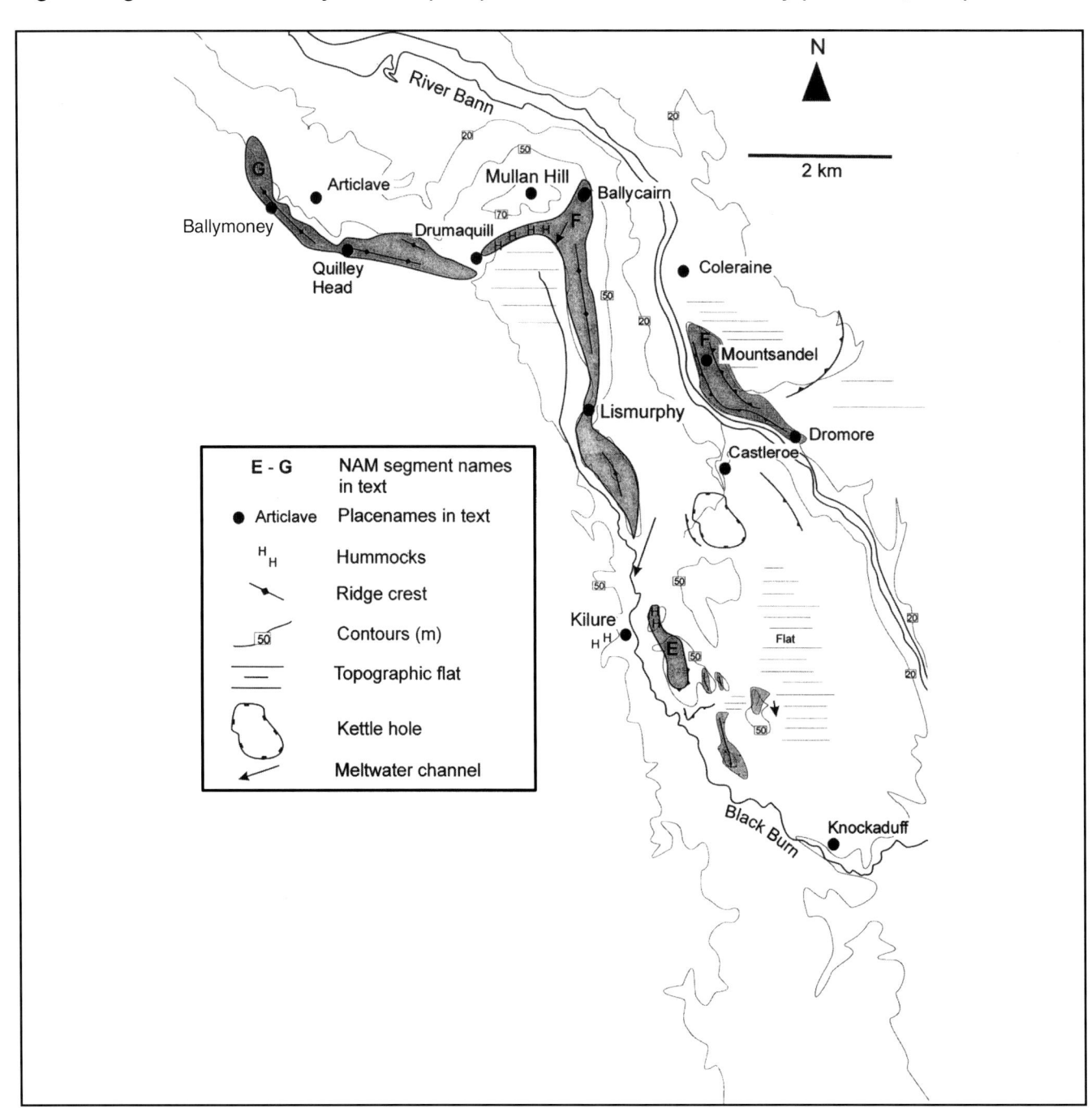

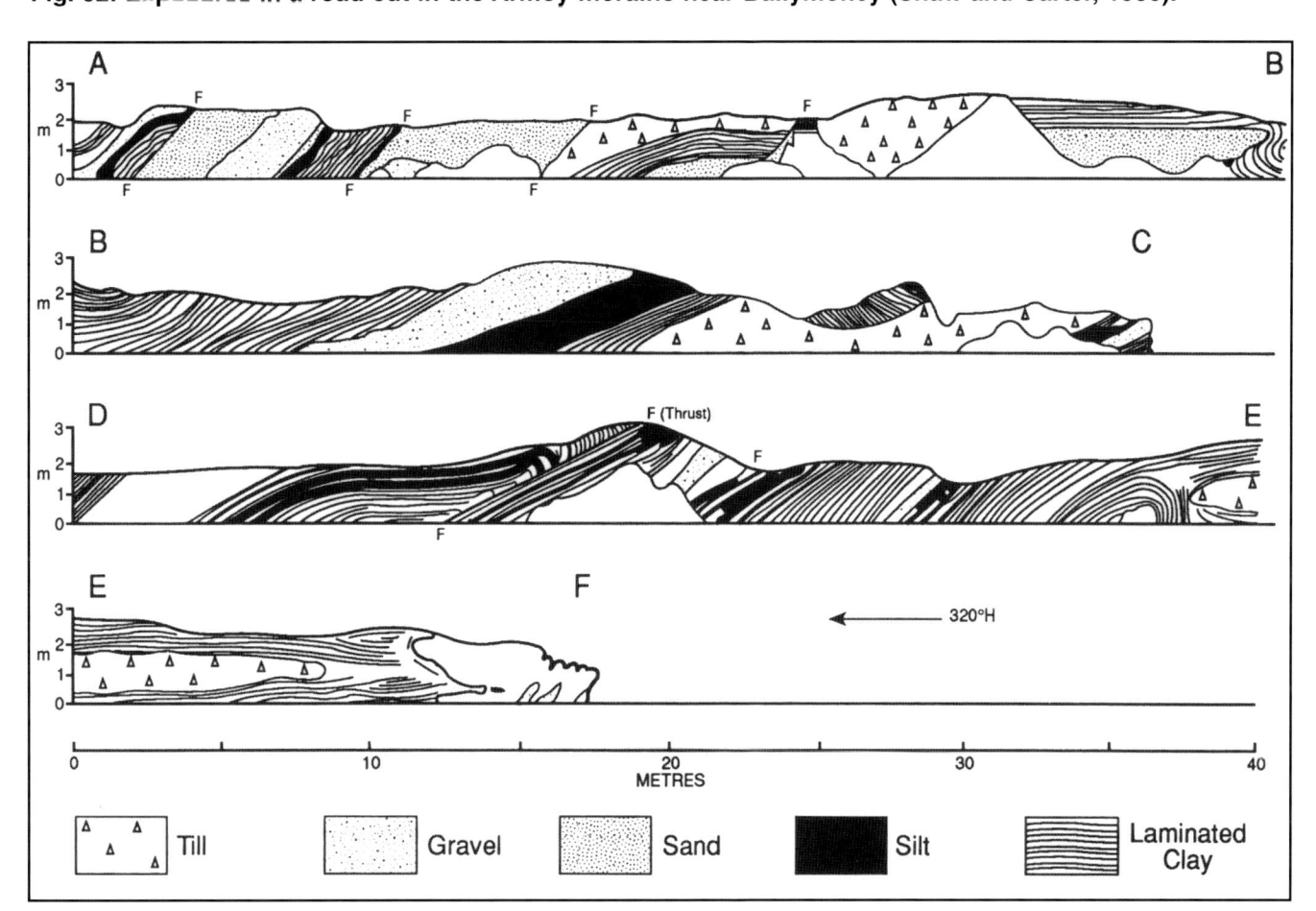

Fig. 52: Exposures in a road cut in the Armoy moraine near Ballymoney (Shaw and Carter, 1980).

movement probably represents the main ice sheet advance to the LGM in this specific ice sheet sector.

Deglacial sea levels

Stephens and Synge (1965) recognised that Arctic marine transgressions occurred in the Bann valley and in the North Channel and suggested that the transgression was contemporaneous with the maximum extent of ice in Lough Foyle at the Moville moraine and at Malin Head and Lough Swilly. Between Fair Head and the mouth of the river Bann the marine transgression occurred somewhat later and after withdrawal of ice from the coastal lowlands (Stephens and Synge, 1965). This model of high RSL during deglaciation is well-founded because it is based on three critical field observations. These are the deposition of red marine clay in inter-drumlin hollows, late-glacial marine notches which were cut into areas vacated by ice, and raised shoreline features which are associated with a succession of morainic systems (Stephens et al., 1975). These workers (e.g. Stephens and Synge, 1966; Stephens, 1968) also used the tilts of the reconstructed strandlines to recognise shorelines of different late-glacial ages. They also pointed out that this method of analysis is flawed because the older late-glacial shorelines are metachronous regardless of the height at which they are found.

Along the north coast, a wide range of raised glaciomarine deposits (Eyles and McCabe, 1989) and raised beach features postdate the last termination when ice withdrew from the continental shelf for the last time after 14 kyr BP. However the environmental signature of the deglacial and early late-glacial period was one of extremely rapid local environmental change driven by rapid rates of isostatic rebound, differential tectonics, meltwater events and wider eustatic changes. In many instances factors such as wave climates, available slopes and coastal configuration were overprinted on the general isostatic and eustatic controls. The preservation potential of a complete facies succession is therefore very low.

Along the north coast large raised extraglacial deltas occur in the Carey valley (McCabe and Eyles, 1988) which may indicate RSLs up to 100 m OD immediately the area was vacated by ice (~ 14 kyr BP). Lower notches and a marine delta at Fruitfield (Limavady) record RSLs around 20 m OD when the ice had retreated south from the Roe valley into the Sperrin Mountains (Fig. 46). The moraine at Ballykelly is notched by a further staircase of successively lower shorelines. Only the relative ages of these features is known, though a date from beach shells on Rathlin Island suggests a sea level of ~ 10 m OD at 12.1 kyr BP (Carter, 1993). It is therefore likely that the late-glacial beaches span the time period between 14 and 12 kyr BP.

In northwestern Britain most exposures of deglacial deposits consist of diamict (subglacial or glaciomarine till) overlain directly by raised beach sand and gravel. In most cases the diamict upper surface is strongly erosional. Clearly there is a missing facies here because idealised emergent facies would be expected to show progression from ice-contact glaciomarine or diamict to shallow marine and wave-influenced facies and finally upper shoreface sand and gravel. Commonly, because of imbalances between transgressional and erosional spikes, we find that erosion surfaces occur between glacigenic deposits and overlying raised clastic beaches. Exposures, preserved in a horseshoe embayment at Portballintrae, preserve an emergent facies sequence (Figs. 53, 54) (McCabe et al., 1994). Three lithofacies assemblages are present and have not been described from any other site in northern Britain. At the head of the bay longitudinal s-forms are cut into basalt and record ice flow onto the continental shelf. At the base of the section a massive muddy diamict was formed by resedimentation from debris released by ice marginal processes and slumping of adjacent beds of stratified mud/sand forming irregular pods. Rhythmically-bedded sand and mud couplets contain a wide range of wave-influenced structures and laterally extensive ripple trains and are separated from the underlying diamict by both transitional and wave-eroded contacts. The range and preservation of boreo-arctic foraminifera present are typical of a lower-shoreface, storm-influenced setting. The fourteen sand/mud couplets are resolved into well-defined facies sequences (Fig. 55) which are explained by relative energy levels of variable wave agitation during the course

Fig. 53: (A) Location of Portballintrae, north Co Antrim. (B) Generalised ice flows onto the continental shelf at the last glacial maximum (Bowen *et al.*, 1986).

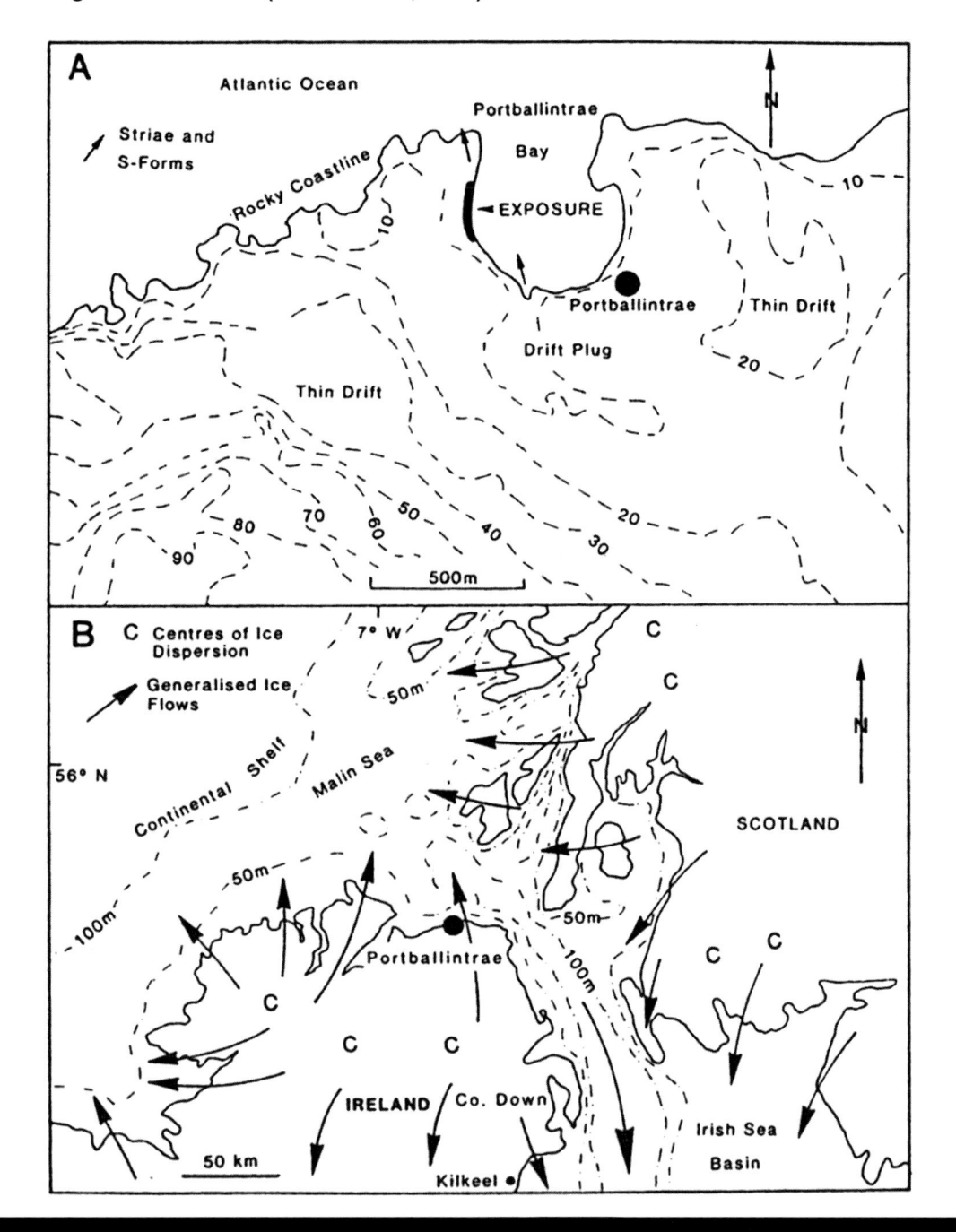

Fig. 54: Lithofacies succession exposed along the western margin of Portballintrae Bay, Co Antrim. Clast fabrics are based on 25 clasts at sites F1 to F5 in the massive diamict. Note the relatively weak strengths of clustering around V1.

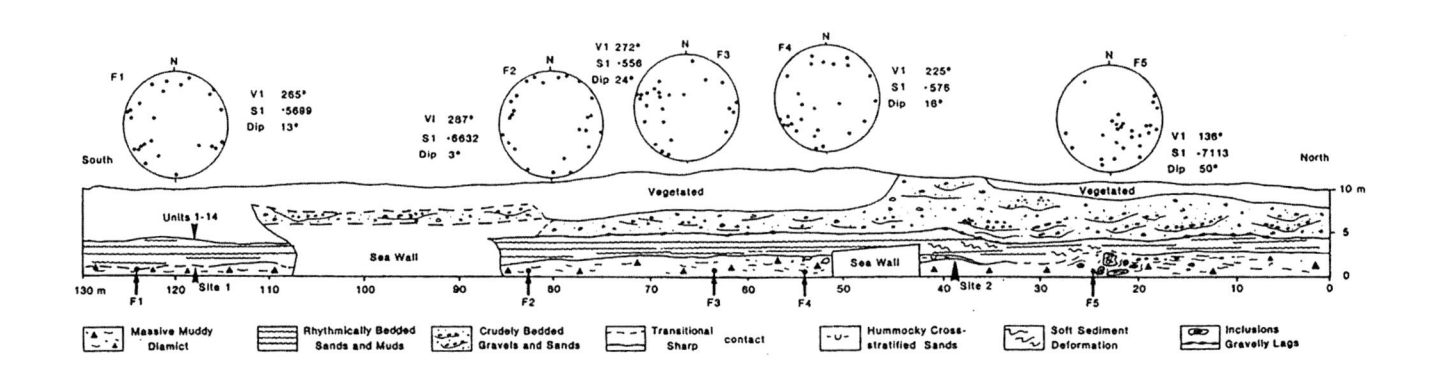

of a single storm event (Fig. 56). The rhythmites are truncated by a planar wave-cut surface and overlain by crudely-organised beds of gravel within cross-cutting scours. These may be associated with offshore-directed, storm-induced sediment pulses. Overall the coarsening upwards succession is explained by tidewater sedimentation during ice wastage, rapid isostatic rebound and isostatic deceleration in the late-glacial.

It is stressed that facies successions of this type have a low preservation potential due to reworking during emergence. All of the sea-level data presented here may not be well-constrained by absolute dates but they record high RSL during a time of very rapid environmental change during final deglaciation. Whether or not current rheological models can fully describe or take account of these rapid changes during the last deglacial is extremely doubtful (e.g. Lambeck and Purcell, 2001).

Fig. 55: Detailed vertical section of rhythmically bedded sand and muds, Portballintrae, site 1. The fourteen rhythmically bedded units and granulometric trends (coarsening upwards) form the basis for the storm-influenced setting. Note the well-developed laminated mud drapes capping each sandy unit with preservation of the dominant ripple train (McCabe et al., 1994).

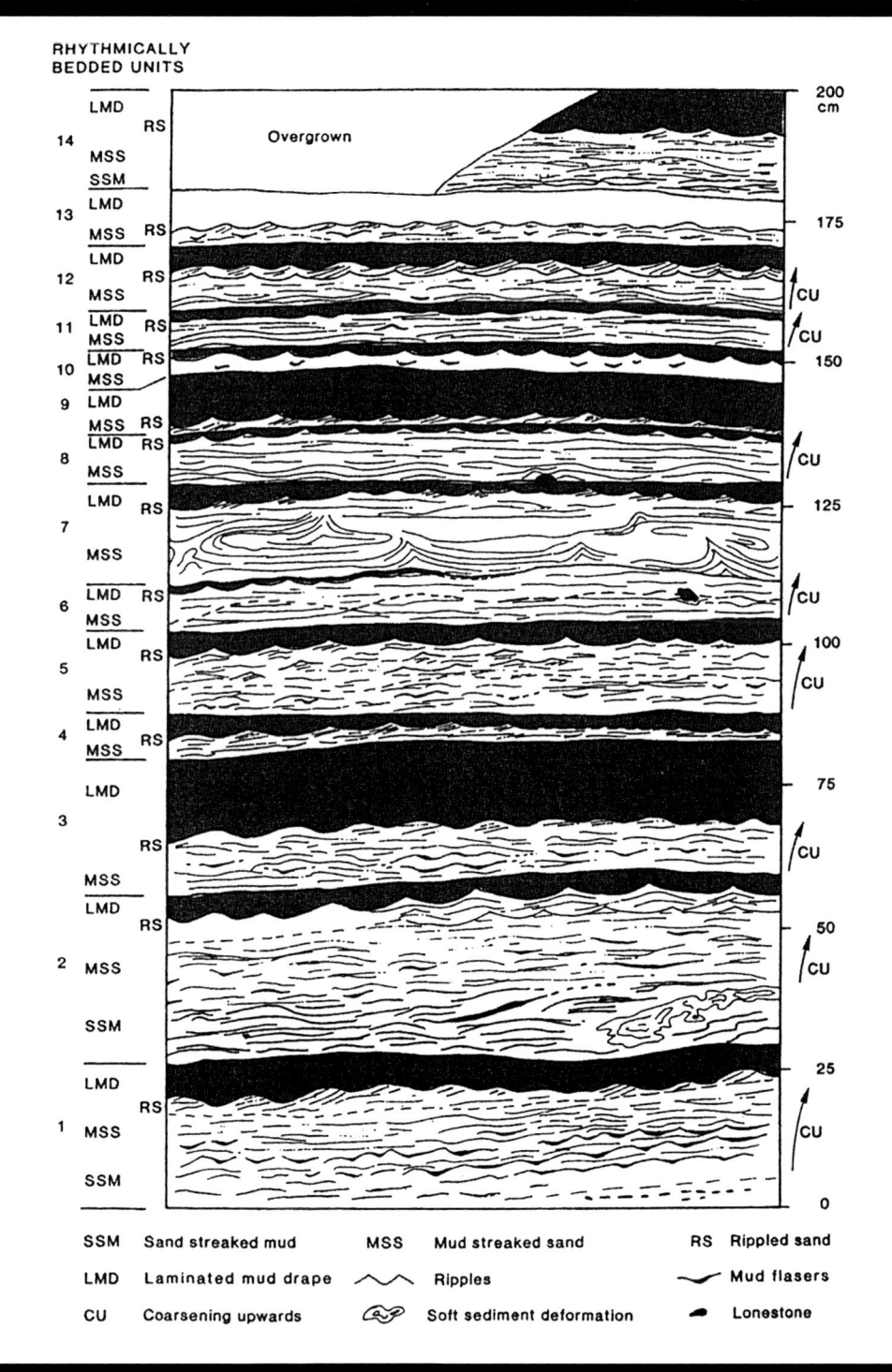

Fig. 56: Processes and postulated relationships between the facies successions in an idealised unit and relative energy levels of variable wave agitation during the course of a single storm (McCabe *et al.*, 1994).

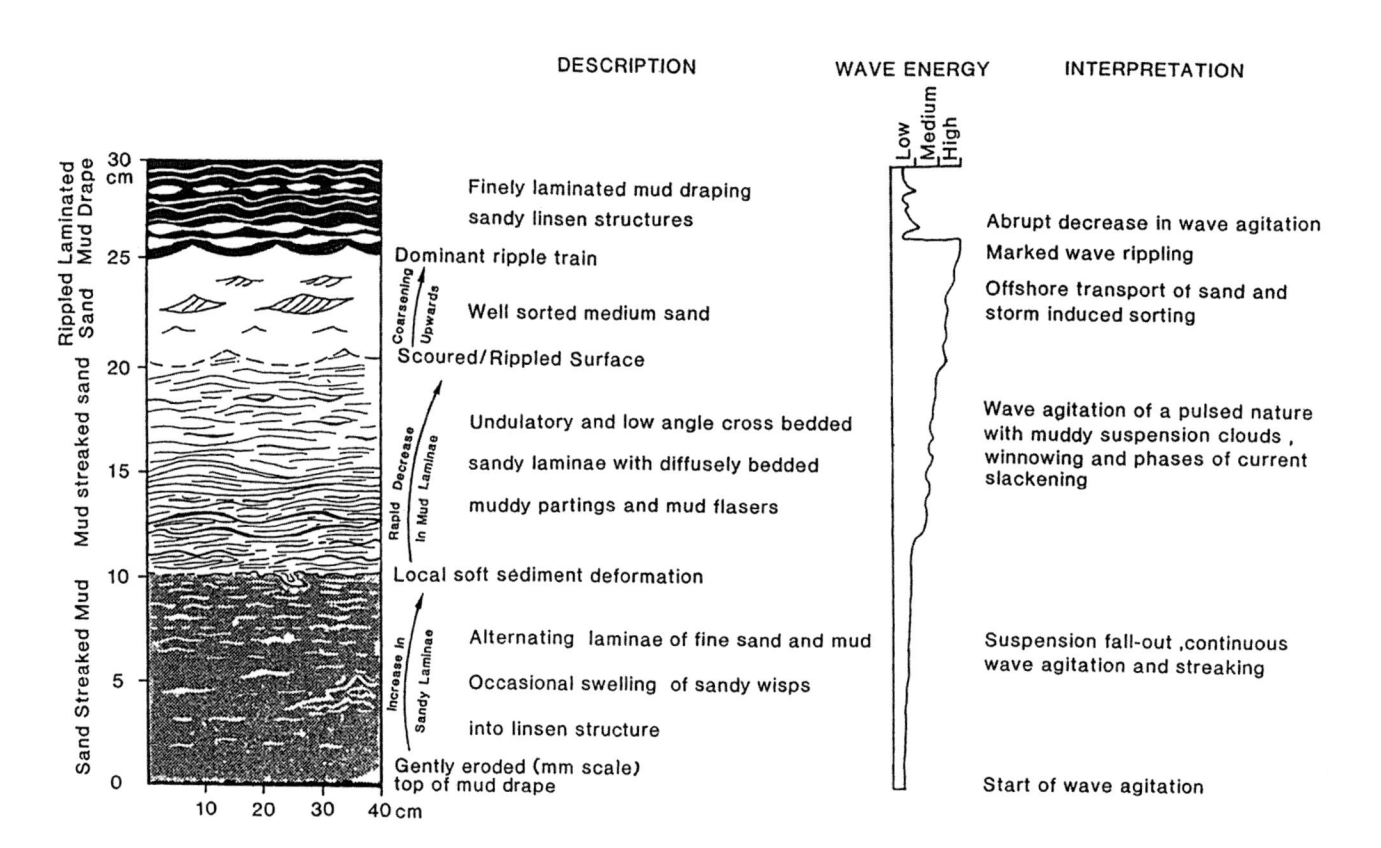

Shelf sediments and stratigraphy

Andrew Cooper

The sea floor bathymetry off the Northern Ireland north coast exhibits a gently sloping inner shelf and a generally shallow outer shelf punctuated with several deep depressions (Fig. 57).

The offshore zone of the Northern Ireland north coast is affected by a high energy wave regime (modal deep water wave heights > 2 m, period 8-9 s) and by strong tidal currents. Spring tidal range reaches 2.5 m at Magilligan Point but falls to 1.0 m at Ballycastle. Strong tidal currents are generated

Fig. 57: Generalised bathymetry off the Northern Ireland north coast. Note the wide shallow zone offshore of Lough Foyle and the deep depressions north of Rathlin Island and between Benbane head and Islay

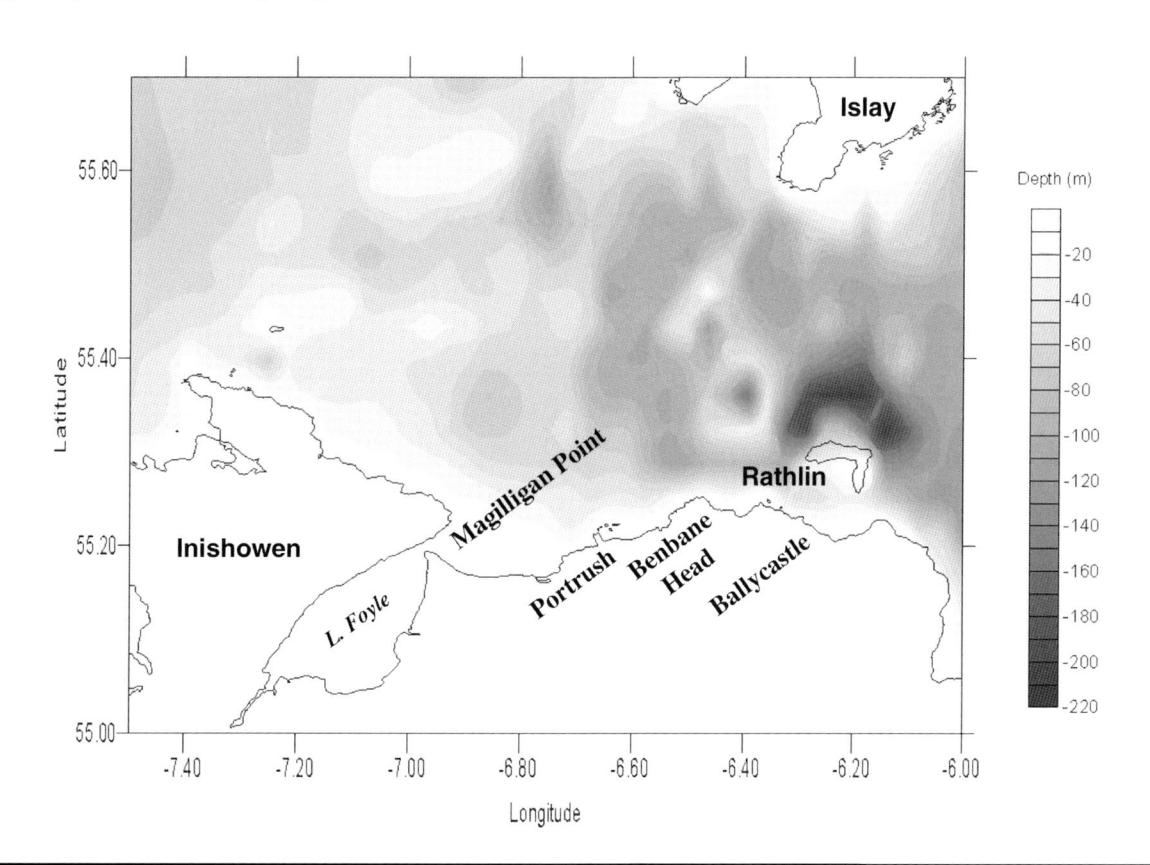

Fig. 58: Shore-normal inshore seismic stratigraphic profile at Portballintrae. The sequence, which is interpreted largely by reference to onshore exposures, comprises a basement of glacial sediment or bedrock overlain by glacio-marine sediments, a regressive sand unit and a transgressive sand unit. A marked change in seafloor character is evident at a depth of c. 30 m where the inner shelf sediment wedge gives way to an scoured relict glacial surface.

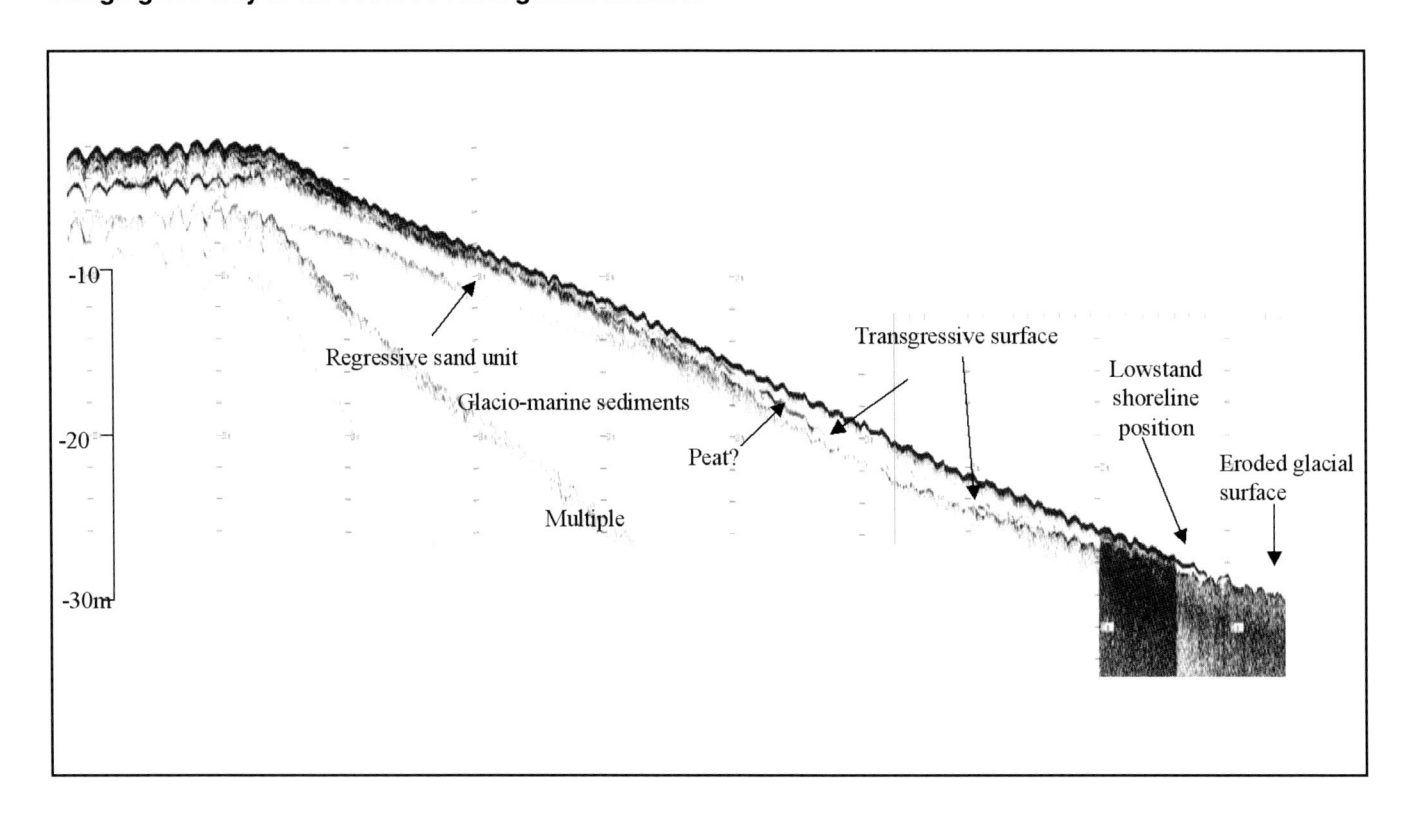

under this comparatively low tidal regime because of the location onshore of an amphidromic point which produces a tidal edge wave around which tides rotate and at which strong tidal currents are generated in the absence of large tidal range. Flows are locally accelerated by the presence of constrictions and coastal promontories. Around Rathlin Island, for example, near-bed tidal currents reach 1.5 m s^{-1} on spring tides. The tidal currents exhibit an easterly residual which drives sediment transport toward the Irish Sea.

The distribution of sediments on the shelf is strongly related to sea-level history. Sediment in the outer shelf comprises an eroded glacial surface on which localised accumulations of tidally-transported sandy sediment occur. The inner shelf in contrast, which was traversed by sea level during the past 10 kyr, contains a distinctive stratigraphy related to erosion and deposition in the littoral zone. By comparison with onshore exposures, particularly those at Portballintrae (McCabe *et al.*, 1994), the inshore stratigraphy (Fig. 58) is interpreted as

Fig. 59: Sonographs of the sea floor showing A. contact between planar inshore sand sheet and scoured glacial deposits; B. rippled crest crest of sandwave on gravel substrate; C. Large scale tidal sand waves with rippled surfaces.

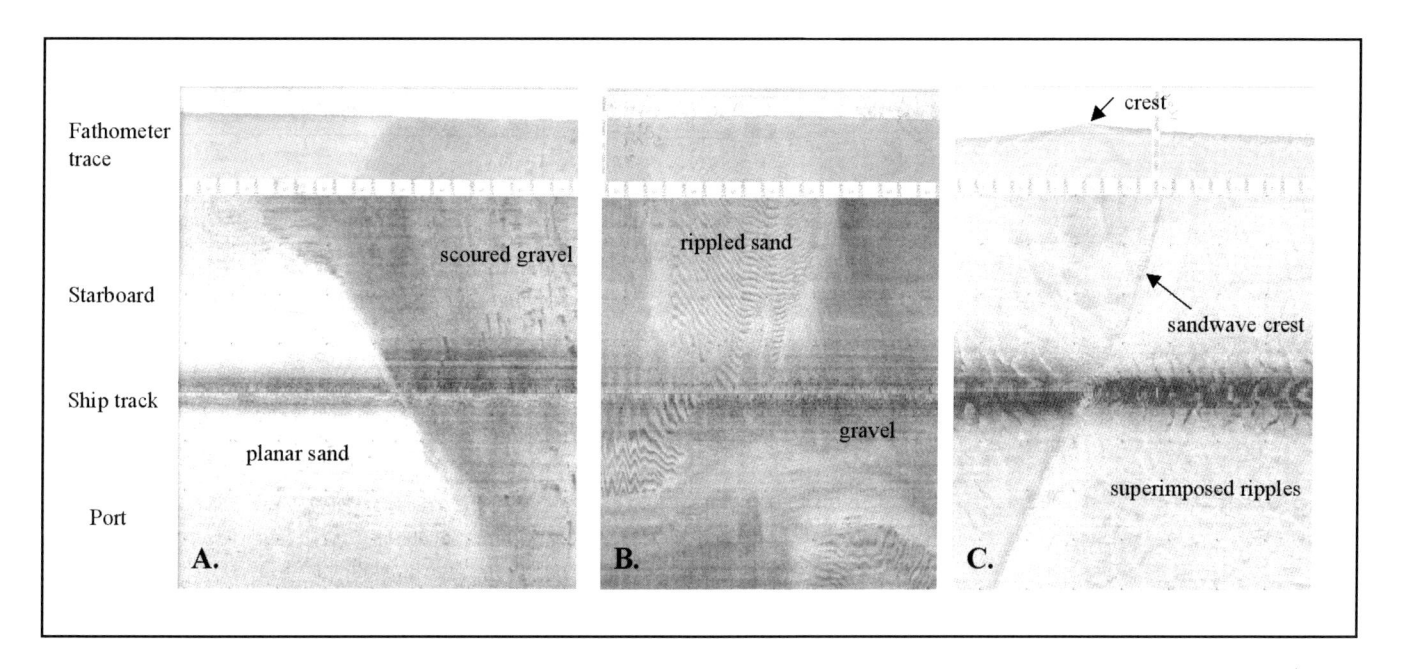

comprising a glaciomarine unit overlying a basement of glacial sediment or bedrock. This surface is overlain by a regressive sandy unit associated with sea level fall from a late-glacial high level of about + 20 m to a lowstand of about - 30 m (Cooper et al., 2002). Subsequent transgression across the sediment-rich sectors led to development of a barrier backed in places by paralic sediments that are now partially preserved on the shelf as peat.

Sediments on the shelf comprise sand with minor amounts of gravel. Mud is absent. Sand forms a surface veneer in depths greater than 30 m whereas in shallower depths sand thickness may exceed 5 m. Fine sand is the dominant grain size in shallow depths (< ~ 30 m) while medium sand is the dominant grain size in deeper water. The skeletal carbonate content of shelf sediments is typically ~ 20% in shallow water and > 40% in deeper water. Substantial inshore sand accumulations occur between Magilligan and Portstewart, at Portrush east strand and at Whitepark Bay where they are associated with major onshore beach/dune accumulations.

Modelling of wave-induced bottom currents and of tidal currents (Lawlor, 2000) shows that the shelf may be divided into an inner, wave-dominated zone and an outer tidal-current-dominated zone. The inner, wave-dominated zone is characterised by planar sand sheets in embayments with bedrock exposed adjacent to headlands. Occasional wave ripples are evident. In the tidal-current dominated zone a variety of bedforms exists. These include sand ribbons, sand streaks, asymmetric sand waves and megaripples (Fig. 59). Asymmetry on these bedforms indicates a dominant easterly transport.

The presence of sediment-starved features (sand ribbons) to the west of the area coupled with the large thicknesses of sand offshore of Portballintrae is suggestive of long-term sediment depletion in the west with accumulation in the east (Fig. 59). The deep depression between Benbane Head and Islay (Fig. 57) provides an impediment to continued eastward transport that renders shelf areas to the east comparatively sediment poor.

Offshore archaeology of the north coast

Colin Breen, Wes Forsythe and Rory Quinn

Introduction

Ireland's insular position on the edge of western Europe was one of the primary factors in the development of the nation, and one of the governing factors in its relations with the rest of the world. Its comparatively small size meant that the sea has played a great part in the economy and politics of the island. Consequently a significant maritime tradition developed, which is today reflected in a wide range of maritime monument types, industrial, secular and religious, around the coast and on the seabed.

The archaeological wealth of maritime sites was demonstrated by the investigation in the late 1960s and early 1970s of three Spanish Armada wrecks off the coast. The excavations of the *Girona, Santa Maria de la Rosa* and the *Trinidad Valencera* produced a valuable insight into everyday life on board late Medieval ships as well as providing invaluable details on the armaments that were carried. While the importance of such sites was realised, there was a popular misconception in Ireland that these wrecks were unique. It was thought that the vast majority of wrecks would not survive in the inhospitable underwater environment, whilst anything that did survive would be of limited importance; important wreck-sites would only be found in the warmer waters of the Mediterranean; and that the Northern world was sadly lacking in these remains. There was also a prevalent attitude within Irish archaeology that sites were viewed from a terrestrial perspective and that maritime traditions had little part to play in the Irish archaeological record.

Responsibility for the protection of the archaeological resource in Ireland has lain with government since 1882 under the first Ancient Monuments Protection Act. However, it was not until recent years that the government in Northern Ireland has concerned itself with maritime archaeology. *'This Common Inheritance'*, a White Paper on environment and archaeology, was published in 1990. This paper announced proposals for dealing with historic wrecks. As a result of this paper an Agency Agreement was signed with the Department of National Heritage in August 1992, under which the Department of the Environment for Northern Ireland accepted responsibility for wrecks in Northern Ireland's territorial waters under the Protection of Wrecks Act, 1973.

To date, only one wreck in Northern waters, *La Girona*, has been designated under this act. The Historic Monuments and Archaeological Objects (NI) Order 1995 extends legal protection to archaeological sites and objects below high water mark and on the seabed. Under this legislation, sites can be scheduled on land and the seabed to 12 nautical miles offshore. A number of sites in the intertidal zone in Strangford Lough have recently

High Energy Coasts

Fig. 60: SMR wreck distribution off the north coast. Each data point represents a single wreck site. Note the concentrations around historically important ports and navigation hazards

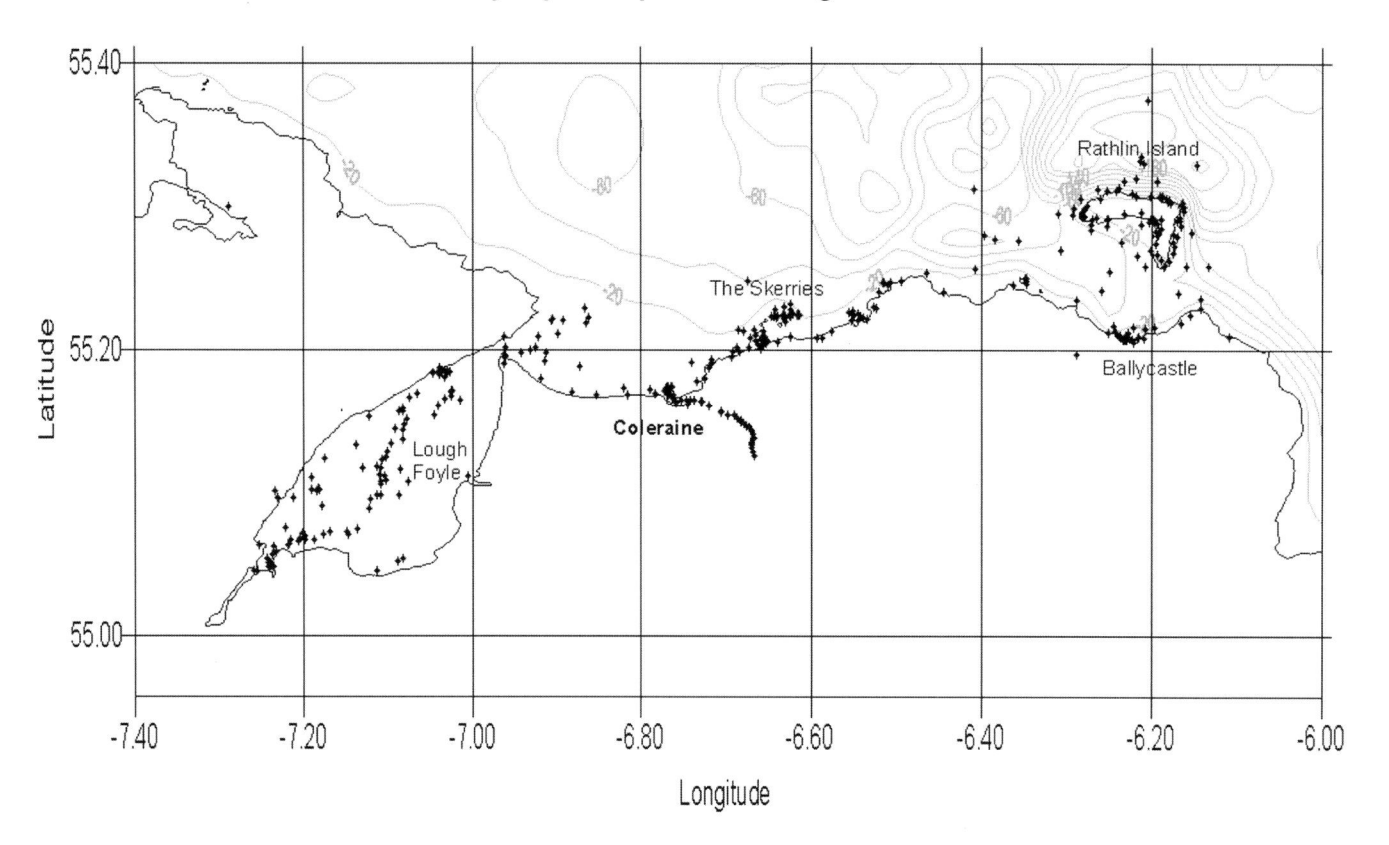

been scheduled under this order. It is recognised, however, that legislation is only one aspect of dealing with the maritime archaeological resource.

The Maritime Sites and Monuments Record (MSMR)

In 1993, The Maritime Sites and Monuments Record (MSMR) was established by the Environment and Heritage Service (and agency within the Department of the Environment in Northern Ireland) to create a comprehensive database of all wreck sites in Irish waters in order to quantify the nature and extent of the resource. To carry out this task a complete desk-based study of sources relating to shipwrecks was undertaken. The resulting database contains reference to some 6,000 shipwrecking incidents in Northern Ireland, of which about 1000 occur off the north coasts of counties Donegal, Derry and Antrim (Fig. 60).

Documentary sources were of primary importance to the survey, although cartographic and illustrative material was also examined. The majority of sources related to post-medieval wrecks, and included the papers of the High Courts of the British and Irish Admiralties, Lloyd's List, national and local newspapers and British Parliamentary papers. Although providing invaluable information, one major limitation recognised in this approach was the lack of significant documentary information pertaining to pre- 18th Century wrecks in Ireland. For this reason the Environment and Heritage Service (EHS), in partnership with the Coastal Studies Research Group at the University of Ulster, embarked on a programme of seabed mapping in an attempt to record submerged and buried archaeological resources. The seafloor-mapping programme of the inshore coastal waters of Northern Ireland employed a side-scan sonar, an echo-sounder, a Chirp sub-bottom profiler, and a proton precession magnetometer with the aim of providing comprehensive and detailed archaeological and geomorphological information on targeted areas around the coastline. Further information can be accessed at: http://www.ulst.ac.uk/faculty/science/crg/marine.htm. Data from the geophysical surveys are constantly being fed back into the MSMR and a GIS database is currently under construction, combining natural and cultural data.

Case Study I: Taymouth Castle

In 1995, EHS was asked to examine the wreck-site of *Taymouth Castle* (Figs. 60, 61), located near Cushendun on the coast of County Antrim (Breen, 1996). The wreck-site contained large quantities of pottery which were being systematically plundered by divers. In the course of the following months, large-scale plundering took place. EHS took the decision to conduct a survey and excavation of the site in order to investigate it in a controlled manner and to retrieve a representative sample of artefacts before they were lost. This decision was taken in line with EHS's management role in maritime archaeology. Their responsibility does not end with location and survey of a site; decisions are taken in the light of any factors on the sea-bed that may affect it. In this instance *in situ* conservation measures coupled with protective legislative measures would not have been effective in preventing further interference.

Lloyd's Register shows that the *Taymouth* was built in 1865 at Glasgow by the Connell Company. The vessel was owned by T. Skinner & Company of the Glasgow and Asiatic Shipping Companies. She was a fully rigged ship measuring 172 ft long, with a 29-ft beam and a weight of 627 tons. The vessel was a composite ship, one of the first of its kind, built with iron framing and wooden planking. This planking was sheathed with copper and yellow metal, as the problem of iron fouling had yet to be solved.

The Belfast Newsletter of the time contains a detailed account of the vessel's final days. The ship left Scotland for Singapore in January 1867. She was carrying a valuable general cargo, valued at £50,000. This included large quantities of brandy, wine and spirits, as well as pottery and iron materials. After only a few days at sea the vessel was caught in very heavy weather off the Antrim coast and was subsequently wrecked between Torr Head and Cushendun. The crew was drowned. Some of the cargo was salvaged at the time by the coastguard. Oral tradition recounts that the ship was again partially salvaged by hard hat divers in the early 1900s. No records have been found about this exercise so the extent of salvage is unknown.

During the initial wrecking incident the ship appears to have been driven onshore stern-first. The vessel was visible for a number of days enduring a heavy beating, before finally submerging. The remains of the ship currently lie below steep sea cliffs at the bottom of an underwater boulder slope

Fig. 61: Site plan of Taymouth Castle (Drawing: Maire Ni Loinsigh)

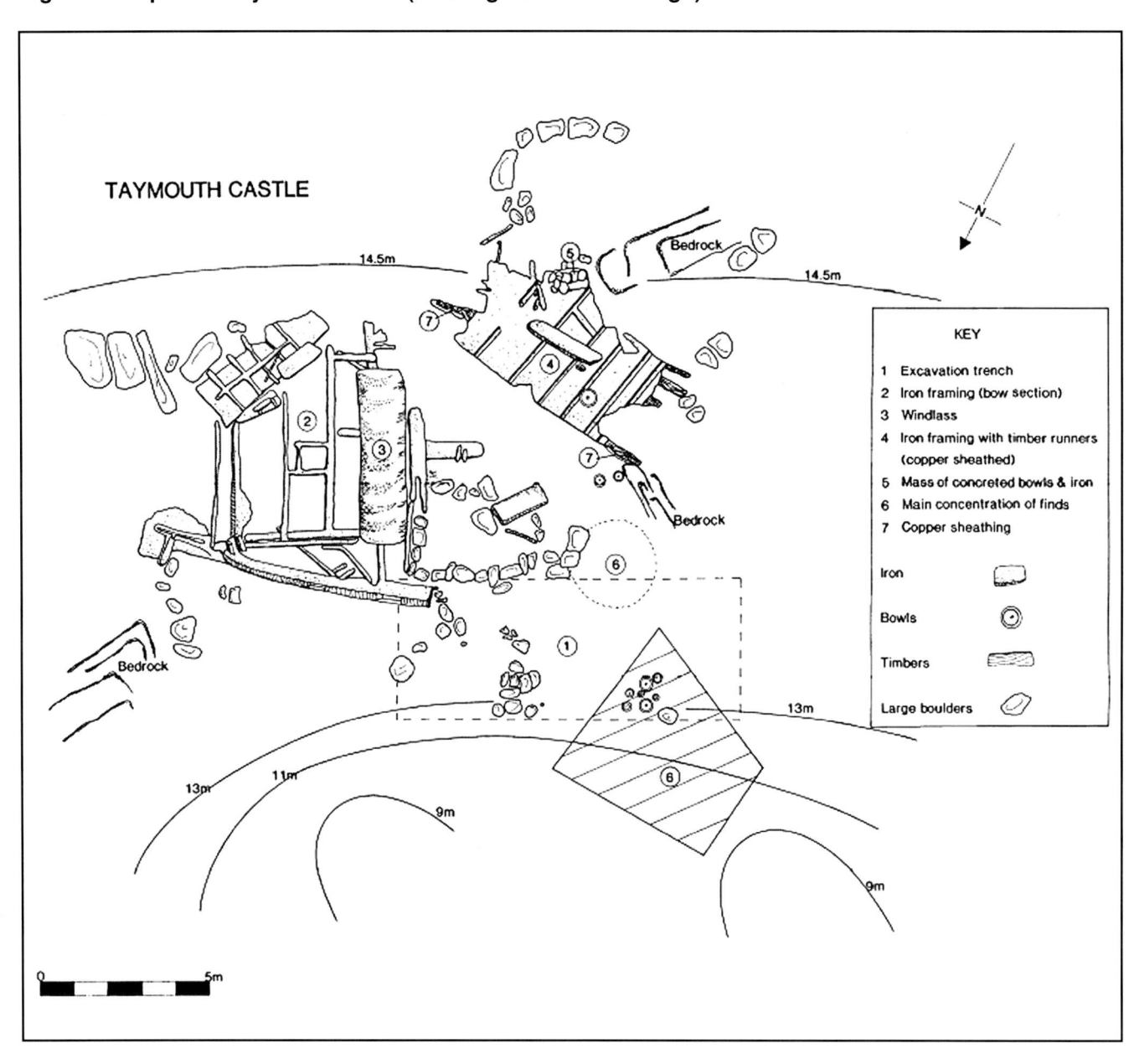

in 14 m of water (Fig. 61). A section of iron framing from the bow lies a short distance from the slope. A large windlass can be seen *in situ* on top of this framing. This consists of a large iron drum laid horizontally. Intact links of the anchor chain remain concreted onto the windlass and lead off from the bow section to the starboard side. This would suggest that the anchor was dropped during wrecking, possibly in an attempt to keep the ship off the rocks. A large portion of intact hull planking lies behind the windlass on the starboard side. This consists of a large rectangular iron frame with external timber members, which are copper sheathed. A large concentration of artefacts was found at the bottom of the slope. It appears that during the wrecking process a large amount of cargo was deposited in this area. Boulder collapse and natural depositional processes seem to have covered much of this material, ensuring its survival. The ship was also carrying quantities of iron bowls stacked inside each other. Straw packing was evidently placed between each bowl. These bowls have concreted together forming a further protective layer over the underlying material. Recent diver activity resulted in the destruction of this concreted mass, revealing thousands of sherds. The pottery was identified as Glaswegian Sponge Ware dating from the late 1850s. Items recovered include dinner plates and various sizes of bowl. A number of glass and stone-ware bottles still corked were also recovered from beneath this artificial layer. Some of the dark glass bottles had 'Cooper of Portobello' visible on their underside. Fragments of bottle heads were also found with lead seals protecting the corks. Other finds included five deadeyes. One of these had steel cordage still intact. A series of small timbers from a wooden case were uncovered associated with a heavy cluster of sherds. This appears to be an original packing case for the pottery. It is interesting to note the level of preservation on the site given that this area of the coast is regarded as being highly dynamic. Not only did natural depositional factors aid in the preservation but the archaeological site formation processes also helped.

The *Taymouth Castle* site provided an ideal opportunity to study an important pottery and artefact assemblage from the 1800s as well as providing an opportunity to examine an early example of the composite ship-building technique.

Case Study II: La Girona

One of the most notable wrecks to have occurred of the north coast of Ireland was *La Girona*, a galleass of the Spanish Armada which sank near the Giant's Causeway in 1588. The vessel was discovered in 1967 by Robert Sténuit, a Belgian salvage expert. On his first dive around Lacada Point, Sténuit recovered a number of Spanish coins and noted the presence of a range of other artefactual remains including the distinctively shaped lead ingots, which were common items carried on-board the Armada vessels. These ingots would have been melted down later to make lead shot once the invasion force had landed. Sténuit returned the following year, in 1968, with a dive team and a range of equipment that would enable him to carry out a large-scale salvage job.

By Sténuit's final season in 1969, an incredible assortment of objects had been recovered. The vessel itself had been completely broken up by the exposed north coast seas. A lack of sediment around the site (which would have aided preservation) led to objects such as ordnance or personal items being either covered by stones or buried into pockets of sand and shingle below large boulders. The continual movement of these stones over the centuries allowed many artefacts to become even more deeply buried. The largest items recovered from the site were three guns, including one bronze half-saker and one bronze esmeril. The muzzle of a third gun was also recovered. The ship had an original complement of up to 50 guns but many of these were salvaged at the time by local chieftains and by an English salvage operation mounted soon after the wrecking.

An impressive assortment of personal items was found including religious crosses, jewellery and kitchen utensils. Recent work by a licensed diver, under the conditions of the Protection of Wrecks Act (1973), has recovered further personal items and located two more iron cannons and part of an anchor.

Onshore archaeology and human habitation in the coastal zone

Peter Wilson

Introduction

The north coast of Northern Ireland (Fig. 62) has been a favoured location for habitation, exploited for its natural resources, utilised for ritual purposes, and has served as a means of communication since the first colonists arrived *c.* 7000 years BC. This long history of human activity is evident from the

Fig. 62: The north coast of Northern Ireland showing major settlements and locations of archaeological sites mention in the text.

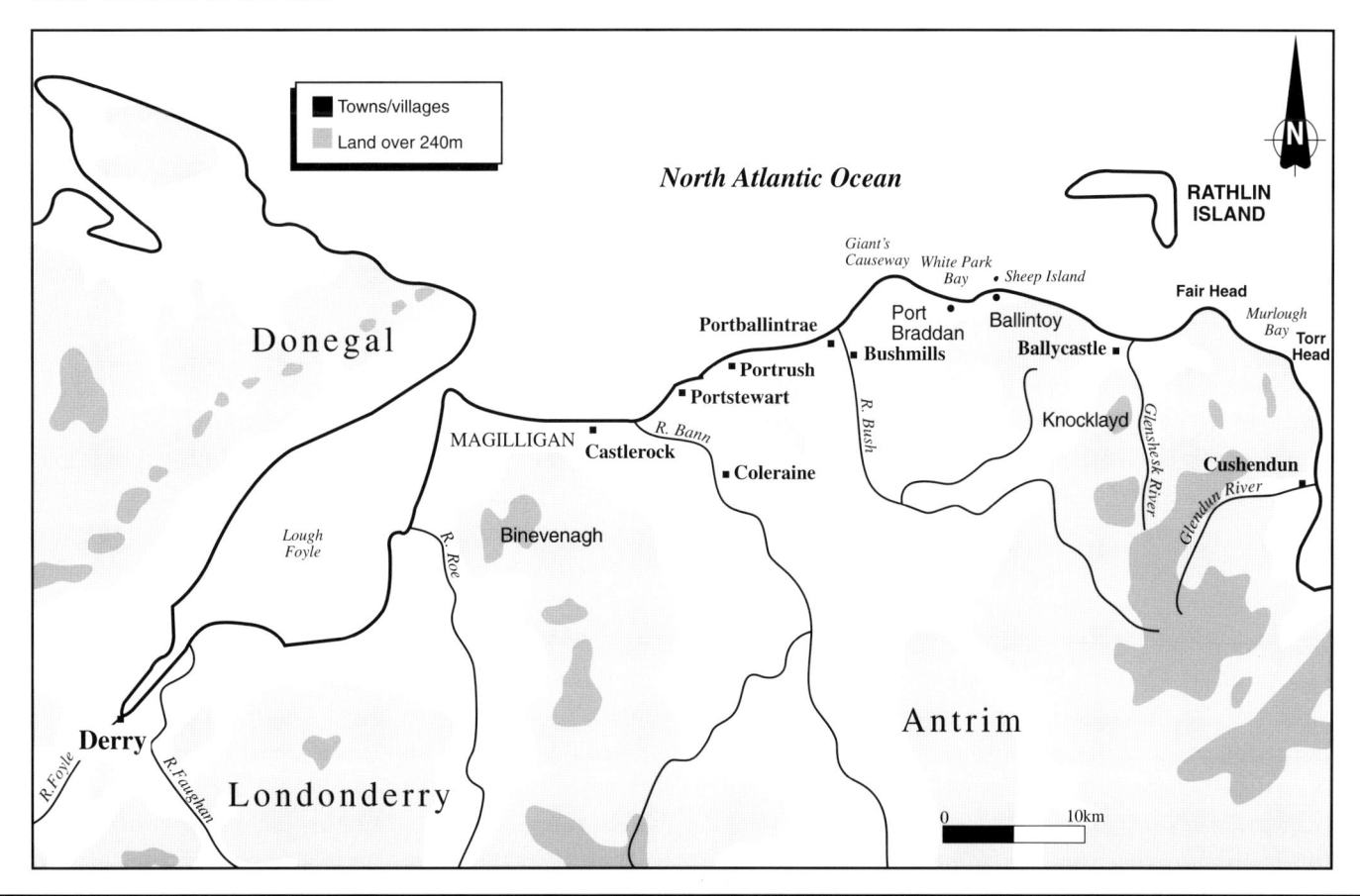

richness of materials and artefacts recovered from archaeological excavations and the numerous and partly ruined stone and/or earthen structures.

Excavation and recovery of artefacts began in earnest during the latter part of the 19th Century when a number of amateur collectors or 'hobbyist antiquarians' focussed their attention on the sand dunes adjacent to the Bann estuary, and those at Portrush, Portballintrae and White Park Bay. Prominent amongst these people was William J. Knowles of Ballymena, who published several lengthy and detailed descriptions of the finds he amassed on his frequent visits to the coast (Knowles, 1878, 1885, 1887, 1889, 1891, 1895, 1901). Around the same time, William Gray and Leonard Hassé were also involved in collecting and documenting the evidence for human activities in sand dunes (Gray, 1879; Hassé, 1890). Investigations of dune archaeology continued during the 20th Century with reports by Coffey and Praeger (1904), Hewson (1934), May and Batty (1948), Collins (1977), Mallory and Woodman (1984), Mallory et al. (1988) and Yates (1985-86). Together, these publications are testimony to an abundance of sites, materials and artefacts, and indicate that the sandy coastal landscapes of Northern Ireland were an important resource for humans during several periods of history and prehistory.

In the 1930s, a series of excavations was undertaken in caves that occur in basalt cliffs at Port Braddon (May, 1934) and in chalk cliffs at Ballintoy (Jackson, 1933, 1934, 1936, 1938). At Port Braddon, fire hearths were encountered along with numerous bones (mainly animal, but some human ones) and shells, but nothing by which to date the occupation. Similar materials were recovered from the Ballintoy caves and, in addition, pot-sherds of the Late Bronze Age, Iron Age and Early Christian periods were found and suggest cave occupation may have spanned the first millennium BC and the first millennium AD.

The cliff top promontory fort at Larrybane and stone castles such as those at Dunluce, Dunseverick and Kenbane have also attracted considerable attention (e.g. Childe, 1936; Proudfoot and Wilson, 1961-62; O'Neill, 1983) and provide evidence for the continuity of human occupation in the coastal zone throughout the Early Christian and Medieval periods. The castles indicate a defended coastline and are a reminder that shifts in Medieval political and military power occurred at that time.

Mesolithic (c. 7000-3500 years BC)

Evidence for communities of Mesolithic hunter-gatherers in Northern Ireland is concentrated along the coast and in the lower Bann valley. Accumulations of flint artefacts and debitage ascribed to these settlers have been found at a number of sites. One early report of flint flakes and cores is from the inter-tidal peat on Mill Strand, Portrush (Patterson, 1896). In recent years this peat has yielded ^{14}C dates of 5920 ± 80 years BP (peat top) and 7310 ± 100 years BP (from 1.37 m below peat top) (Wilson and McKenna, 1996), placing it securely within the span of Mesolithic activity.

Mount Sandel, overlooking the River Bann on the south side of Coleraine, is one of the very few locations at which Mesolithic settlement is attested in Northern Ireland. Flint artefacts were first reported from around this site by Gray (1888) but thorough excavation was not undertaken until the 1970s. The site produced a wealth of evidence for Mesolithic settlement, including arcs of post-holes delimiting hut sites, hearths, charcoal, burnt bones (predominantly of pig and fish) and hazel nut shells, as well as an abundance of worked flint (Woodman, 1985). Several ^{14}C dates place occupation of Mount Sandel around 7000 years BC, making it the earliest settlement yet found in Ireland. The nature of the food remains indicates the site was well placed to allow exploitation of the terrestrial, riverine and marine/estuarine resources by hunting, fishing and gathering. It is not known whether the site was occupied all year round or only on a seasonal basis, but the pattern of hearths and post-holes suggests the huts were rebuilt over a number of years.

Neolithic (*c.* 4000-2000 years BC)

Although there is evidence for Neolithic activity at Mount Sandel (Woodman, 1985), and numerous pot-sherds and flint artefacts have been recovered from the coastal dunes (see above), the remains of early farming settlements are not abundant along the north coast of Northern Ireland. One site of possible Neolithic settlement is White Park Bay where a linear group of 20 round houses was identified near the centre of the bay and a further nine at the eastern end of the bay (Knowles, 1885, 1901). There is also the rather enigmatic site of Goodland, near Murlough Bay east of Ballycastle, where numerous pits filled with stones, charcoal, flint and pot-sherds were found below blanket peat (Case *et al.*, 1969). From detailed investigations of the sub-peat soils, Proudfoot (1958) proposed that the gradual deterioration of soil quality was a direct result of Neolithic agricultural practices.

Outcrops of porcellanite at Tievebulliagh, near Cushendall, and Brockley, on Rathlin Island, were quarried during the Neolithic for the manufacture of polished stone axes. These are believed to have been used for tree clearance in order to create areas for cultivation and pasture, and for ceremonial purposes. Examples of these axes have been found throughout Ireland and Britain and indicate the existence of exchange networks.

Probably the most prominent and enduring evidence of Neolithic activity in the coastal zone is the megalithic tomb. These are principally passage tombs, although wedge tombs, court tombs and portal tombs also occur. Current thinking suggests that in addition to being repositories for the deceased, they functioned as territorial indicators. Gray (1884) and Hobson (1907) provided early descriptions of some of the north coast tombs. Three tombs occur on high ground above White Park Bay (Fig. 63) and along with tombs on hilltops near Ballycastle – Carnanmore (379 m), Greenanmore (297 m) and Knocklayd (514 m) – occupy spectacular situations overlooking the coast. Few of the tombs have been excavated but Neolithic pot-sherds, flint artefacts, and porcellanite axes, along with cremated bone, have been recovered from the excavations that have been conducted. If it is assumed that the distribution of tombs reflects the distribution of Neolithic settlement, then agricultural activity must have been widespread in this part of Northern Ireland.

Bronze Age (*c.* 2000-300 years BC)

Various remains, both artefactual and human, provide the evidence for activity in the Bronze Age. The coastal dunes have yielded much of the artefactual material, and at White Park Bay there are indications that continuity of settlement from the Neolithic into the Bronze Age may have occurred. Many of the finds from coastal dunes are of ceramics and lithics, but also bronze pins and casting moulds for swords and spearheads are known. In additions, cist burials have been reported from sand dune contexts (Gray, 1879; Collins, 1977), and although wedge tombs are believed to have been erected during the later Neolithic, there is evidence that they continued to be built and utilised for burials during the early Bronze Age.

One of the best-preserved Bronze Age monuments in the region is at Lissanduff, Portballintrae. On a hilltop overlooking the estuary of the River Bush are two adjacent enclosures surrounded by earthen banks. One of the enclosures is centred on a spring and had been lined with clay to retain water and thus forms an artificial pool. The site has been interpreted as of ritual significance because it is similar to certain other ritual structures, and is located at the northern end of an important route from the south.

Iron Age (*c.* 300 years BC-431 years AD)

In contrast to some other areas of Ulster, there are only slight traces of Iron Age settlement along the north coast of Northern Ireland. Iron Age finds from the sand dunes and the caves at Ballintoy, and a hearth and pit at Mount Sandel indicate some coastal activity was taking place, but the scale of

Fig. 63: Magheraboy passage tomb, near White Park Bay

such activity is unknown. The most recent excavation of an Iron Age context is that at Ballymulholland 1, Magilligan Foreland (Mallory et al., 1988). From a shell midden in eroding sand cliffs evidence for an economy based on cattle, pigs, sheep and shellfish was documented, and the presence of metal (iron) slag was taken to indicate local ironworking. In the absence of detailed evidence for other Iron Age sites, Ballymulholland 1 may or may not be typical of the period.

Early Christian (c. 431-1177 AD)

Records indicate that the first Christian bishop sent by Rome to Ireland arrived in 431 AD. This event defines the start of the Early Christian period. Numerous structures and artefacts dating from this time are known from the north coast of Northern Ireland. Secular society was essentially rural (dispersed) and based in a variety of settlement types. Probably the most ubiquitous settlement was the rath or ringfort – a roughly circular earthen enclosure formed by digging a ditch and using the ditch material to form a bank on the inner side of the ditch, and thus affording the enclosure some measure of defence. One such site is Dunboy rath overlooking White Park Bay. The number of concentric ditches/banks included in the construction distinguishes variations on the basic rath. Where stone was abundant in the landscape, roughly circular drystone-walled enclosures, known as cashels, were built, as at Altagore, near Cushendun. Associated with many raths are souterrains, man-made underground passages and chambers, stone-lined and roofed. Similar structures have also been recorded within the thick walls of cashels. Souterrains are abundant along the north coast of Northern Ireland with a particularly dense distribution between Coleraine and Ballycastle (Mallory and McNeill, 1991), and have been found at many sites where there is no longer any clear surface expression of a rath. The purpose of souterrains has generated much debate: they are usually explained as having been places of refuge during times of conflict and/or places of storage for food and household possessions. A truncated souterrain can be seen in the disused sandpit at Drumnakeel, on the A2 road from Ballycastle to Cushendun.

Another Early Christian settlement structure is the man-made island in a lake – the crannog. The situation of these settlements and their relative inaccessibility clearly indicates their defensive nature. Although some crannogs were constructed as early as the Late Bronze Age, dendro-dates from excavated timbers show that many were built or strengthened in the Early Christian period. The best example of a crannog from the north coast area is at Lough na Cranagh on Fair Head (Fig. 64). This crannog is roughly oval in plan and has a drystone revetment that rises 1.5 m above the waterline.

Excavations at the coastal promontory fort of Larrybane, undertaken in 1935 and again in 1954, revealed that settlement had probably occurred around 700-900 AD (Childe, 1936; Proudfoot and Wilson, 1961-62). A rock-cut ditch, and a rampart formerly 2 m high and 5 m wide, defended the fort site. Thus, some of the surviving settlement types of Early Christian secular society indicate a defensive element to their location and construction.

The broad economic context of the Early Christian period was discussed by Mallory and Woodman (1984) based on material recovered from a shell midden at Oughtymore, Magilligan Foreland, and finds documented in earlier reports of coastal excavations. The combined evidence suggests a mixed arable and pastoral economy with

Fig. 64: Lough na Cranagh crannog, Fair Head

the exploitation of rye, barley and wheat, and cattle, sheep, pig, horse and red deer. Coupled to this, the great variety of fish and shellfish remains at certain sites indicates the added importance of marine food resources.

Several Early Christian ecclesiastical sites are well represented within the north coast area. At Armoy, 9 km south of Ballycastle, the remains of a round tower (Fig. 65) stand adjacent to St. Patrick's Church. The site was reputedly granted to St. Patrick in 470 AD and the resulting ecclesiastical centre (monastery) is reported to have been attacked several times in the later Early Christian period. The round tower, and a souterrain discovered as a result of road widening in the 1980s, lends support to those reports. The earliest record of an Irish round tower is from the first half of the tenth century and they continued to be built until the early thirteenth century. They are usually interpreted as bell towers and/or defensive structures. Many towers were 25-35 m high, with windows, a conical roof and a door situated some distance above ground level. The Armoy tower is now about 12 m high and is all that remains visible of the monastic foundation.

Fig. 65: The remains of the round tower at Armoy

Other Early Christian ecclesiastical sites along the north coast include those of Drumnakill Church, at Murlough Bay, and Templastragh, near Port Braddon. The former site is associated with a nearby ballaun (ritual) stone. At the latter site, an inscribed cross-slab, believed to date from the earliest Christian foundation is built into the ruined walls of a later church. Another Early Christian cross-slab (Broughanlea Cross) stands alongside the A2 road, 1.5 km east of Ballycastle.

Medieval (*c.* 1177-1700 years AD)

The advance into Ulster by the Anglo-Normans in 1177 AD was quickly followed by the appearance of fortified constructions – the so-called 'mottes' – steeply-sloping and flat-topped earthen mounds crowned with wooden towers. Some mottes had an associated 'bailey' - a defended courtyard at a lower level than the motte and intended for domestic and workaday purposes. Several somewhat degraded mottes can be seen close to the north coast: the mound at Ballycairn, on the hill overlooking Coleraine on the west side of the River Bann, has been considered a former motte and the Broom More and Cloughanmurray mottes are a short distance inland from Ballycastle. The large earthwork at Mount Sandel (Mountsandel Fort), adjacent to the Mesolithic site has also been regarded as an Anglo-Norman motte. Some sources have identified this as the site of Kil Santain – a fortification built by John de Courcy in 1197 AD – but the age and origin(s) of the mound have been disputed.

Stone-built castles of Medieval age are present at several locations along the north coast. The best preserved and most dramatically situated of these is undoubtedly Dunluce Castle, 2.5 km west of Portballintrae. Occupation of the basalt stack, prior to construction of the first castle, is evident from the presence of a rock-cut souterrain that contained Early Christian pottery. The earliest castle dates from the 14th Century and has been attributed to the MacQuillan family who held power in the region until displaced by the Scottish MacDonnells in the 16th Century. Most of the present remains date from MacDonnell occupancy in the late 16th and early 17th Centuries (Fig. 66).

Fig. 66: Dunluce Castle

The castle was captured by in 1565 by Shane O'Neill, and badly damaged and captured again in 1584 by forces under the command of Sir John Perrott. However, following each of these events the MacDonnells resumed residency and, under the leadership of Sorley Boy MacDonnell and his son James, the castle was rebuilt and extended. The MacDonnells also gained extensive territories and were granted the Earldom of Antrim. In 1639 part of the castle and some of its occupants fell into the sea and after the 1641-42 conflict the castle was gradually abandoned and a new house built on the mainland. In 1928 the 7th Earl of Antrim passed the ruins over to the Government for preservation as a monument. The castle is now open to the public for a small admission charge and a guidebook is available.

In a field adjacent to the castle the remains of a deserted village can be seen. The village was destroyed in the 1641-42 conflict, although the residents were spared. With appropriate low lighting the house-platforms are visible in pasture. The ruins of the village church stand about 0.4 km from the castle. Several of the gravestones carry 17th Century dates.

Lough Foyle

Andrew Cooper and Jeremy Gault

Environmental setting

Lough Foyle (Fig. 67) is a wide, shallow embayment located in a glacially incised fault valley. The western shoreline comprises outcrops of Dalradian (Precambrian) metasediments of high relief while the geology of the eastern shore comprises Mesozoic sediments topped by the Tertiary basalts of the Antrim Plateau. The Lough is a semi-enclosed marine embayment in which salinity averages 15-20 ppt. The tidal prism is about 300×10^6 m^3 and comparison of bathymetric charts indicates that the total volume of the estuary has increased since 1840. The Lough thus appears to be a net exporter of sediment. Dominant waves within the Lough approach from the southwest, and the water surface is afforded a degree of shelter from winds from other directions by high ground on both western and eastern shorelines. The ocean shoreline is affected by large Atlantic swell waves which, through refraction, influence the seaward plan form of Magilligan Foreland which has developed a concave, swash-aligned equilibrium form.

Evolution

A number of late glacial shoreline features are exposed around the Lough as emergent cliff lines, raised beaches and tidal flats that indicate late glacial shorelines at about + 20 m OD. Sea level fell below the present by about 12,500 ^{14}C yr BP to a lowstand of about – 30 m (about 10,000 ^{14}C yr BP) during which time the river valleys were incised.

Carter (1982) reported a change from marine to estuarine conditions in a borehole at Magilligan Point at about – 30 m.

The Holocene evolution of the Lough comprised a phase of initial drowning as sea level rose from a Holocene lowstand of – 30 m to about + 3 m by 6500 ^{14}C yr BP whereafter sea level fell to the

Fig. 67: Locality map of Lough Foyle showing shorelines subdivided into four zones related to antecedent topography, sediment supply and contemporary dynamics

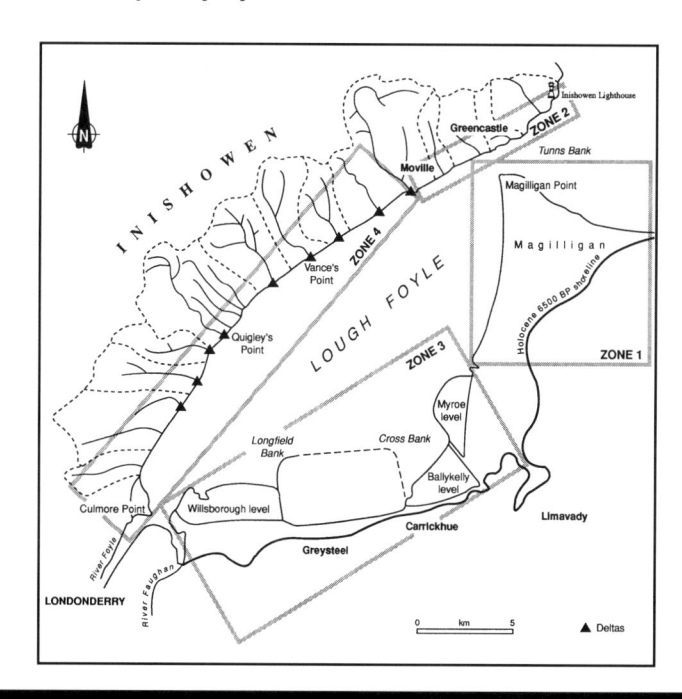

present. The fall in sea level was accompanied by the landward transport of shelf sands into the initially wide estuary mouth. The 6500 yr BP shoreline is exposed along the eastern and western shores as a series of scarps, terraces and sediment bodies (Fig. 67). The earliest depositional feature associated with this shoreline is a gravel ridge exposed adjacent to the modern Roe estuary. The fall in sea level saw the progressive accumulation of a series of beach ridges along the eastern margin of the Lough and the tidal channel was fixed against the resistant rock outcrops of the western shore. These beach ridges accumulated to form the present day Magilligan Foreland and its adjacent tidal flats.

Contemporary geomorphology

The contemporary Lough comprises several discrete sub-environments. Magilligan Foreland acts as a barrier to oceanic wave influences and although its seaward margin attains swash-alignment with long period swells, its Lough Foyle shoreline is affected by short period wind waves. Most of the Lough consists of shallow (> 2 m deep) areas of mobile sandy sediment into which a main tidal channel and several subsidiary branches are incised (Fig. 68). Although the ebb-delta is located in a high energy swell environment, it achieves a high degree of shelter from Inishowen headland to the west. The upper surface of the ebb-tidal delta is intertidally exposed and when submerged is a zone of wave shoaling and occasional breaking. (Its name (the Tunns Bank) refers to the sea god whose hair was seen in the breaking waves). Changes in the ebb-tidal delta morphology were linked by Carter *et al.* (1982) to changes in shoreline configuration on the seaward margin of the Magilligan barrier as wave refraction changed in response to changes in offshore bathymetry. A substantial portion of the intertidal flats in the upper part of the Lough were reclaimed in the early 19th Century. These are maintained as agricultural land at present although periodic pumping is required for drainage and the sea defences on the Lough shore have recently been substantially upgraded.

Shoreline environments within the Lough vary markedly and several distinct sub-environments may be identified. These are here designated zones 1-4 and are discussed below.

Shoreline Zone 1: Magilligan Foreland

Magilligan Foreland is composed almost entirely of unconsolidated sand (with intercalated peat beds) in which no natural headlands occur other than localised zones of salt marsh accretion. It is a zone of unimpeded littoral sand transport. As such the shoreline has evolved a distinctive morphology both in plan and profile. The ocean margin is characterised by a wide dissipative beach fronted by multiple bars and on which spilling breakers persistently characterise the shoreline. The beach sand is sufficiently well packed to permit access by normal road vehicles at Benone.

The most dynamic zone of this sector is at Magilligan Point (Fig. 69A) where ocean and estuary waves interact to produce alternating, but long-lived periods of beach ridge erosion and accretion. The present erosional phase, which began about 1980, followed a phase of persistent accretion (marked by beach ridge accumulation) between 1950 and 1979 that was documented by Carter (1975b, 1979). The process of beach ridge formation during accretionary phases is linked to two mechanisms (Carter, 1986). One involves onshore transport of sediment and berm development in the intertidal zone through swash action, while the other involves extension

High Energy Coasts

Fig. 68: Spot satellite image of Lough Foyle, 1988. Note the extent of mobile sand bodies in the estuary, the multiple flood-tide channels and the ebb-delta. Magilligan foreland forms a barrier at the mouth of the lough.

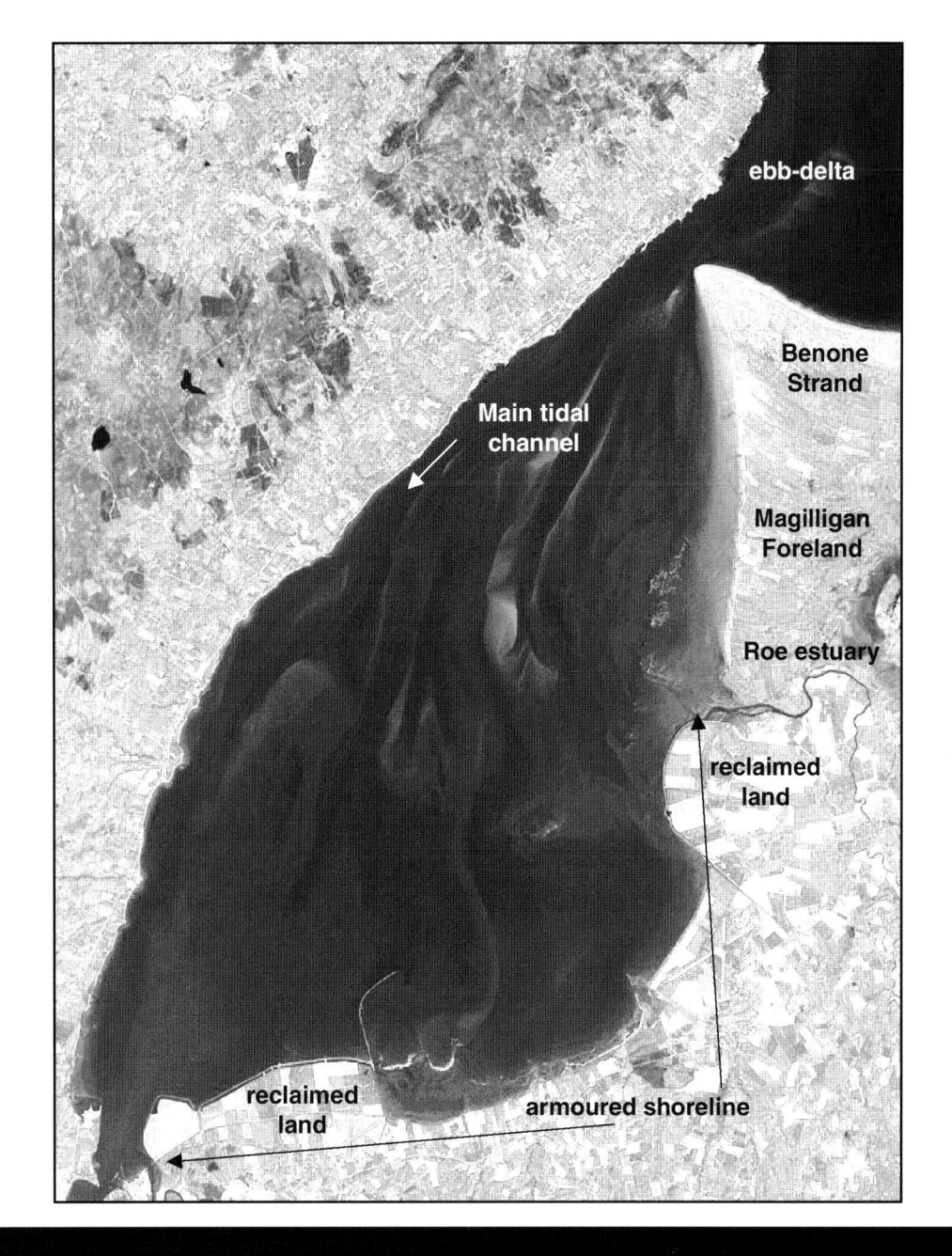

High Energy Coasts

Fig. 69: Photographs illustrating main features of sandy shoreline of Magilligan Foreland (Zone 1). (A) Oblique aerial view of Magilligan Point (November 2001) showing contemporary beachridges. Note Martello Tower, 1812 (arrowed). (B) Vertical aerial view of northern section of Magilligan shoreline. Note intersecting bedforms on intertidal flat and narrow high tide beach. (C) Vertical aerial view of southern section of Magilligan shoreline. Note coastal cell development on shoreline and relationship to salt marsh development.

alongshore of submerged bars which become detached and then migrate onshore where they weld to the beach. The beach ridge accretion of 1955-1979 (Fig. 70A) contrasts markedly with the recession measured between 1996 and 1999 (Fig. 70B).

The Lough Foyle margin of Magilligan Foreland is characterised by an intertidal flat that narrows seaward and which is backed by a persistently retreating scarp cut into sandy sediments of the beach ridge plain. The intertidal flat exhibits a persistent series of low amplitude, long wavelength bedforms with two distinct orientations that intersect at right angles (Fig. 69B). This shoreline has retreated persistently at rates of about 1 m per year for the past two centuries. The tidal flats support large beds of Mussels (*Mytilus edulis*) and Eelgrass (*Zostera spp*). Several scattered stands of saltmarsh vegetation occur along the foreshore. The lower saltmarsh consists of a community dominated by *Puccinellia maritima*. As tidal influence declines up the shore, this gives way to a community characterised by *Festuca rubra* and *Juncus gerardii*. A number of small-scale coastal cells (zeta bays) have developed along the shoreline (Fig. 69C) in which salt marsh outcrops form headlands for cell planform development.

Shoreline Zone 2

The western, rocky shoreline adjacent to the tidal inlet is characterised by a series of small headland-embayment beaches (Fig. 71A) within each of which a fixed sediment volume appears to respond to seasonal changes in the wave regime by profile adjustment. These beaches are confined on the Lough side by the deep tidal channel which precludes longshore sediment transport between beaches.

Shoreline Zone 3

On the southeastern margin of the Lough most of the shoreline has been extensively modified by reclamation of former intertidal flats (Fig. 71C) and the entire shoreline has been armoured. Between Greysteel and Carrickhue, however, which is the only sector not to have been extensively reclaimed, the shoreline morphology comprises wide intertidal flats of mixed sand and mud upon which shell-rich ridges are formed (Fig. 71D). These ridges migrate landward at rates influenced by wave energy and basement slope (Lowry, 1982).

Shoreline Zone 4

On the southwestern shore which is predominantly rocky, several small streams flowing from the steep Inishowen hinterland have deposited a series of small fan deltas (Fig. 71B) from which coarse-grained and relatively poorly sorted sediment is reworked to form narrow beaches of mixed sand and gravel. These beaches are bounded by the deep tidal channel.

Discussion

The variability in shoreline forms within Lough Foyle may be attributed to the antecedent topography and contemporary dynamics. The steep topography of the western (Inishowen) shoreline owes its origin to its resistant lithologies which were relatively less eroded by ice than the Mesozoic and Tertiary lithologies to the east. This steep topography is responsible for formation of the Foyle river channel and present tidal channels along the western shoreline. In the east, a wide, gently sloping basement provided a focus for deposition of glacially-derived and wave-reworked sediment during the Holocene.

Contemporary processes within the Lough are dominated by southwesterly wind-generated waves that are progressively eroding the sandy Lough shoreline along Magilligan Foreland, which is exposed to maximum fetch distances and faces the dominant wind direction. Low wave energy and low sediment supply in the southeastern sector is responsible for relatively fine-grained intertidal flats and the dominance of biogenic particles (shells) in the ridges that develop there. The steep hinterland of the southwestern shoreline is responsible for the fast-flowing streams that have deposited fan deltas in the Lough while low wave energy on the southwestern shore impedes the dispersal of fan delta sediment. The tidal channel effectively isolates western and eastern sections of the Lough. Higher wave energy toward the mouth of the Lough, coupled with a lowering of the topography, has led to the development of a series of isolated headland-embayment beaches.

Management issues

Lough Foyle straddles the UK-Republic of Ireland border (which runs along the shipping channel on the western side of the Lough). A number of areas of its management are handled by a unique cross-border institution now known as the Loughs Agency (formerly the Foyle Fisheries Commission). The responsibilities of the Loughs Agency extend to fisheries (including shellfish), recreation and the promotion of economic development on Lough Foyle and Carlingford Lough which also spans the border. Other management issues are dealt with on a sectoral basis by the relevant government departments and local authorities.

Lough Foyle supports up to 40,000 migratory birds each winter. It supports internationally important populations of three species in particular; Whooper swan *Cygnus cygnus* (around 900 individuals or 5.6% of the international population), Light-bellied Brent Goose *Branta bernicla hrota* (around 3700 individuals or 18.7% of the international population), and Bar-tailed Godwit *Limosa lapponica* (around 1900 or 1.9% of the international population). The Lough consequently has a number of conservation designations that seek to limit and control the range of human activities that potentially threaten the environment. Among its designations are the national designation of Area of Special Scientific Interest (ASSI), European Designations of Special Protection Area (SPA) and Special Area of Conservation (SAC) and international recognition as a Ramsar site. In addition, mudflats in the southeastern shoreline are held by the Royal Society for Protection of Birds (RSPB) as a nature reserve and salt marsh at the roe estuary is owned by the Foyle Wildfowlers' Association. Some of these designations are discussed more fully in Appendix 1 at the end of this section.

The SPA (> 2200 hectares) includes the whole of the Lough Foyle ASSI and the intertidal area of Magilligan ASSI in Lough Foyle extending south of Magilligan Point. The boundary of the SPA

Fig. 70: Shoreline changes at Magilligan Point during an accretionary phase (A), after Carter (1979) and erosional phase (B). Diagram A shows dated beach ridges formed through accretion between 1955 and 1977. Diagram B shows surveyed high water marks between May 1996 and March 1998

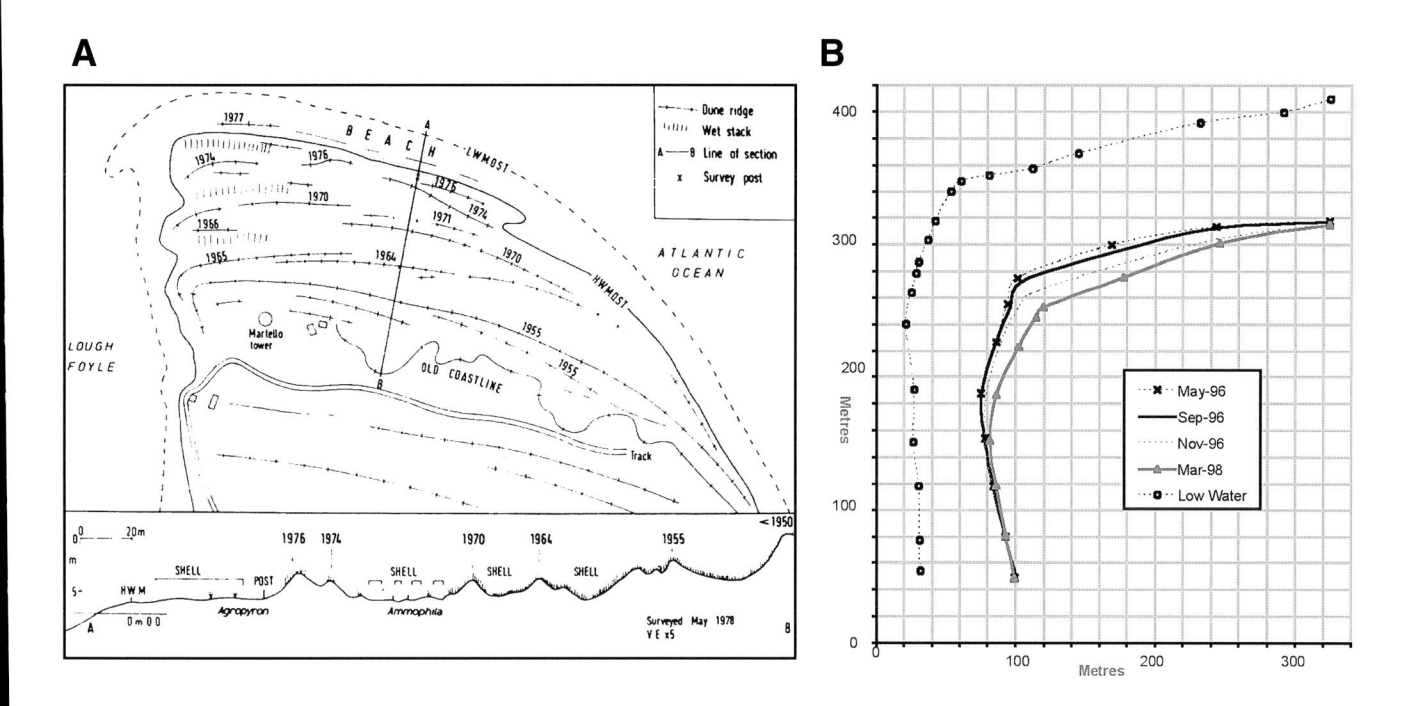

coincides with that of the Lough Foyle Ramsar site and it overlaps with Magilligan SAC.

In addition, 1000 hectares at Magilligan Point is designated as a SAC by virtue of being one of the largest dune systems in the UK and providing a representation of several habitat types (dunes with *Salix arenaria*, humid dune slacks, and fixed dunes with herbaceous vegetation (grey dunes)) in Northern Ireland.

Lough Foyle's qualification as a Ramsar site is based on several criteria of the Ramsar Convention. It is a representative example of a wetland complex including intertidal sand and mudflats with extensive seagrass beds, saltmarsh, estuaries and associated brackish ditches. It also plays a substantial hydrological, biological and ecological system role in the natural functioning of a major river basin which is located in a trans-border position. The site also supports an appreciable assemblage of rare, vulnerable or endangered species or sub-species of plant and animal. These include Allis Shad *Alosa alosa*, Twaite Shad *Alosa fallax fallax*, Smelt *Osmerus eperlanus* and Sea Lamprey *Petromyzon marinus*, all of which are Irish Red Data Book species. In addition, important populations of Atlantic Salmon *Salmo salar* migrate through the system to and from their spawning grounds.

Several issues of concern presently exist for the management of Lough Foyle. These are summarised below:

1. Erosion of the Magilligan shoreline has given cause for concern to local farmers and several informal coastal defences have been emplaced to try and halt the erosion. An assessment of the potential for salt marsh as protection concluded that it was unlikely to succeed. Ironically, the sea defences on the reclaimed section of the shoreline have recently (1995-6) been upgraded.

2. Plans have been submitted for the extension of the runway of Derry City Airport onto about two hectares of the intertidal flat. There are concerns over the likely effect on birdlife.

3. A small car ferry is to run between Magilligan Point and Greencastle. The ferry terminus and piers are presently under construction. There are concerns over the impact on sedimentation and coastal processes.

Appendix 1

Special Protection Areas (SPAs) are designated under the European Commission Directive on the Conservation of Wild Birds (79/409/EEC). All European Community member States are required to identify internationally important areas for breeding, over-wintering and migrating birds and designate them as Special Protection Areas (SPAs). The United Kingdom practice is to protect these areas under domestic legislation before classifying them as SPAs. Classified SPAs and candidate SACs together form the European wide network of sites known as Natura 2000. Eleven SPAs have been designated in Northern Ireland.

The Loughs Agency is an agency of the Foyle Carlingford and Irish Lights Commission. The Commission was established following the Agreement between both Governments which has been facilitated by the North/South Co-operation (Implementation Bodies) (Northern Ireland) Order 1999 and the British-Irish Agreement Act 1999. It has a Board with 12 members who in exercising the functions of the body are required to act in accordance with, any directions given by the North South Ministerial Council, to whom it also reports. The Commission's sponsoring Departments are the Department of Agriculture and Rural Development and the Department of the Marine and Natural Resources.

Functions and areas of responsibility

The Loughs Agency is responsible for exercising the following functions in the Foyle Area and the Carlingford Areas:

- The promotion of development and management of Lough Foyle and Carlingford Lough for commercial and recreational purposes in respect of marine, fishery and aquaculture matters;

- The conservation, protection, management and development of the salmon and inland fisheries of the Foyle and Carlingford Areas;

- The development and licensing of aquaculture;

- The development of marine tourism in the Carlingford and Foyle Areas.

Fig. 71: Photographs illustrating the main morphological characteristics of the shoreline in zones 2, 3 and 4. (A) Pocket beach on rocky northwest shoreline (Zone 2). Note raised shoreline features of Holocene and late glacial age. (B) Fan delta at stream outlet on south western shoreline (Zone 4). (C) Reclaimed land fronted by drainage channel and sea defences (Zone 3). (D) Shell/gravel ridge overlying mixed sand/mud intertidal flat on unaltered shoreline (Zone 3)

Native oysters - a problem for fisheries and conservation in Europe

Tony Andrew

Background

Since the advent of man, oysters have provided an important protein source and have assumed major cultural and socio-economic importance in western European countries. The antiquity of oyster harvesting is evidenced in megalithic and neolithic middens and shell (cultch) is found as building and flooring materials from mediaeval site through to the last century along the western European seaboard. As a source of protein oysters provided a significant contribution to the diet to the point that the poor complained that they were getting too much at the expense of other traditional fish and meats – "It's a wery remarkable circumstance, Sir," said Sam, "that poverty and oysters always seem to go together." (*Pickwick Papers*, Charles Dickens). The situation has changed markedly during the past century and now oysters realise a high price as a luxury food. A parallel is found in the salmon (*Salmo salar*) market where salmon has moved from being cheap protein to a luxury item and back again.

European oysters comprise two species, the flat oyster and the Portuguese oyster, the latter being distributed along the coast of Portugal and in the Gironde estuary in France. The native flat oyster, *Ostraea edulis*, is found commonly around the coasts of Western Europe and the Mediterranean (see Fig. 72). The flat oyster has been the major market oyster from all other European coasts and has been cultured for a number of centuries in

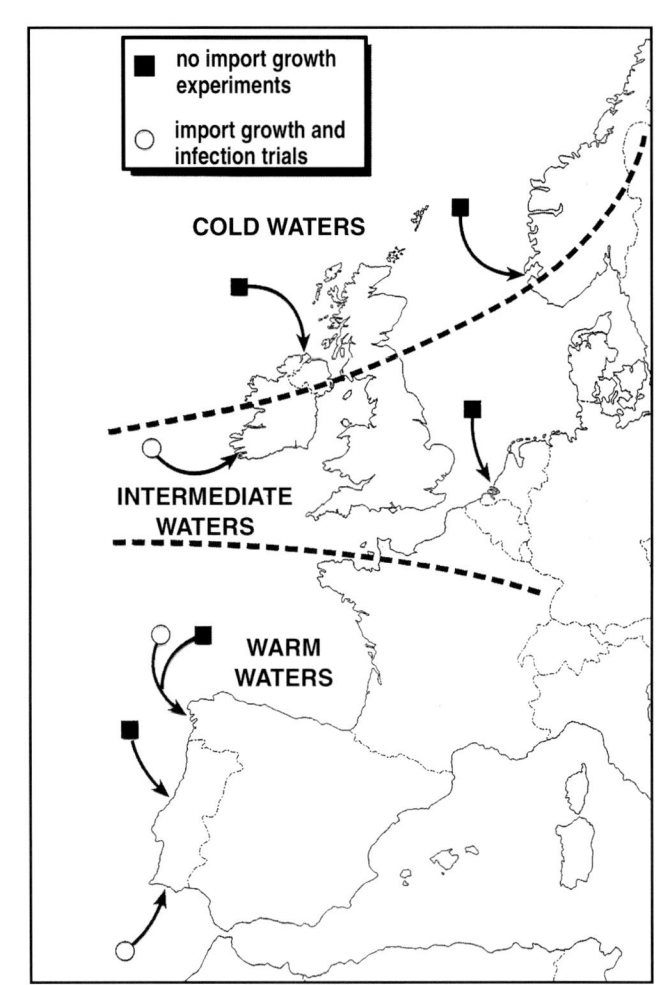

Fig. 72: Waters in western Europe where the native oyster - *Ostrea edulis* - is distributed together with relative water temperatures. Also shown are the Portuguese and Spanish fisheries together with the major Irish fisheries. Upper dotted line delimits the extreme limits of distribution.

France, Holland, Spain, Portugal and Norway using techniques where young settled oysters are grown up to maturity on rafts or ropes in natural environments. These techniques are still used. However the bulk of oysters are harvested from naturally-occurring "wild" populations with natural recruitment and settlement on the oyster beds. The growth of these populations depends upon mature oysters for larval production, suitable substrates – clean oyster or mussel (*Mytilus edulis*) shell – for settlement, and food availability and temperature for growth. The most important pressure for adult population regulation is human harvesting.

This situation changed dramatically from 1979 onwards with the introduction of a protozoa disease, *Bonamia ostraeae*, into the populations. This disease was accidentally introduced from North America where it is endemic in native *Crassostrea* spp but is not especially harmful. In the flat oyster populations it causes 80-90% mortality. *Bonamia ostraeae*, in simple terms, is a blood parasite transmitted when stocks are re-laid in uninfected situations. It affects the musculature of immediately, pre-sexually maturing oysters causing them to gape, silt-up and die. The transmission pathway is not fully understood. The progress of this disease has been to invade the major traditional oyster fisheries of Europe and the only significant Bonamia-free fisheries are to be found in Lough Foyle in the north of Ireland and some Norwegian waters. Oysters suffer from two other principal diseases, *Marteilia* and *Herpes*, but these are not such virulent killers as *Bonamia*.

The current situation is that wild fishery production has fallen from more than 20,000 tonnes per annum to less than 2000 tonnes in the space of 20 years. The current major "wild oyster" fisheries are restricted to north-west Ireland. A corresponding

Fig. 73: The life cycle of the native oyster – *Ostrea edulis*

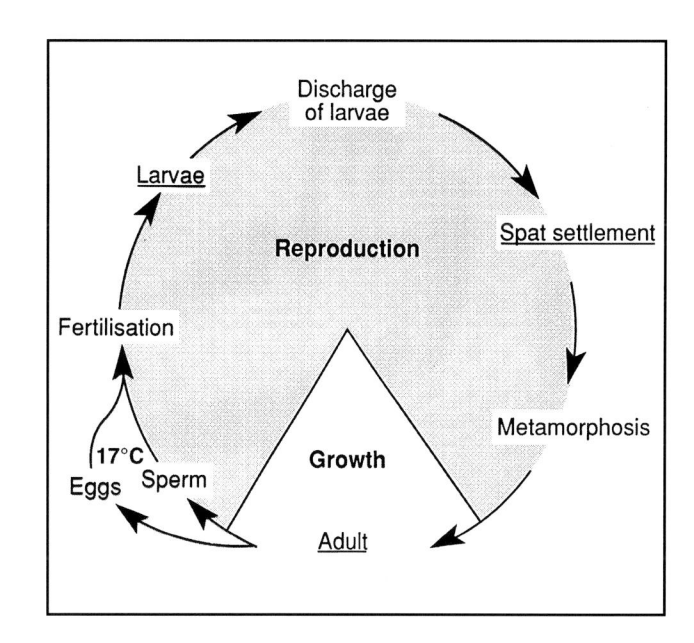

fall in Portuguese oyster production has also occurred in the Gironde, not *Bonamia* driven. This is compensated to an extent by the culture of flat oysters in the Galician waters of north-west Spain to bring them to market size before the onset of the disease. Other limited production by culture takes place in limited operations. The main production effort of oysters has been replaced by the mass culture of Pacific oysters, *Crassostraea gigas*, an exotic species with a faster growth rate, which is not disease susceptible to the same extent. The volume of production has more than matched the original production levels of native oysters but the gourmand still prefers the native flat and pays a significant premium for this species (O'Connor et al., 1992; Gardner and Elliott 2001).

Life cycle and growth of Ostrea edulis

The important features of the life cycle follow but it is essential to note that a proper understanding of the biology and ecology of the species is necessary for any potential for enhancement or control of oyster production. A simplified life cycle is presented in figure 73.

Adult oysters produce sperm and eggs sequentially, as the animals are hermaphrodite but maturation of the sexes is not concurrent. Eggs are fertilised in the mantle cavity and released as larvae at appropriate conditions of tide and lunar cycle. The free-swimming larvae grow and metamorphose in the planktonic waters and then settle as spat on suitable substrates where they filter feed on organic material and grow to adult size. This growth phase is food and temperature dependent and to reach adult size takes between two and five years dependent upon water temperatures. The maturation cycle requires temperatures in excess of 17°C according to the literature and usually occurs between May and September depending upon latitude.

Spat settlement success depends upon the availability of suitable substrate in the form of clean cultch, old mussel or oyster shell. Mortality to this stage is very high in the plankton, in the alighting on suitable substrates and in the early phase of attachment to this substrate.

Growth is determined by food availability in the environment. Although oysters may be found in many coastal marine locations, they are a mildly low-salinity tolerant species and estuaries provide food rich environments with reduced interspecific competition. Therefore the most productive areas of population production are to be found in rias and estuaries increasing in a southerly direction along the coasts (Fig. 72).

Lough Foyle and oyster production

Lough Foyle is an extensive estuary located in the north of Ireland (Fig. 74). A relatively small wild oyster fishery, producing 500-1500 tonnes of oysters a year, it is one of two fisheries still unaffected by bonamial disease. The fishery has a short season and provides part of the income of local fishermen and farmers who move on to other species or occupations after the September to November season. The reasons for the limited size of the fishery are several and complicated (McKelvey and Andrew, 1996; McKelvey et al., 1996).

Recruitment to the population is limited to warm years. The location of Lough Foyle is at the limit of the European distribution of oysters because the Gulf Stream, bringing warmer water, misses the estuary. Although a mild maritime climate prevails, summers tend to be coolish and wet resulting in ambient water temperatures rarely exceeding 15°C (Fig. 75) which is below the threshold for successful maturation to take place. Figure 75 shows the environmental temperatures during the late summer for more than twenty years and, although it is suspected the local oysters are cold adapted, successful recruitment probably only takes place every five years. The critical period for recruitment in Lough Foyle occurs in late September during the fishing season.

Recruitment is also dependent upon available substrate for spat settlement. This is limited to four main areas in the lough. The smll area furthest north-east is thought to be import for larval production although not very important as a fishery site. Population recruitment may be sustained.

Temperature also affects the growth rate and this has two consequences for Lough Foyle oysters. Firstly the growth rate is slower than other

High Energy Coasts

Fig. 74: The distribution of the oyster beds in Lough Foyle and the main fishing ports.

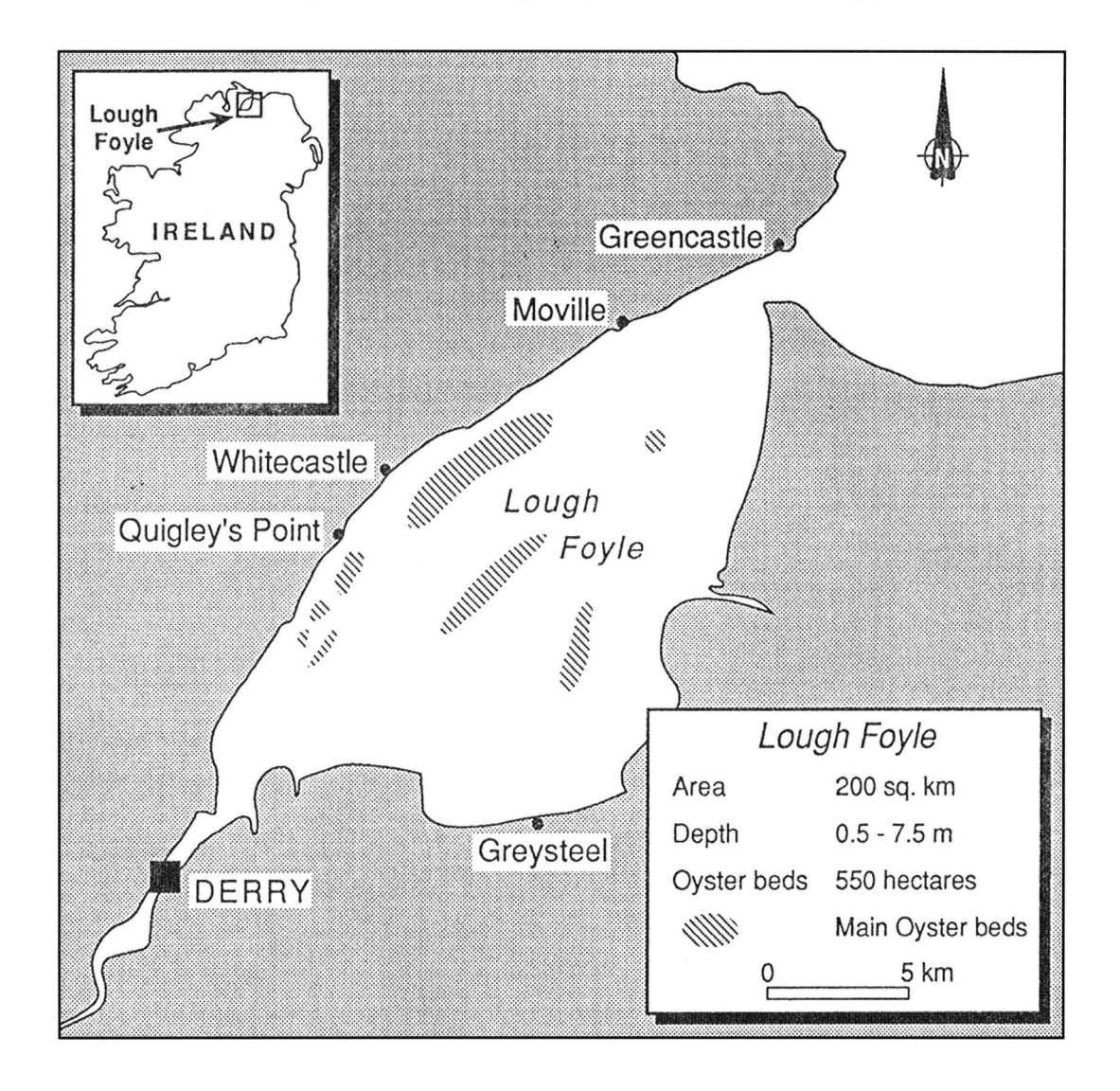

Lough Foyle
Area	200 sq. km
Depth	0.5 - 7.5 m
Oyster beds	550 hectares

Fig. 75: The summer temperature regime in Lough Foyle from 1970-1993 showing the periods when ambient temperature exceeds 15°C. Also shown is the successful recruitment years (spat settlement) and the developing cohorts of the oyster population.

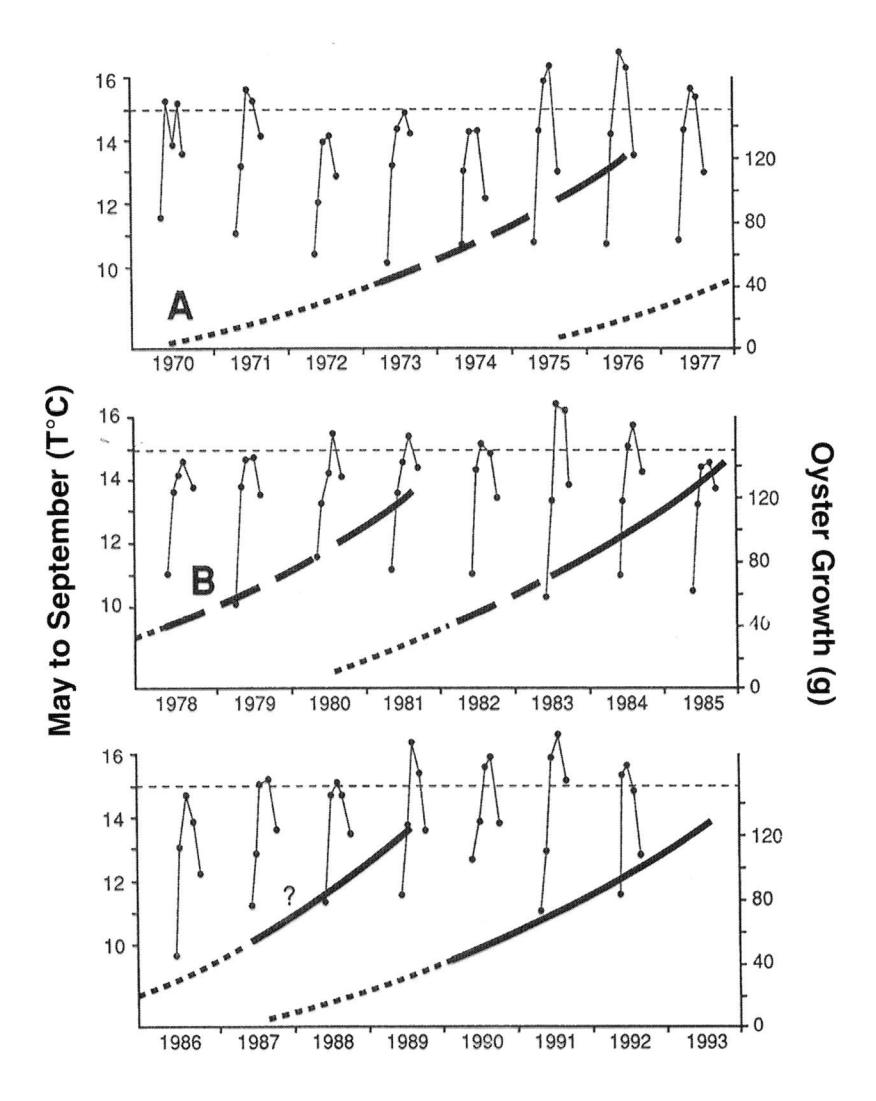

Fig. 76: (a) Allen curve calculating production of oysters in Lough Foyle comparing size at harvest with those in Spanish fisheries. (b) The generalised effect of environmental temperature on the final growth size in oysters. In colder waters, oysters grow slower but achieve a larger final size.

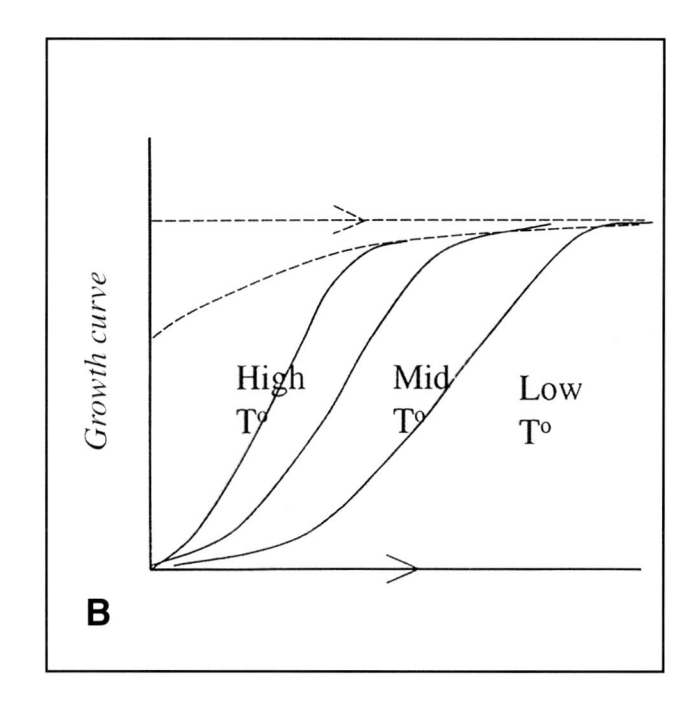

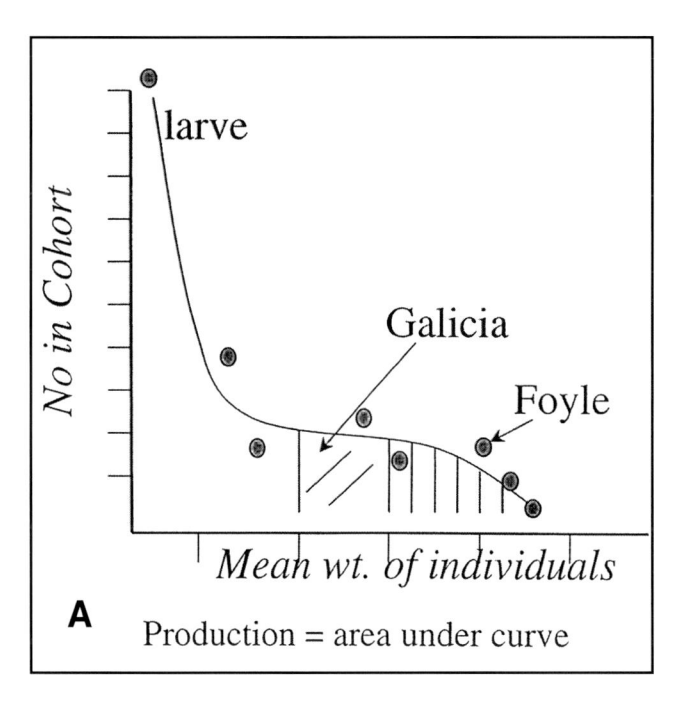

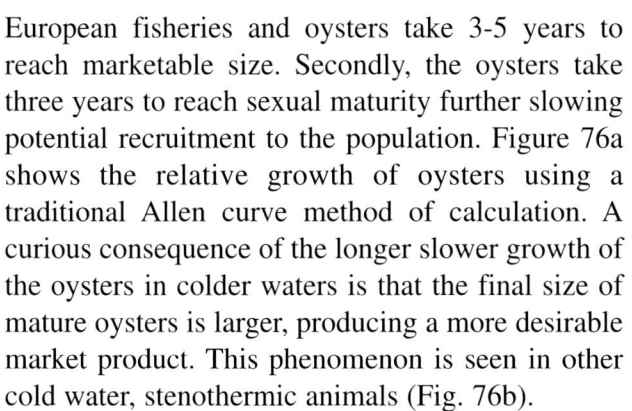

European fisheries and oysters take 3-5 years to reach marketable size. Secondly, the oysters take three years to reach sexual maturity further slowing potential recruitment to the population. Figure 76a shows the relative growth of oysters using a traditional Allen curve method of calculation. A curious consequence of the longer slower growth of the oysters in colder waters is that the final size of mature oysters is larger, producing a more desirable market product. This phenomenon is seen in other cold water, stenothermic animals (Fig. 76b).

The future of native oyster fisheries

The incidence of bonamial disease and its catastrophic effect on the European oyster fishery has propelled Lough Foyle to a position of prominence and importance in the European context. It is desirable to protect this disease free population. It is also desirable to increase the population if at all possible.

Conservation of the population needs to be carried out on two fronts. Firstly it is essential that there is no introduction of oysters from other environments by relaying "foreign" stock from other waters. This involves acceptance of this practice by all parties and adequate policing of the fishery. The fundamental mechanisms are in place from the local oyster co-operatives and the regulatory body the Foyle Fisheries Commission. Secondly the same groups must be involved in the sensible regulation of the fishery to prevent over fishing and maintenance of the wild fishery. This may involve artificial spat generation to increase recruitment – using local breeding stock – and the increase of the available shell for spat settlement. More shell may be added and existing shell may be cleaned.

In other fisheries alternative strategies have been adopted. The Norwegian fisheries have been based on artificial spat production for more than 150 years. Oysters are then seeded on to trays and grown to adult size from there. The Galician fisheries use a similar strategy in *Bonamia* infected waters and market the oyster at two years before they become infected. The size of product is considerably smaller but acceptable in the Spanish market.

Concluding remarks

The unique importance of the Foyle oyster fishery cannot be stressed although an alternative wild native fishery is being reintroduced into Strangford Lough (1997) (Gardner and Elliott, 2001), which had been a previously productive fishery until the early 1900s. Lough Foyle has become of vital conservation significance as the remaining disease free stocks in Europe. Its fate as a fishery will be determined by the following factors: remaining disease free, continuing recruitment success, continuing residence of sufficient breeding stock (by controlling fishing practice) and the availability of suitable settlement areas. The condition implies the restriction of competition for substrate space with other species such as mussels.

Magilligan Foreland

Peter Wilson

Introduction

The triangular beach-ridge plain of Magilligan Foreland is the largest coastal accumulation feature, and probably the most intensively researched coastal sediment body, in Ireland. Magilligan Foreland is that area of land extending south from Magilligan Point to the estuary of the River Roe and east from Lough Foyle to the foot of the steeper ground that rises to Binevenagh (the 10 m contour from Downhill in the north to Ballycarton in the south may be regarded as the eastern limit). It covers an area of 32 km^2 and comprises 250-300 northeast-facing swash-aligned beach ridges that have evolved in response to land/sea-level changes within the Holocene stage of the late Quaternary. The beach ridges are overlain locally by aeolian, lacustrine and/or alluvial sediments (Fig. 77).

Early Reports

Aspects of the natural history and human utilisation of Magilligan are documented in several 'early' publications. In a letter to the Bishop of Derry, dated 1725, Robert Innes described many of the area's 'curiosities' and recognised "that this land was formerly sea" (Innes, 1794). The use of the sands as rabbit warrens during the 17th, 18th and early 19th centuries is commented on by Sampson (1802), Dawson (1835) and Lewis (1837). At one time Magilligan was regarded as the most profitable warren in Ireland with an annual cull of 36,000- 60,000 rabbits for both meat and skins. Portlock (1843) mentioned that interbedded sands and peat were visible in cliffs along the Lough Foyle shoreline, and Kilroe (1913) was the first to offer an explanation for the presence of "so much sand", believing it to have been transported by wind from newly exposed beaches as sea level fell. Charlesworth (1924) regarded Magilligan as the re-sorted moraine of a Scottish ice lobe. However, although it is likely that the sands do represent reworked glacigenic sediments, there is no evidence that a moraine extended across the area now occupied by the foreland. Plant macro-fossils from peat, and shells from marl, obtained from exposures in sand cliffs along the Lough Foyle shoreline of Magilligan, were reported on by MacMillan (1957) and, although undated, the peats and marls were recognised as being the products of marshy ground or lagoons that developed in depressions between the beach ridges.

Recent research

Studies at Magilligan concerned with coastal dynamics and geomorphology were initiated by the late Bill Carter. His DPhil thesis (Carter, 1972) provided the basis for many papers over the next two decades, several of which contained the results of regular ground surveys pertaining to rates of shoreline progradation, foredune growth and

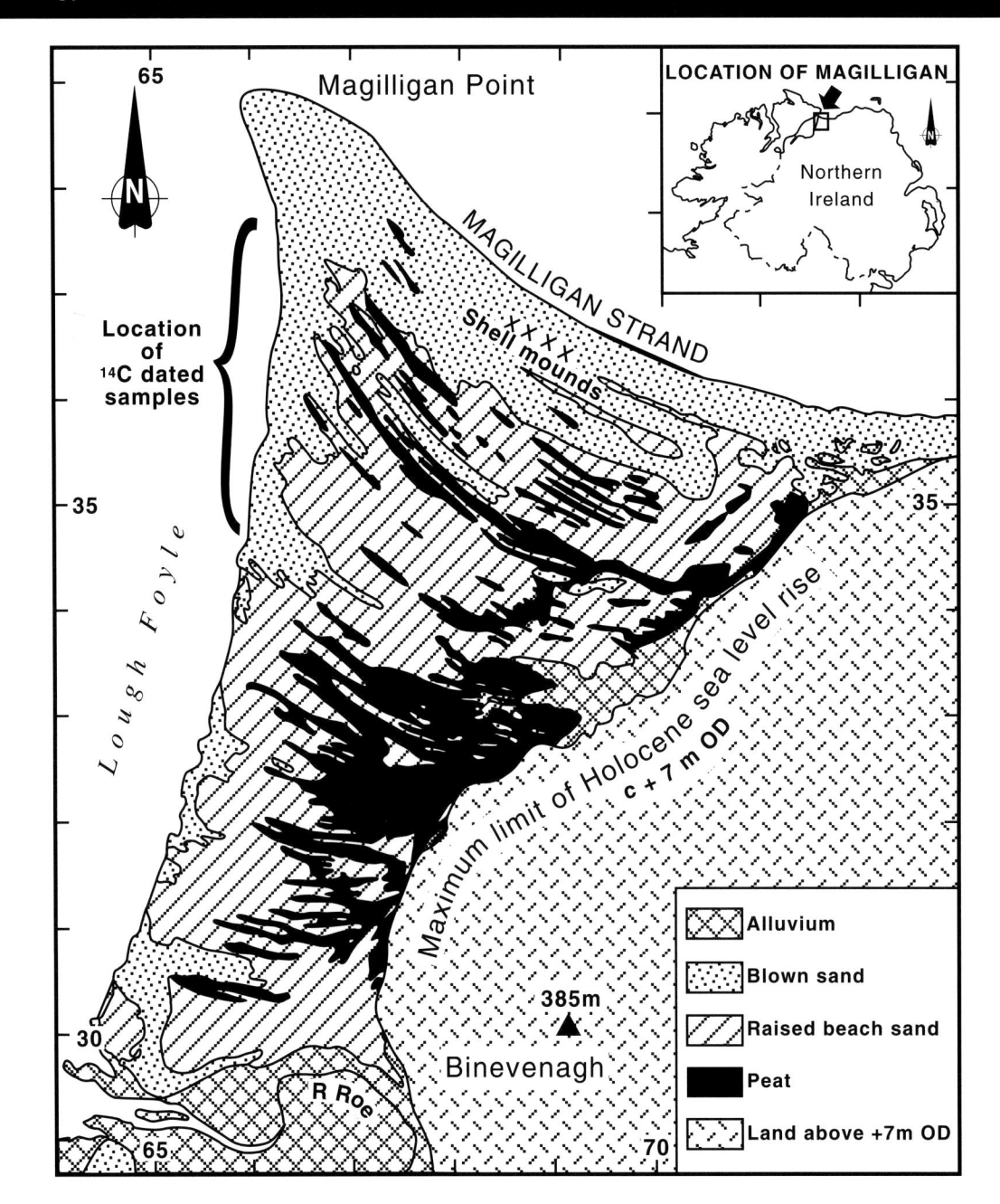

Fig. 77: Holocene sediments of Magilligan Foreland (based on 1:50,000 Northern Ireland Geological Survey map) and locations of ^{14}C-dated samples and sub-dune shell mounds. Marginal grid is at 1 km intervals.

erosion. It was with Bill's encouragement and support that I developed an interest in the Holocene evolution of Magilligan and its soils and palaeosols.

Holocene evolution

The early and mid-Holocene evolution of Magilligan is still conjectural, as none of the ^{14}C dates so far obtained is older than 4500 BP. However, it has been proposed (Carter, 1982a) that the foreland accumulated following development of an early Holocene shoreline at +7 m to +8 m OD around Lough Foyle. A possible maximum age for this shoreline is provided by a ^{14}C date of 6955 ± 100 BP from wood sealed beneath shingle at Drumskellan, in the southwest corner of Lough Foyle (Colhoun et al., 1973). The Magilligan beach ridges are thought to have accumulated after construction of a gravel barrier, trending east-west just north of the estuary of the River Roe, that probably formed at the time of the maximum Holocene transgression (c. 7000-6500 BP; Carter, 1982a). These gravels do not crop out at the coast: they have only been recorded in excavations, and shells reported to occur within the gravels have not been collected for dating.

Following the development of this barrier, a series of swash-aligned beach ridges formed, supplied by offshore sediment sources, and gradually extended northwards towards the present northeast-facing coast. Carter (1986) identified three principal sets of ridges: sets I and II being related to the Holocene progradation of the foreland, and set III representing recent deposition at the distal margin (Magilligan Point). The ridges in sets I and II are 100-300 m wide and crestal elevations decline in altitude from +7 m to around +2.5 m OD. Internally the ridges are characterised by seaward-dipping (1-2°) parallel laminae composed of mixed quartz and carbonate sand and occasional large lamellibranch valves.

The sand-cliff exposures along the Lough Foyle shoreline of Magilligan have provided evidence for the late Holocene evolution of the foreland. These exposures demonstrate three phases of sand accumulation and subsequent topographic stability, each marked by a period of pedogenesis (Fig. 78). The earliest palaeotopography is the beach-ridge plain. Podzolised soils occupy the crests and slopes of the beach ridges and peats occur in the inter-ridge depressions. Marine shell valves collected from the beach-ridge sands exposed along the northern part of the shoreline produced ^{14}C dates indicating ridge construction occurred in that area about 3000-2500 BP. Peat bed initiation in the inter-ridge depressions began at different times (between 2500-1000 BP), probably due to variations in the depths of the depressions, their elevations relative to the water table, and rate of progradation. The shallower inter-ridge depressions are thought to have stabilised first encouraging peat formation earlier than in deeper depressions that remained flooded. Soil development on beach-ridge crests and slopes resulted in the formation of humus podzols. These strongly colour-differentiated soils have yielded ^{14}C dates between 1700-1300 BP and confirm that the soils and peats were contemporaneous and formed across the same topography, together constituting catenary sequences (McMorris, 1979; Wilson and Bateman, 1986; Wilson and Farrington, 1989; Wilson, 1996).

As development of the beach-ridge plain neared completion, prominent aeolian dunes formed on the seaward side of the beach ridges near to the present-day Magilligan Point. Peat developed between the dunes and soils formed across their slopes and crests. Dating of the soils and peat suggest these

High Energy Coasts

Fig. 78: Stages in the late Holocene evolution of Magilligan Foreland (modified from Wilson and Farrington, 1989).

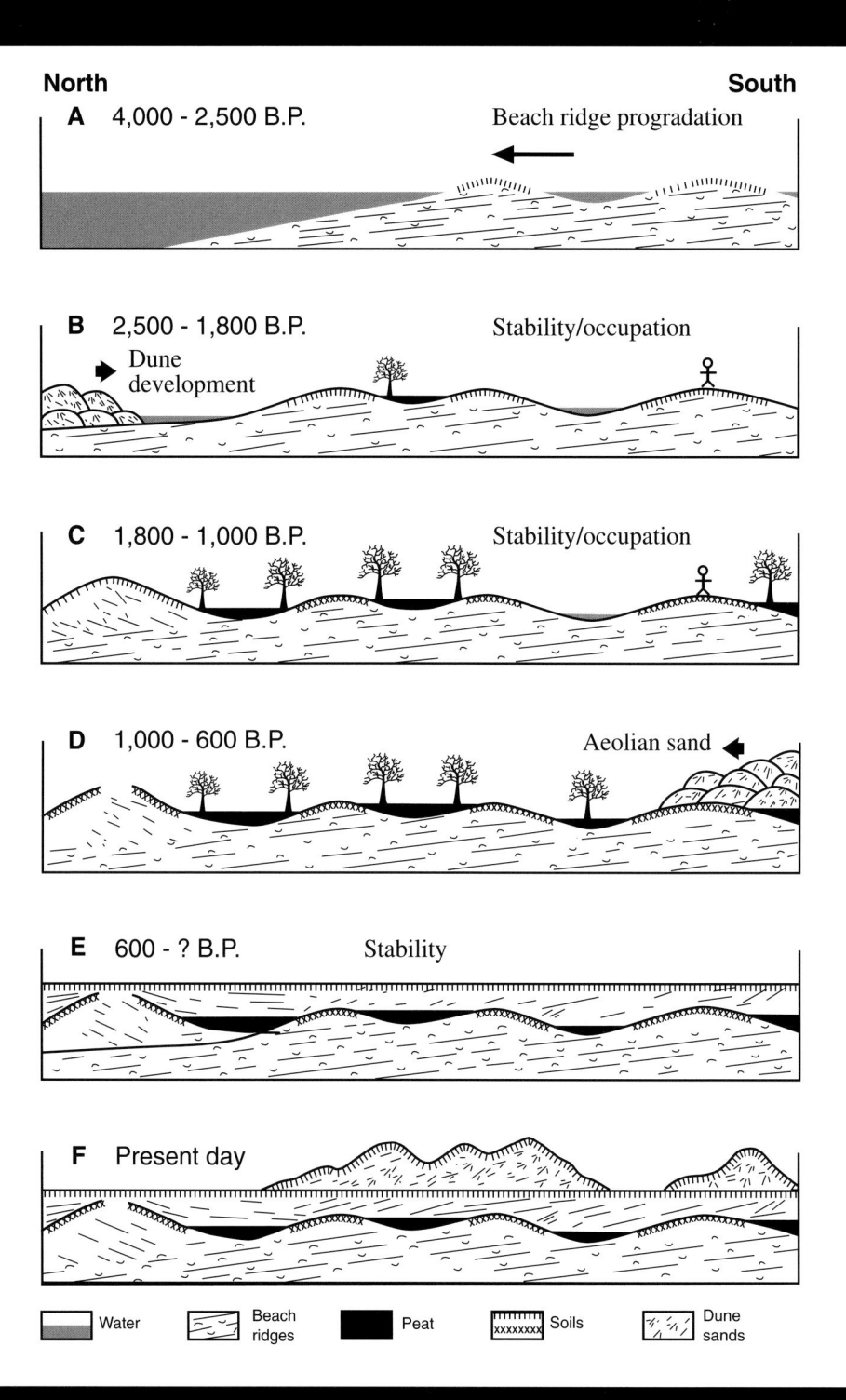

Fig. 79: Pattern of foredune ridges at Magilligan Point, based on air photos and ground surveys (modified from Carter and Wilson, 1990).

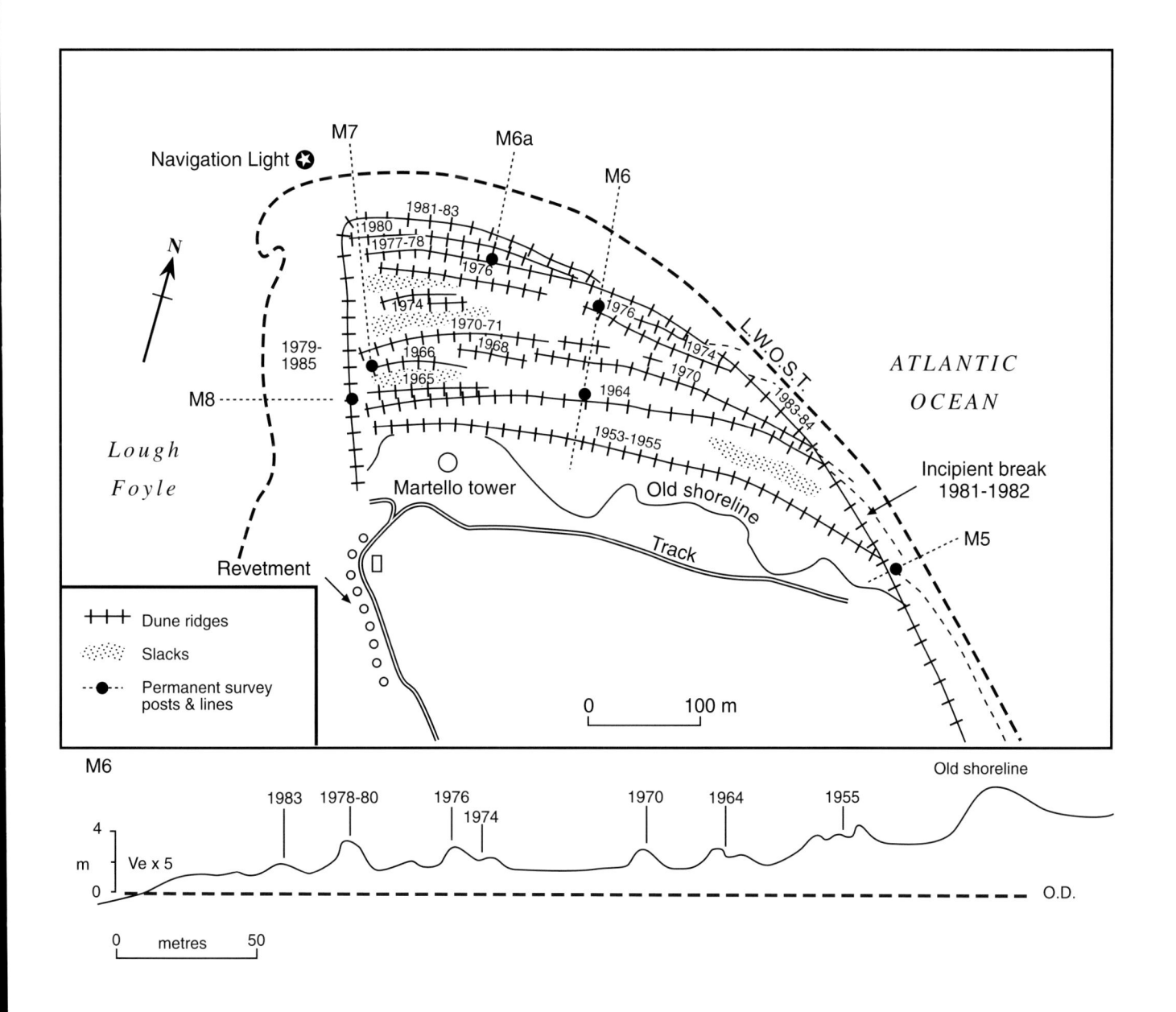

dunes are penecontemporaneous with the beach-ridge topography to the south (Wilson and Bateman, 1987). Thus, the earliest palaeotopography is a complex one of both beach ridges and aeolian dunes.

Human occupation of the beach ridge/aeolian dune topography is attested by the occurrence of shell middens dating to both the Iron Age and Early Christian periods (Mallory and Woodman, 1984; Mallory et al., 1989). These remains indicate permanent settlement of Magilligan with an economy based on both arable and pastoral agriculture, and fishing and shellfish collection.

The Lough Foyle margin of Magilligan was subsequently buried by up to 2.5 m of aeolian sand. Dates from the top of the inter-ridge peats give maximum ages for burial by aeolian sand and suggest that burial was time transgressive from the south between 1200-600 BP. Soil development occurred on this aeolian sand but the degree of pedogenesis is less than that on the underlying beach ridges, suggesting a shorter soil-forming interval. A final phase of sand deposition created the modern discontinuous dune topography (Fig. 78).

Aeolian dunes also occur along the northeast coast of Magilligan. The maximum width of this dune belt exceeds 1 km and they rise to c. +17 m OD; they are much more prominent features than the dunes alongside Lough Foyle. Unfortunately, there is little information available concerning the evolution of these dunes (access is denied because of military activities). However, their morphology (multiple shore-parallel ridges) suggests they developed from landward redistribution of beach sands by on-shore winds. A ^{14}C date of 780 ± 60 BP obtained on shell fragments from shell mounds (Fig. 77) beneath the dunes provides a maximum age for dune development (Carter, 1975a; Wilson and Farrington, 1989).

Recent coastal dynamics

The small area of dunes at Magilligan Point has generated considerable interest because of the rate of coastline progradation, dune building, and the accompanying evolution of the soil and vegetation communities (Fig. 79). The beach ridges and dunes have been dated by reference to air photos and ground surveys, and detailed explanations of their origin, growth, pedogenesis and vegetation dynamics have been presented in several papers (Carter, 1975b, 1979; Wilson, 1987; Carter and Wilson, 1990). The present dune system dates from the mid-1950s and followed the destruction of earlier dunes by a series of storms. Dune growth has been linked to erosion of adjacent cliffs and longshore transport of sand in nearshore bars which 'weld' onto the beach. Deflation of these bars provided sand for the dunes. Stabilisation by vegetation has been rapid as have been the changes brought about by pedogenesis. The Magilligan Point dune system is unique in Northern Ireland in terms of the rapidity of dune growth and stabilisation.

Erosion of the coastline has also figured as a prominent research theme with observations and measurements from both the west- and northeast-facing coasts (Carter, 1975; Carter et al., 1982; Carter and Stone, 1989; Carter and Bartlett, 1990). Data compiled by Carter (1991b) indicate erosion rates of over 3 m yr^{-1} are commonplace and that some parts of the shoreline have receded by over 160 m since the first air photos were taken in 1949. Carter et al. (1982) examined the effects of sub-tidal ebb-shoal elongation on the erosion of the

Magilligan coast. The results indicated that changes in the size and shape of the offshore shoal (Tuns Bank) were critical in governing erosion. As the shoal expanded, erosion rates increased; as the shoal contracted shoreline accretion occurred.

Over shorter timescales, erosion rates are probably controlled by climatic factors – in particular wind direction and strength – which concentrate wave energy and thus erosion at selected locations. Carter and Stone (1989) described three types of dune-eroding events resulting from particular wave/wind/tide combinations. A continuum of slope failure forms was recorded, but with three principal members: avalanche, slide, and slump. The role of vegetation, and in particular root systems, was highlighted as a vital factor influencing mode of failure, and that storm erosion of dunes was required to maintain beach and nearshore equilibrium.

Future research

Although much information concerning the Holocene evolution and contemporary dynamics of Magilligan Foreland is now available, there are still opportunities for further research. Detailed knowledge of foreland development during the mid-Holocene is lacking, and the construction of a jetty at Magilligan Point in 2001, to facilitate a ferry link with Co. Donegal, may be anticipated to impact on local shoreline dynamics. Research directed towards these issues will undoubtedly provide a fruitful field of enquiry.

Other aspects

Other interesting aspects of Magilligan Foreland include:

1. The Martello Tower at Magilligan Point. This was built in 1812 and had a gun mounted on top to protect against invasion during the Napoleonic Wars. During World War II it was again used for a gun emplacement. The tower is now a protected monument.

2. Magilligan was selected as the baseline for the first topographical survey of Ireland in 1834. The small base towers can still be seen at Ballymulholland and Minearny.

3. The prison and military training area – a prominent sight from the Gortmore viewpoint and of some significance during the rather turbulent years of Northern Ireland's 'troubles'.

4. An important area for carrot production. Magilligan carrots are famous throughout Northern Ireland.

Bann estuary dunes

Peter Wilson and John McGourty

Introduction

Three small but distinctive dune systems occur adjacent to the estuary of the River Bann: Castlerock and Grangemore, to the west and south of the estuary respectively, and Portstewart to the north (Fig. 80). The Castlerock (*c.* 1 km^2) and Portstewart (*c.* 1.5 km^2) systems are fronted by broad, north-facing sand beaches exposed to high-energy Atlantic swell and sea waves. The Grangemore dunes (*c.* 0.7 km^2) are within the confines of the estuary, 2.5 km from the open sea. Although these dune systems are separated from one another by the River Bann and the Articlave River, they may be considered as part of the same single physiographic unit (beaches, dunes and estuary) that has evolved during the last 6000 ^{14}C years BP.

The Grangemore dune system has a relatively subdued appearance, rising to slightly in excess of 10 m OD, and, except for a few small active blowouts, is dominated by mature pasture and heathland species. This may be due to dune position within the estuary that has effectively isolated the system from modern beach sediment sources and/or an extended usage for sheep and cattle grazing. Unlike the neighbouring dunes, there is no calcium carbonate (shell fragments) within the Grangemore sands. This probably reflects a long history of stability and pedogenesis, rather than an initial absence of carbonate.

At Castlerock and Portstewart the dunes rise to 20+ m and *c.* 30 m OD respectively. Both systems have been modified extensively for golf courses, more so at Castlerock than Portstewart. Beyond the limits of the golf courses the dunes are dominated by *Ammophila arenaria* (marram grass), and dense stands of *Hippophae rhamnoides* (sea buckthorn)

Fig. 80: Sand dune systems adjacent to the Bann estuary. Locations of GPR image transects A, B and C (Fig. 81) and the site of the former Strand Hotel are shown.

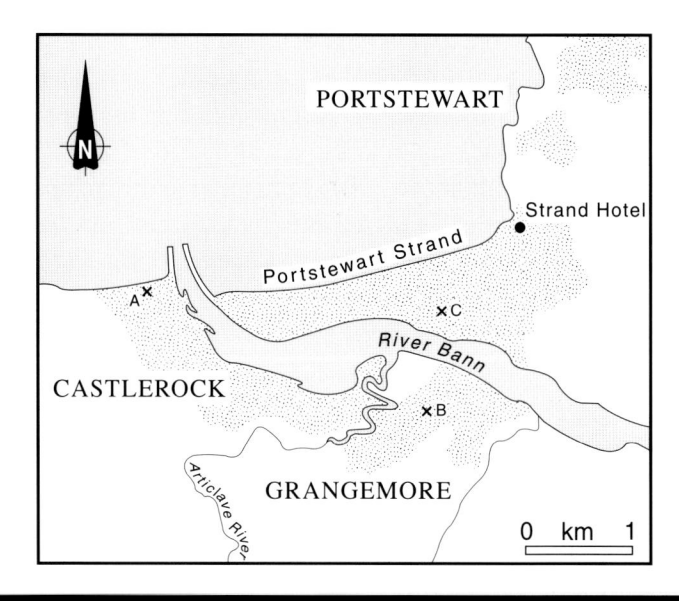

that was introduced in the 1930s. Both systems have been subjected to severe impacts over many years from recreational visitors (Carter, 1988a). Since 1982 the National Trust has managed the dunes at Portstewart and deterioration of the dune environment has been halted.

History and scope of scientific investigations

Scientific interest in these dune systems developed in the 19th Century. Portlock (1843) reported an occurrence of estuarine clays beneath the Grangemore dunes and this was confirmed by Praeger (1893) who described bluish clay, containing foraminifera, interbedded with sands in the banks of the Articlave River. The clay was noted as being slightly above the high water mark. In the banks of a small stream 1.3 km west of the Articlave River, Praeger described a sequence of alternating sands and clays. The clays were regarded as estuarine because of their contained fossil fauna. The surface of the uppermost clay unit was 3 ft (0.9 m) above the high water mark and was buried by blown sands.

Symes *et al.* (1888) and Coffey and Praeger (1904) noted the existence of a ridge of raised beach gravels beneath the Portstewart dunes. These gravels may be seen today at several places between the dunes and consist of well-rounded basalt and flint clasts, with the former lithology predominant. The elevation of the gravels ranges from 4.4 m OD in the east to 1.4 m OD in the west (Wilcock, 1976). One hundred and thirteen species of marine mollusca were recorded in association with the gravels (Fisher, 1935) including *Scrobicularia plana*, a species now extinct in north-eastern Ireland, and *Paphia decussata*, which is extremely rare. Also present within the gravels are basalt ventifacts that were abraded by sand either before the dunes developed or within transport corridors between the dunes that were regularly swept by wind-blown sand (Wilson, 1991a).

From about 1870 the dunes at the Bann estuary were visited regularly by antiquarian collectors who found numerous examples of worked flint, hearth stones, bones, shells and pottery (Gray, 1879; Knowles, 1887, 1889, 1891, 1901; Hassé, 1890). Finds continued to be reported during the 20th Century (Coffey and Praeger, 1904; Hewson, 1934; May and Batty, 1948) and embrace cultures spanning the Neolithic to Medieval periods. Only Coffey and Praeger (1904) and May and Batty (1948) provided stratigraphic details of the sites they investigated: two distinctive 'black bands' (occupation surfaces / buried soils) were recorded, the lowermost containing Neolithic/Bronze Age artefacts and the uppermost containing Iron Age materials.

In the last 20 years a number of ^{14}C dates have been obtained from buried organic materials at both Grangemore and Portstewart and provide age constraints on periods of dune stability and, by inference, periods of dune development. Hamilton and Carter (1983) described a silt/organic-rich interdune deposit exposed in a meander of the Articlave River and obtained a ^{14}C date of 5315 ± 135 years BP. The aeolian sands below the dated horizon represent the earliest Holocene dunes so far identified in Ireland. Two undated soil units with immature podzolic development were recorded within the overlying sands by Hamilton and Carter (1983). A ^{14}C date of 2580 ± 60 years BP was obtained by Wilson (1994) on the organic matter of a buried podzolic soil from elsewhere within the Grangemore dunes. More recently, another six ^{14}C

Fig. 81: Example radar images and annotated interpretative sketches for dunes at A: Castlerock, B: Grangemore and C: Portstewart. Numbers indicate sedimentary packages and are explained in the text.

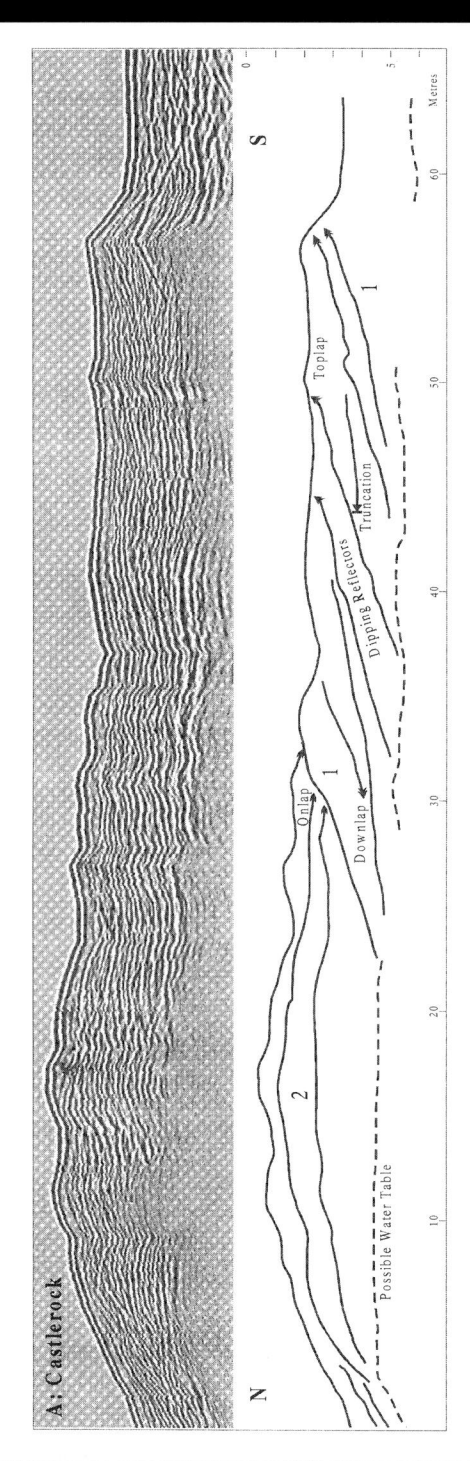

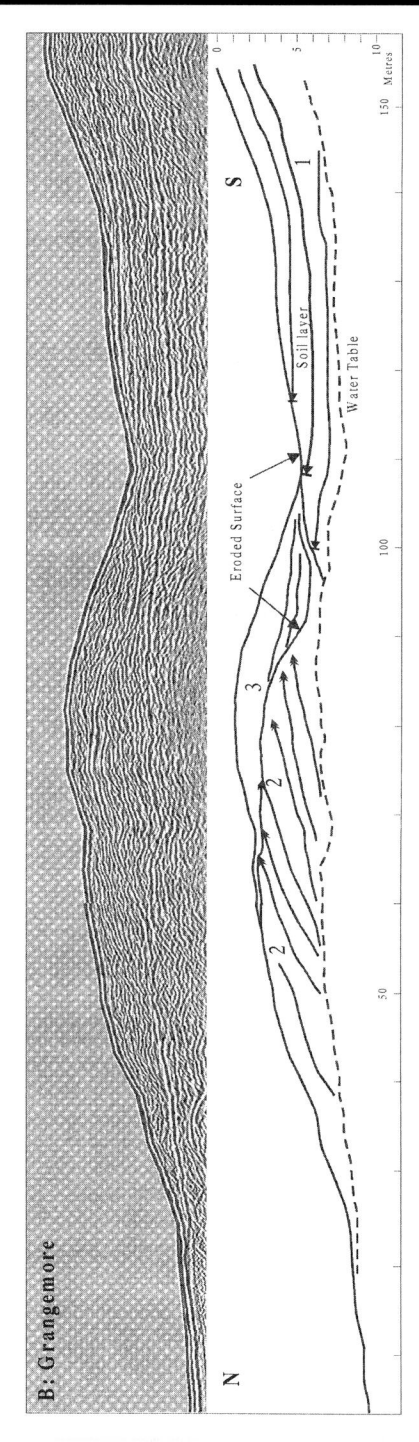

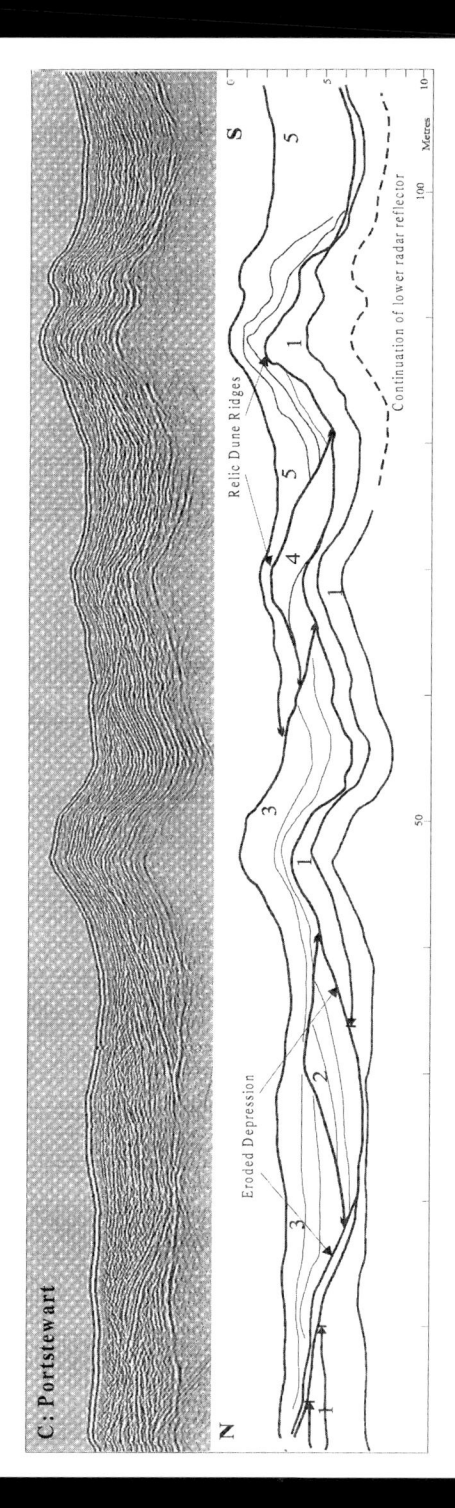

dates (as yet unpublished) have been obtained on buried organic materials from Grangemore. Four of these are consistent with the date reported by Wilson (1994) and indicate the presence of a stable dune landscape around 2500-2200 ^{14}C years BP. Two dates suggest stability phases prevailed around 1200 and 1000 ^{14}C years BP.

Only two ^{14}C dates have been obtained from the dunes at Portstewart. From a surface scatter of broken marine shell and small pebbles in an inter-dune depression a date of 1050 ± 80 years BP on fragments of *Arctica islandica* was reported by Wilson and McKenna (1996). These materials and the date, uncorrected for either isotopic fractionation or marine reservoir effects, were thought to indicate and constrain barrier overwash prior to closure of the dune depression at its seaward end by the development of shore-parallel dune ridges. A charcoal-rich horizon beneath 9 m of dune sand, and with at least 2 m of dune sand below, has recently been dated to *c*. 1500 years BP.

From the higher ground around the former Strand Hotel, east of the Portstewart dunes, Wilson (1991b) reported a date of 4780 ± 45 years BP from soil organic matter buried by sand and, from within the sand, a date of 525 ± 45 years BP from the organic matter of a buried podzolic soil. This sand forms part of a discontinuous cover of aeolian sand that underlies the town of Portstewart and was previously regarded by Wilcock (1976) and Wilson and Manning (1978) as of mid-Holocene age and related to a higher stand of sea level. However, the stratigraphy at the Strand Hotel indicates two phases of sand accumulation occurred and the earlier date indicates initial accumulation occurred after sea level had fallen from its mid-Holocene peak (Wilson, 1991b; Wilson and McKenna, 1996).

Sand accumulation after 525 ± 45 years BP at this site was noted by Wilson (1991b) and Wilson and McKenna (1996) as having occurred within a period of well-documented climatic deterioration and increased storminess in north-western Europe – the Little Ice Age (LIA) (cf. Lamb, 1995), but caution was expressed about attributing sand accumulation to climatic forcing mechanisms because there was limited evidence (dating or otherwise) from dunes elsewhere in the north and west of Ireland. However, it now seems that coastal dune building occurred in Donegal during the LIA (Wilson and Braley, 1997) and a series of optically-stimulated luminescence dates (unpublished) from dunes at Castlerock, Portstewart, Portrush, and Portballintrae indicate substantial dune activity during that interval.

Ground Penetrating Radar (GPR) has been utilised recently as a tool for mapping the internal structure of the Bann estuary dunes and providing information concerning their geomorphological development (Wilson and McGourty, 1999; McGourty and Wilson, 2000). A total of 17 transects (total length 3000 m) has been surveyed in this way. Example radar images and annotated interpretative sketches (one from each system) are shown in Figure 81. The Castlerock image (Fig. 81A) shows two sedimentary packages. Package 1 consists of seaward-dipping reflectors with evidence of truncation and downlap: the latter resulting from differences in reflector gradients. Thus, this package displays some internal complexity. Package 2 lies seaward of 1 and consists of broad anticlinal reflectors that mirror ground surface topography and onlap package 1. This second sedimentary package is thus younger and displays a less complex structure/origin than package 1.

A radar image for the Grangemore dunes is shown in Figure 81B. Three sedimentary packages are evident. Package 1 (oldest) shows shallow concave-up reflectors truncated on their northern margin by the modern ground surface. One of the reflectors represents the organic horizon of a buried soil and indicates a stable phase (= soil development) during emplacement of the package. Package 2, seaward of 1, displays moderately to steeply inclined reflectors truncated by a former ground surface. Both packages are overlain in part by package 3 (youngest).

Five sedimentary packages have been identified in the Portstewart radar image (Fig. 81C). The oldest package (1) occurs throughout the 110 m transect as an undulating dune topography with maximum amplitude of $c.$ 6 m and wavelength of $c.$ 20-25 m. This is overlain in part by package 2, which occupies a depression in the package 1 topography. Package 3 covers 1 and 2 as far as $c.$ 65 m from the origin and exhibits both planar and hummocky relief. Package 4 overlies the southern limit of 3 and part of 1, and package 5 represents the most recent phase of sand accumulation as it overlies packages 1, 3 and 4. Package 5 is thickest where is has infilled depressions in the topography created by packages 1 and 4 and thinnest where it covers crests of earlier dune ridges.

Application of GPR is providing detailed information about phases of dune development and is complementing data previously gained from exposures containing buried soils.

Management issues

In a number of publications, the late Bill Carter discussed issues pertinent to the management of the Bann estuary dunes and beaches. In particular, he highlighted problems arising from unrestricted human access to the dunes, the practice of allowing vehicles onto Portstewart Strand (Fig. 80), the removal (mining) of beach sand for various purposes, and the channelization and dredging of the river mouth. Although some of these practices are now more carefully controlled than formerly, they serve to indicate the potential fragility of 'soft' coasts to a range of human activities and therefore the need for integrated management strategies.

Practices such as motorbike scrambling and barbecue fires have been banned, and access to the dunes is restricted to pedestrians. Even though many of the scars of the worst excesses of recreational activities have now healed, vegetation trampling and erosion of the foredunes continues because pedestrian access is unrestricted (Wilcock, 1976; Carter, 1988a). Vehicles are still permitted onto Portstewart Strand for a fee. This leads to sand compaction and reduces beach-to-dune sediment transport (Carter, 1991b), and increases the amount of litter left behind by visitors. However, the National Trust (the current beach manager) is aware of the latter problem and has provided receptacles for litter and dog waste. Small-scale sediment removal (sand mining) has a long history on beaches in Northern Ireland and has been undertaken by both farmers and builders (Carter *et al*., 1992). Although sand removal has almost stopped at Portstewart, the occasional reports of clandestine activity are usually met by strong objections from concerned residents groups. Carter and Bartlett (1990) and Carter (1991b) discussed erosion around the Bann estuary as part of a wider survey of coastal erosion in the north of Northern Ireland. They highlighted the dredging and dumping offshore of sediment from the river mouth. The need for continued dredging was interpreted as indicating sediment replenishment, probably from nearshore bars and/or erosion on both sides of the lower estuary. Concern was expressed about the vulnerability of the dunes to erosion should dredging continue to occur.

Although small in area, the Bann estuary dunes contain a wealth of information relating to their evolution and human utilisation since the mid-Holocene. The popularity of the area for recreation has led to concerns about the deterioration of local environmental quality and a number of management strategies have been put in place to address some of those issues.

Nearshore sediment dynamics of the River Bann estuary: some preliminary results

Lyn McDowell, Jasper Knight and Rory Quinn

Introduction

The north coast of Ireland is a glaciated shelf environment which has been subject to significant fluctuations in relative sea-level (RSL) during the late-glacial and Holocene (Carter, 1982a; Wilson and McKenna, 1996). Consequently, coastal and nearshore geomorphology, sediment supply and shoreline position have undergone relatively rapid changes during these periods. Reconstruction of the development of such shelf environments requires high quality, reliable data on surficial geology, sediment stratigraphy and energy vectors along with reliably dated index points to constrain RSL change. However, little detailed mapping or investigation of the shelf environment of Northern Ireland has been done, and questions remain. Of these, two questions are of interest here. Firstly, what is the fate of debris produced during the cutting of shore platforms in the late Pleistocene and early Holocene (Wilson and McKenna, 1996); and secondly, is there any surviving seabed and sub-bottom evidence – such as palaeo-shorelines – for RSL lowstand, highstand and transgressive phases? Offshore mapping to answer these questions requires the use of high-resolution marine acoustic data.

The estuary of the River Bann, Northern Ireland's longest river, shows good geomorphic, stratigraphic and dating evidence for changes in RSL and sediment supply during the late Pleistocene and early Holocene (Carter and Wilson, 1990a; Wilson and McKenna, 1996). At present the river discharges to the sea at the western side of the estuary via a pair of jetties, 150 m apart, built in the 1870s and modified to their present form in the 1890s (Fig. 82). The easternmost three-quarters of the re-entrant is separated from the sea by a mid-Holocene gravel barrier (Carter and Wilson, 1993) on which is anchored the Portstewart Strand/dune complex (2.7 km long). The dune and beach system on the western side of the river mouth has prograded significantly since the construction of the jetties, reflecting west to east longshore drift. Both beaches feature wide, dissipative profiles.

Methodology

A range of marine acoustic methods was used to map bathymetry, surficial sediments and stratigraphy. These were:

1. A *Nautech* ST50 single beam echo-sounder, used to map bathymetry with a sampling interval of approximately 6 m horizontal spacing;

2. A side scan sonar suite, comprising an *Edgetech* 272-TD towfish and *Edgetech* 260-TH data logger/printer, to map surficial geology. Three surveys were conducted between August 2000 and August 2001, the

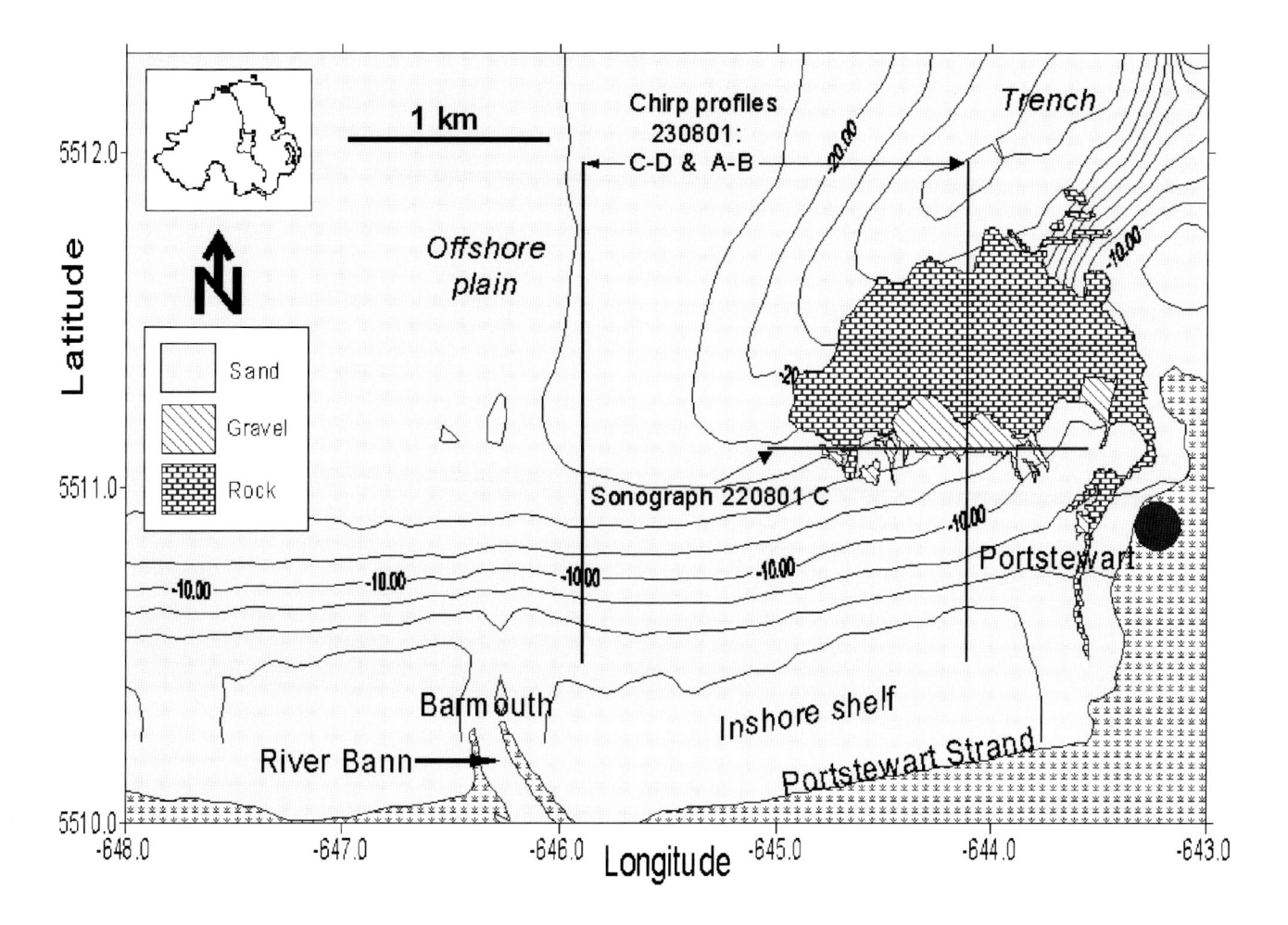

Fig. 82: Study area showing surveyed bathymetry (2 m contour interval); distribution of surface sedimentary facies as interpreted from acoustic data and ground-truthed by sediment sampling; and sites mentioned in the text. Inset shows the course of the River Bann in Northern Ireland

first yielding complete spatial coverage of the study area followed by two specifically targeted surveys, totaling 170 km of survey lines. Survey parameters were in the ranges: 100-500 kHz frequency, 150-250 m line spacing and 200-300 m total swath width. Side scan sonar evidence was ground-truthed by bucket dredge sediment sampling;

3. An *Edgetech X-Star* SB 216-S towfish, allied with an *Edgetech Midas* processor and recorder were used to image sub-surface stratigraphy. The towfish was deployed at a 3 m water depth using a 2-10 kHz pulse rate, chosen for its higher resolution;

4. All marine positional data were acquired with a *Litton Marine* LMX 400 dGPS with a horizontal accuracy of ± 5 m;

5. A further program of diver sampling is planned for spring 2002. Tide gauges and wave recorders will also be deployed at that time.

Results

Echo-sounding revealed three main bathymetric features (Fig. 82):

1. An inshore shelf, present just seaward of the surf zone in 5-10 m water depth;

2. A break of slope, marking the edge of the inshore shelf, shelves down to a largely featureless offshore plain which lies at 14-15 m water depth;

3. A north-east trending, flat floored trench which is cut into the offshore plain.

Side scan sonar results from the first two surveys were compiled to produce the simplified facies map in Fig. 82 which depicts the main sedimentary facies boundaries. Three distinct acoustic facies were identified and sediment sampling confirmed these to be sand, gravel and rock. These can be considered as end members of a continuum where sediments may contain 2 or 3 of these components. Fig. 83 shows a sonograph from an east-west transect across the southern margin of the bathymetric trench (location shown in Fig. 82), and shows each of the facies and their typical spatial relationships to one another.

Overall, the area is dominated by sand, except for the floor and eastern flank of the bathymetric trench and the bedrock shelf paralleling the hard coast. These geological constraints are likely to control tidal current vectors, and thus sediment transport in this area. Tidal scouring has exposed, or maintained the exposure of, a bedrock surface. Individual boulders up to 1 m diameter, which may be glacial erratics, winnowed glacial till or intertidal shore platform debris, are imaged on the bedrock surface. This surface is overlain by rippled gravel beds at its southern margin and both bedrock and gravel are overlain by generally planar sands. The gravel ripples are well defined, with typical amplitudes and wavelengths of 1.0 m and 1.5 m respectively. The ripples are generally west to east trending with sub-parallel crests, but their bifurcation ratio increases eastwards while amplitude and wavelength both decrease in that direction. The sand facies features a series of narrow, north-south trending channels, floored by the rippled gravel. These may be the product of tidal scouring or north-south trending bathymetric highs, albeit of low relief, in the gravel bed which is onlapped from either side by the sand facies. Repeat side scan sonar surveys suggest the channels are seasonally mobile.

Fig. 83: East-west sonograph (220801 C) across bathymetric trench showing the distribution of sand, gravel and rock facies, and their relationships to one another

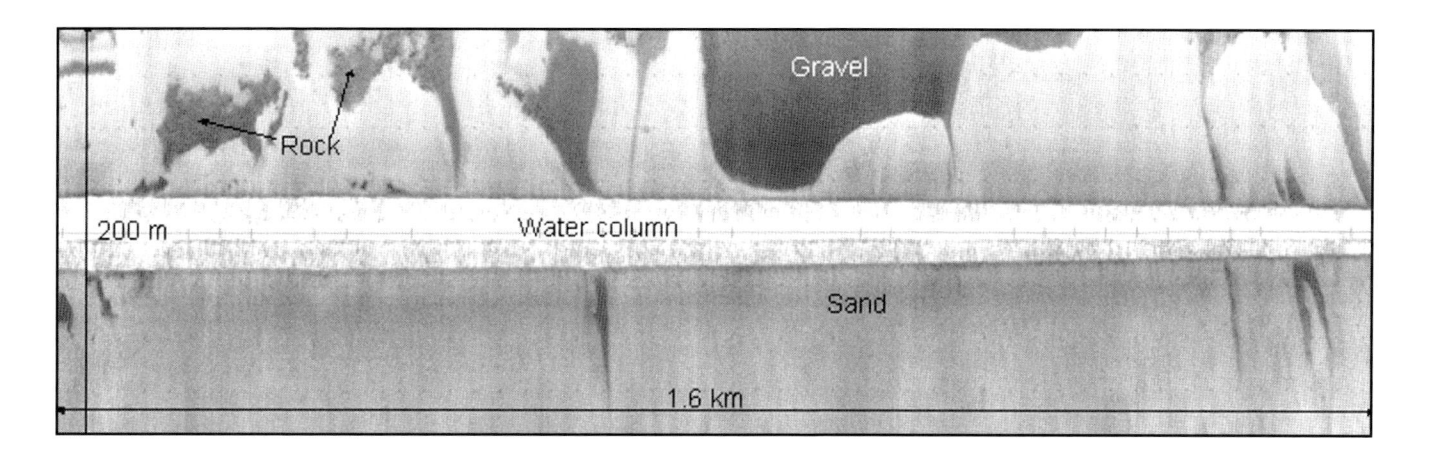

Results from a 1998 Chirp sub-bottom profiler survey (Cooper et al., 2002) were made available and complemented by the 2001 survey. Profile 230801 C-D, oriented north-south along a line 150 m east of the Barmouth, has two main seismic stratigraphic units, here termed offshore and inshore units, overlying the acoustic basement:

1. Offshore unit. Internally this unit is dominated by a low reflectivity matrix. Structures within the unit include a single near-surface and surface parallel, high intensity reflector and a second, diffuse reflector of moderate intensity which lies sub-parallel to the surface of the unit at 5-7 m depth in the sediment pile.

2. Inshore unit. The offshore unit is overlain from inshore by a second unit of greater internal complexity containing 9 internal reflectors in the uppermost 3-5 m. These reflectors are parallel with the uppermost surface of the unit and are generally laterally continuous in the seismic profile, although there are some breaks.

A second profile through the bathymetric trench (Fig. 84) includes a bedrock and gravel surface exposure (marked 3 in Fig. 84) corresponding to the inshore margin of the trench which is onlapped from the north by an offshore unit of sands (1) containing a diffuse internal reflector, probably re-worked glacial debris. The unit is also downlapped from the south by an inshore sand wedge (2) which is internally more complex, featuring one continuous, parallel, near-surface reflector and a sequence of up to six sub-parallel, but less continuous, reflectors in the nearshore zone. The same diffuse reflector that is present in the offshore unit is evident also in the inshore wedge but is neither as extensive nor as well defined.

Interpretation

Results from the north coast inner shelf demonstrate three major controls on Holocene nearshore sedimentation along Northern Ireland's north coast: (1) sediment supply; (2) the configuration of basement geology operating as a constraint on tidal current vectors, and (3) the effect of wave climate.

Late Pleistocene glaciation deposited large quantities of debris further out on the shelf (Carter, 1982a; Wilson and McKenna, 1996) and it is this material that has been the major source of sediment for the construction of the soft coast features described above (Carter and Bartlett, 1990; Wilson and McKenna, 1996). However, prolonged re-working onshore of the contents of this finite store means that net supplies to the present day coast are now dwindling (Carter, 1982a; Wilson and McKenna, 1996), although they are augmented to some degree by west to east longshore drift.

The morphologic constraint imposed on the River Bann estuary and the nearshore zone by basement geology (in the form of the Tertiary basalt outcrops that delimit the coastal re-entrant occupied by the estuary) also constrains the dynamic interaction of fluvial and marine processes. The eastern basalt outcrop is interpreted as a significant control on the role of tidal currents in the down-cutting of the bathymetric trench due to its interference with dominant west to east longshore drift and thus in the localised orientation and operation of those currents.

RSL fluctuations have also been an important control on the timing, location and elevation of effective wave attack. Superimposed on the basic wave climate are frequent storm events which have had, and continue to have, significant effects on the soft coast geomorphology of Northern Ireland's exposed coast (Wilson and McKenna, 1996; Cooper et al., 2002).

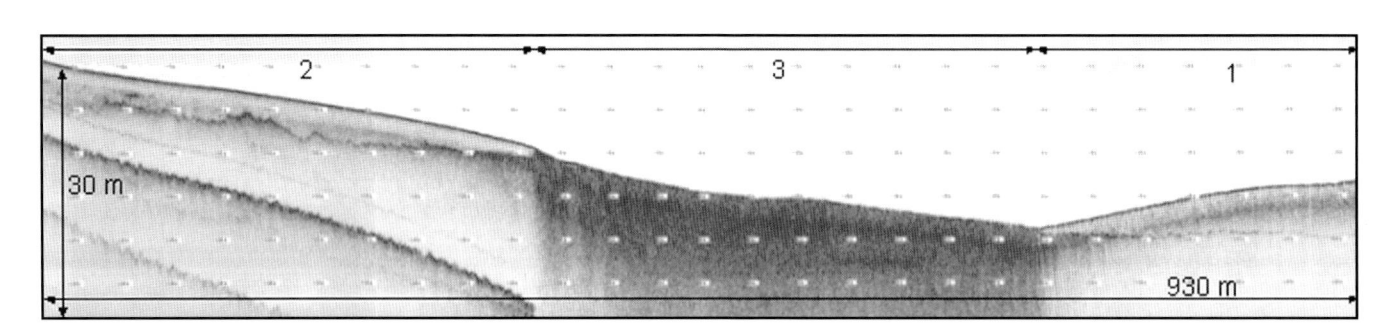

Fig. 84: Chirp sub-bottom profile 230801 A-B oriented north-south through the inshore wedge (2), bathymetric trench (3) and offshore plain (1). The profile is compensated for vessel heave and vertical exaggeration is ~ 4.5

Basalt cliffs and shore platforms between Portstewart (Co Derry) and Portballintrae (Co Antrim)

John McKenna

Basalt cliffs and shore platforms form the major part of the shore between Portstewart, Co. Derry, and Portballintrae, Co. Antrim. The coast has a general WSW-ENE trend, and in plan consists of a series of low amplitude embayments and headlands. The basalt cliffs are in two sections. First, 4 km of cliffs extend between Portstewart and Portrush. For 2 km east of the Curran Strand the shore is formed of vertical chalk cliffs fronted by a narrow, discontinuous, low elevation platform. Second, at Dunluce Castle the basalt cliffs and platforms resume, forming the shore for a further 4 km, finally terminating on the eastern side of the bay at Portballintrae at the mouth of the River Bush. These two sections are termed Portrush and Portballintrae respectively (Fig. 85).

Shore platforms are found flanking the headlands but some of the most extensive examples occupy the inner part of embayments. The topography of the basalt platforms is characterised by its high relative relief and general ruggedness - the signature of a wave-quarrying environment. In many cases the term "platform" is perhaps a misnomer for these uneven surfaces, dotted with residual knobs of rock reaching heights of several metres above the adjacent surface. However, most of the platforms do display a broadly planar surface for at least part of their width. The plan detail is also highly irregular. The orientations of the platforms correspond closely with NNW-trending regional joint sets in the underlying Tertiary basalts, and mesofracture sets. This trend coincides with the direction of maximum fetch and most effective wave attack, and this favourable element of the local geology has clearly helped to optimise shore platform development.

The shore platforms between Portstewart and Portballintrae have plane elevations at ~ 1.0-1.5 m OD. They are broadly sub-horizontal, generally demonstrating minor overall dips of < 3° to seaward (although occasionally landward), and with extensive planar sections (< 1°). These low angle planes may be functions of the narrow tidal range (1.5 m) or may simply reflect the attitude of the basalt bedding. Both of these factors may reinforce each other, although horizontality may also be aided by the unidirectional mode of erosion ("planar swash"). Wave erosion has often scarped the bedded basalts such that within a small area there can be several planar surfaces with differing elevations and amounts and directions of dip. The cliff/platform junction usually coincides with a flow top, which is occasionally notched. The characteristic flow-top control of the cliff base elevation means that the latter rises and falls alongshore (making it difficult to locate a representative platform profile). A shore-parallel cliff base gully with abraded rounded surfaces is also characteristic. High-tide cliff ramps are unusual. Occasionally, as at Holywell Port and Rinagree Point, there is a narrow cliff bench between the cliff and the main platform. Such

Fig. 85: Basalt shore platforms on the north coast of Ireland: Portstewart to Portrush (top) and Portrush to Portballintrae (bottom)

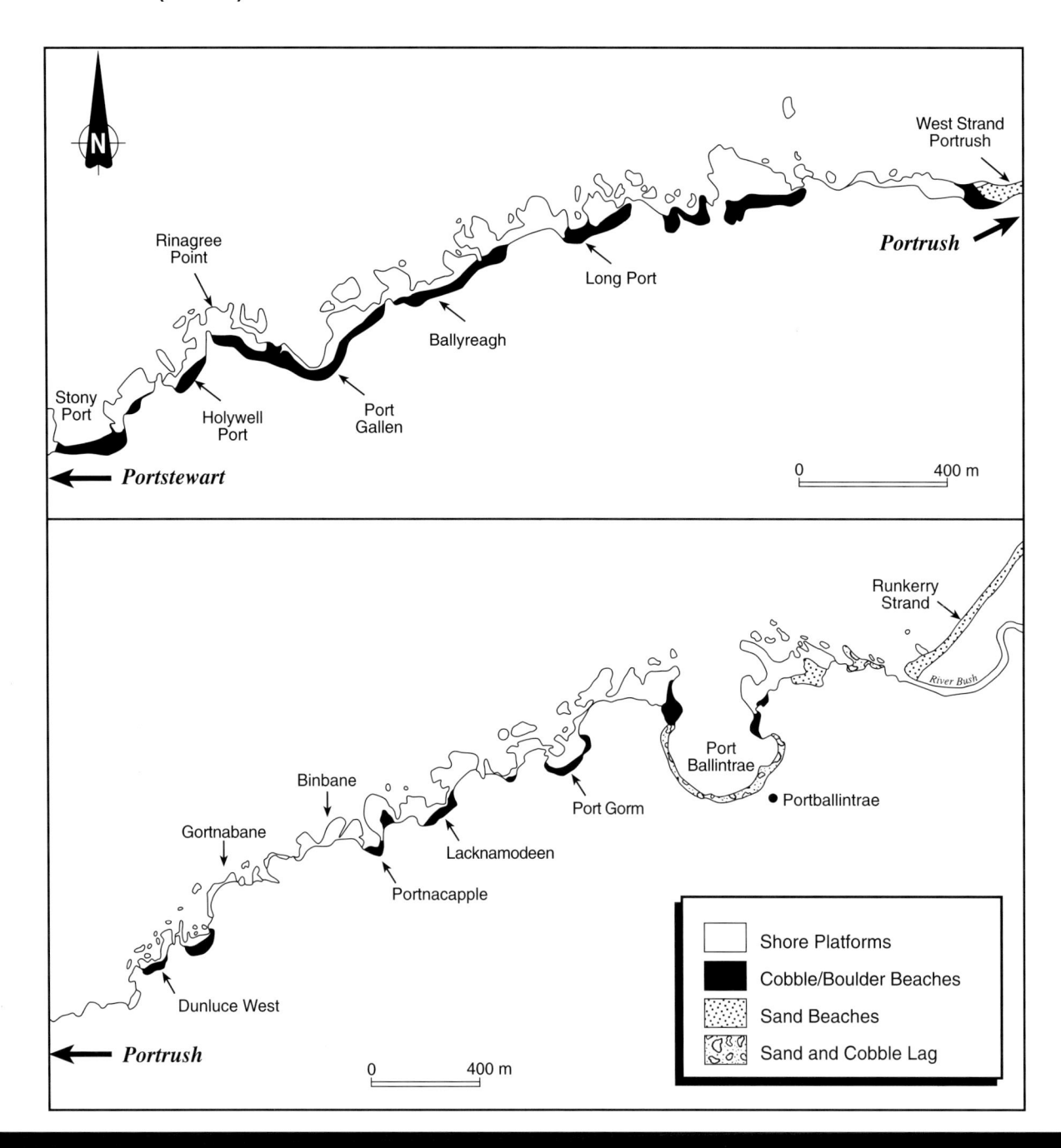

benches are probably formed by occasional, high level storm-wave attack along particularly friable flow tops in the basalts.

The platforms are traversed by many steep-sided channels, their angle of approach relating to that of the controlling joint. Channels are often continuous with an eroded gully on the subaerial platform surface, indicating erosion along the same fracture. Concentration of marine erosion along joints has often fragmented the platforms into shore-attached and offshore sections, and small residual fragments and reefs are also common. On their seaward margins the platforms invariably terminate in a steep, usually vertical, low-tide cliff dropping straight down to ~ 5-10 m depth of water. The substrate below the low-tide cliff comprises sand littered with rounded cobbles and boulders. Frequently, the final few metres of the platform surface consists of a narrow wave-quarried low-tide ramp which links the platform plane to the low-tide cliff. Thus the platforms fit neatly into the micro/meso-tidal group in the classification of Trenhaile and Layzell (1980).

At the head of the re-entrants along the coast there are storm beaches of boulders and large cobbles, reaching a mean elevation of 4.9 m OD on the Portrush coast (maximum 5.7 m OD), and 4.6 m OD on the Portballintrae coast (maximum 6.0 m OD). Several of these storm beaches back extensive shore platforms, although others such as Port Gallen exit directly to the shallow water of the embayment. The major storm beaches give way landward to degraded cliffs, although there are a few small immature boulder beaches in embayments, where the cliffs are vertical and apparently active. Work on these boulder beaches has confirmed the view of Oak (1984) that boulder beaches are sedimentologically unique, e.g. they fine up-beach and demonstrate no shape sorting, in contrast to the general down-beach fining and well-developed shape sorting characteristic of gravel beaches. One interesting puzzle concerns the unbalanced sediment budget. The volume of material in the storm beaches and on the seabed off platform margins comes nowhere near accounting for the huge volume of rock eroded from the basalt cliffs.

The use of shore platforms in RSL studies

Shore platform elevations have been frequently used to establish former, usually higher than present, RSL positions. This approach has been especially popular in the north-west of the British Isles where it has been the basis of an entire school of Quaternary shoreline research. Along the north coast of Ireland the broad picture provided by these studies is that the postglacial shorelines, and higher shorelines of lateglacial age, form tilted strandlines, descending to west and south away from the centre of maximum isostatic recovery in north-east Ireland. While the evidence for lateglacial shorelines is fragmentary, the postglacial shorelines are locally well-defined. Various elevations for these shorelines are given in the literature: Synge and Stephens (1966) describe the highest postglacial shoreline at 9-11 m OD in east Antrim, descending to the west. A well-defined lower shoreline at 4-6 m OD is also identified. Stephens and McCabe (1977) put the highest shoreline for north Antrim at ~ 7-8 m OD. Prior (1966) suggests two shorelines, the higher at 13 m and the lower at 10 m OD, while Orme (1966) describes a postglacial shoreline at Portballintrae at 8-9 m OD.

More recently, misgivings have been expressed about the validity of RSL reconstructions based almost entirely on the elevations and tilts of coastal landforms (Carter, 1983). The shoreline studies may not have taken account of the inherent vertical range and longshore variation of the processes that created the shoreline morphology, e.g. on a storm dominated, high energy coastline wave activity may extend over a vertical range of several tens of metres. RSL reconstructions are bedevilled by the problem posed by process variations at constant sea level. The Quaternary shoreline tradition had a tendency to divorce shore platform morphology from the processes that create it. This led to an over-reliance on morphometry, and to spurious interpretations of process/form relationships. The main problems in using shore platforms in palaeo-shoreline work can be summarised as follows:

1) The platforms may be metachronous;

2) The local relief variation on the platforms is often much greater than the conjectured change in RSL elevation, and the perceived or measured tilts.

In the first of these the issue is the sensitivity of platforms to the process continuum. The rate of development of a shore platform at a given RSL stand is a contentious issue, and there is great uncertainty over the duration of lag times as hard rock landforms adjust to rapidly changing sea-levels. If shore platforms develop well within the time-scale of RSL fluctuations they will be in equilibrium with prevailing morphogenic conditions, and their raised equivalents can be used, at least in principle, to make inferences about the RSL which created them. However, if platform formation is much slower, then much of the morphology is inherited, and so will not exhibit any simple causal relationship with the contemporary marine or subaerial environments. Properties such as elevation, can only be explained in terms of a complex polycyclic model, in which platform development has taken place over long periods of time in the Pleistocene and Holocene. The present form will be essentially independent of any given set of wave and tide processes, and it would be virtually impossible to unravel the elevation/RSL relationships as the platform morphology demonstrates elements deriving from many periods of planation, including the present.

The second point focuses attention on the relationship between morphology and process on contemporary platforms. Many platforms demonstrate a very considerable elevational range in their local relief, and they may also exhibit one or more structurally controlled tilts. This inherent variation is often of sufficient magnitude to effectively mask, or throw doubt on, the effects of claimed low-amplitude RSL changes, and makes precision impossible even where the RSL fluctuation is large enough to be discernible morphologically. Shoreline studies often identify a higher RSL position on the basis of the elevations of narrow rock-cut benches and notches, but these are the very features that demonstrate the greatest vertical range at current sea level. Many of the earlier studies appear to make the simplistic assumption that a given sea level will cut a shoreline bench approximately at MSL (or at least within mean tidal range), and that this shoreline will be laterally consistent. However, on contemporary platforms considerably more regular than those on the north coast of Ireland there can be a variation of over 4 m at contemporary sea level in the elevation of the cliff/platform junction, due to the interplay of geological, marine and topographic variables (Wright, 1970). Comparable variation is to be expected on raised platforms.

Near-cliff elements of rock coast morphology are more likely to survive than the seaward platforms, so there is enormous scope for misinterpretation. Carter et al. (1987) have pointed out that incident storm waves can be modified through interaction with a shore platform to create a stepped shore profile. At low water, waves are largely reflected from the low-tide cliff; then as the tide rises they cross the main platform as turbulent bores. Finally at maximum water depths over the platform the waves reform to break against the high tide cliff, and a narrow platform/bench is eroded above and landward of the main platform. Despite its elevation this high, narrow platform is a product of erosion at contemporary sea level (Fig. 86).

Some cliff-face benches are "high-water lithological ledges", characteristic of storm wave attack on bedded rocks of variable resistance (Trenhaile, 1971). At Holywell Port east of Portstewart the cliff bench reaches an elevation of 3.5 m OD, and is 10 m wide, with the plane of the platform proper lying at 0.5 m OD. Benches can form at constant sea level over a varying non-systematic elevational range, and it would be impossible to correlate any bench elevation with a particular RSL position. During RSL fall it is likely that storm beach sediments would bank up against the outer wall of the bench. Together with mass movement debris from the cliff above, these deposits would modify the bench to create a beach-like terrace adjoining the degraded cliff well above the MSL. The former cliff base position is usually correlated with the break of slope at the base of a raised cliff, so as a result the markers used to identify shorelines may be several metres higher than the true cliff-base positions. Other contemporary platforms have a shore-parallel cliff base gully ("gutter") often well below the mean elevation of the platform plane. The gutter is probably a function of the local landward dip of the bedding, accentuated by the scouring action of reflected waves along the angle at the cliff base, using rockfall clasts as abrasives. The typical shore-parallel faults of the coastal area may also play a part. On the Portballintrae coast there are gutters reaching depths of -1.4 m OD and -0.2 m OD, the latter example being over 2 m below the level of the inner platform plane. Here again the cliff-base elevation is unrepresentative of the level of planation.

Over time the elevation of a wide shore platform might be expected to reflect some equilibrium relationship with contemporary wave processes, and therefore the controlling MSL. This is the ultimate justification for their use in Quaternary RSL studies. However, there is no scientific consensus on the platform elevation/MSL relationship. Some workers believe that all mature platforms are adjusted to low-water level, others favour a mid-tide level equilibrium elevation (Trenhaile, 1987), while a third group contends that wave-formed equilibrium platforms can be found at elevations several metres above MSL. The question arises whether the north coast basalt platforms are in equilibrium with present sea level or an earlier, higher sea level, or whether they are at some intermediate stage of development. Interpretation of raised platforms must be based on process/morphology relationships shown to exist on present platforms. At present not enough is known about these interactions on contemporary platforms for platform elevations to be any more than very general guides to RSL heights. Certainly any chronological interpretations are unlikely.

As knowledge of the process environment on contemporary platforms is scanty, the way has been left open for several highly debatable contentions. Characteristically, shoreline studies have been reluctant to accept that an extensive shore platform can be formed at a single stand of sea-level. This reflects an assumption that narrow benches and notches close to MSL are formed quickly by initially very high erosion rates, but that a "platform" morphology will develop much more slowly into a still-stand as erosion rates decline with time. The question of the time needed for the cutting of a wide platform becomes the crucial point. Shoreline studies tend to take a very conservative stance regarding the vertical range and intensity of contemporary erosion. This has led to the contention that the wider, higher platforms must have been eroded during earlier and higher sea-level stands. For example, Wilson and Manning (1978) assume that the Portrush shore platforms are raised because

Fig. 86: Morphology-process interactions leading to erosion of shore platforms and cliff benches at varying elevations at constant sea level

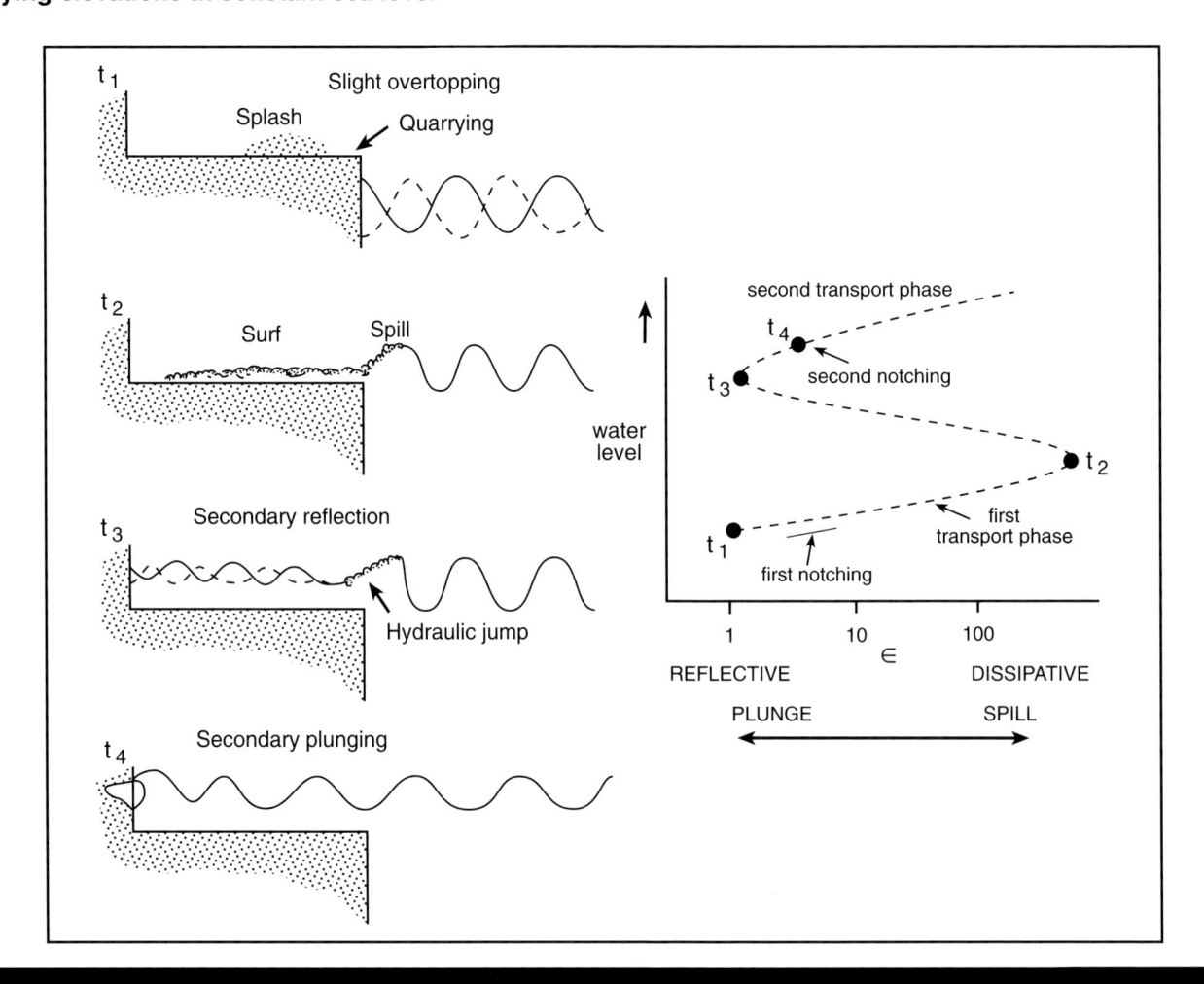

of their elevation; and then assign a pre- or infra-glacial age on the basis that the postglacial transgression was too short to plane platforms of such width.

In fact, the north coast platforms show every indication that they relate to present processes. Erosion is ongoing and active with joint-controlled wave quarrying playing the dominant role. Recent erosion scars are evident on many surfaces several metres above OD. The remarkable scarcity of surficial debris below obviously active cliffs, and the rapid dispersal of tracer blocks, also indicates that high energy wave action regularly sweeps the platforms well above MSL (McKenna et al., 1992). Storm-wave erosion acting at some distance above MSL is the dominant process. Locally, the elevational range of effective erosion is strongly influenced by tidal range, fetch, cliff aspect and bathymetry. The 1.0-1.5 m OD elevations characteristic of the platform planes may indicate the approximate elevation of contemporary erosion, but there is very considerable local variation because the platforms are cut preferentially along flow tops and the less competent basalts over a wide elevational range. Wright (1970) found that structural control of the cliff/platform junction elevation was highly developed where well-bedded limestones had a dip under 8°, a structural condition characteristic of the north coast basalts.

The sea-level curve shown in figure 3, redrawn from Carter (1982a), illustrates that RSL on the north coast has remained in the approximate range 0-4 m OD for the last 5000 years. The shore platform literature contains estimates of very rapid planation rates for platforms up to 200 m wide in similar or shorter time periods. Given the known vertical range of contemporary wave processes, it is clear that the north coast shore platforms have been within the zone of effective wave erosion for a sufficient time to account for their formation. It should also be noted that the local sub-horizontally bedded, medium-hard basalts represent an ideal medium for their development. Thus it is unnecessary to have recourse to inheritance theories to account for the north coast shore platforms, although this possibility is not excluded.

Although the use of raised equivalents of the wider platforms has some theoretical validity in RSL reconstruction, the interplay of structural control and marine processes may still give rise to local relief variations of ~ 5 m at constant sea-level. The platforms on the north coast of Ireland are particularly rugged, with the greatest variation and complexity found near the cliff base, and on outer ramparts. The elevation of the platform plane is probably the most accurate indicator of the controlling MSL in sub-horizontally bedded lithologies, provided that the tidal range is small. However, the area of the platform near the cliff base is more likely to survive later erosion. It is suspected that some of the elevations in the literature are based on only a few randomly chosen points near the cliff-base, which are used subsequently to validate staircases of shorelines.

Even where there is indisputable evidence for a postglacial shoreline there can be many problems in using its elevation to infer any RSL position. At Port Gallen, east of Portstewart, a contemporary platform is being cut into the seaward edges of a dissected raised platform, the latter backed by a degraded raised cliff. The base of the abandoned cliff, actually a vegetated shore platform, falls from 9.3 m to 7.3 m OD in an along-shore distance of 170 m. Thus a raised platform forming a Holocene shoreline can demonstrate the same structurally-controlled along-shore variation as that found on contemporary platforms. As a consequence, the tilt of a raised shoreline cannot be assumed to be due entirely to isostatic influences. Slope deposits will obscure earlier cliff foot positions so the present break of slope at the base of a degraded raised cliff cannot be taken as a reliable indicator of the former cliff base. This probably results in vertical exaggeration of shoreline elevations.

On a storm-wave basalt coast elevational evidence alone is inconclusive, and a limited number of levels taken at long intervals along a stretch of coast could give very misleading results. It is not denied that raised coastal landforms, including shore platforms, are found along the north coast of Ireland. What is at issue is the extent to which these features can be confidently used in shoreline reconstructions. It would clearly be advisable to assign a fairly wide (~ 5 m minimum) margin of vertical error to any claimed shoreline elevation. However, the entire approach is questionable if the total sea-surface oscillation involved had a relative amplitude of < 5 m. Since knowledge of palaeo-wave climate and palaeo-tidal regimes is not usually available, there can be little justification for the precise definition of RSL positions from raised platform elevations.

Management of Co Antrim's sandy beaches

Andrew Cooper and Derek Jackson

Introduction

Sandy beaches on the north coast of Northern Ireland are confined to coastal re-entrants located between resistant rocky headlands. Each embayment contains a fixed sediment volume of relict sand derived largely during the last deglacial cycle. Within each embayment a slow reduction in sediment volume has taken place during the past 5000 years though losses onshore to sand dunes and offshore to the shelf during storm-return surges (Carter, 1991b). This slight natural sediment deficit has led to generally slow rates of coastline recession. Most beaches have achieved a form of equilibrium with the ambient wave field (dominated by long-period swell that is fully refracted at the shoreline). Swash-aligned equilibrium led to the development of crescentic beach plan forms at Portrush east strand, Portballintrae and Runkerry and a cuspate beach plan form on Portrush east strand (also known as Curran (or hook-shaped) strand). A number of human interventions have, however, altered this natural equilibrium and the results of these interventions are well illustrated at each beach.

Portrush west strand

Portrush is a popular seaside destination that mainly caters for Northern Ireland visitors. Its west strand comprises a narrow sandy beach backed by a promenade and landscaped recreational area and has been extensively modified by human activity.

The west strand at Portrush was formerly a wide, smooth, swash-aligned beach backed by a large vegetated sand dune. Modification of the beach began with the construction of the harbour in 1825 which altered wave refraction patterns and caused planform adjustments in the beach that were initially manifest in localised erosion of the shoreline. Damage to dunes was also instigated by visitors with the opening of the Portrush railway in 1855 and the development of Portrush as a holiday resort. Sand extraction for agricultural purposes also reduced the sand volume

The shoreline was stabilised by the construction of a promenade fronted by a sea wall, with the combined intention of providing access and serving a coastal defence function. The beach has lowered substantially (by up to 1.5m) and has narrowed as a result (Fig. 87). The sea defences around the Castle Erin hotel have left it standing as a promontory and have effectively divided the beach into two sections at high tide.

Portrush east strand

Portrush's East Strand, with its close proximity of the Skerries islands offshore, is afforded significant protection from most of the common, major wave attack scenarios from the north and northwest storm directions. The location of the Portrush dune system, owes much of its existence to the sheltering effect of the Skerries, helping to build

High Energy Coasts

Fig. 87: Shoreline changes at Portrush (after Carter, 1991)

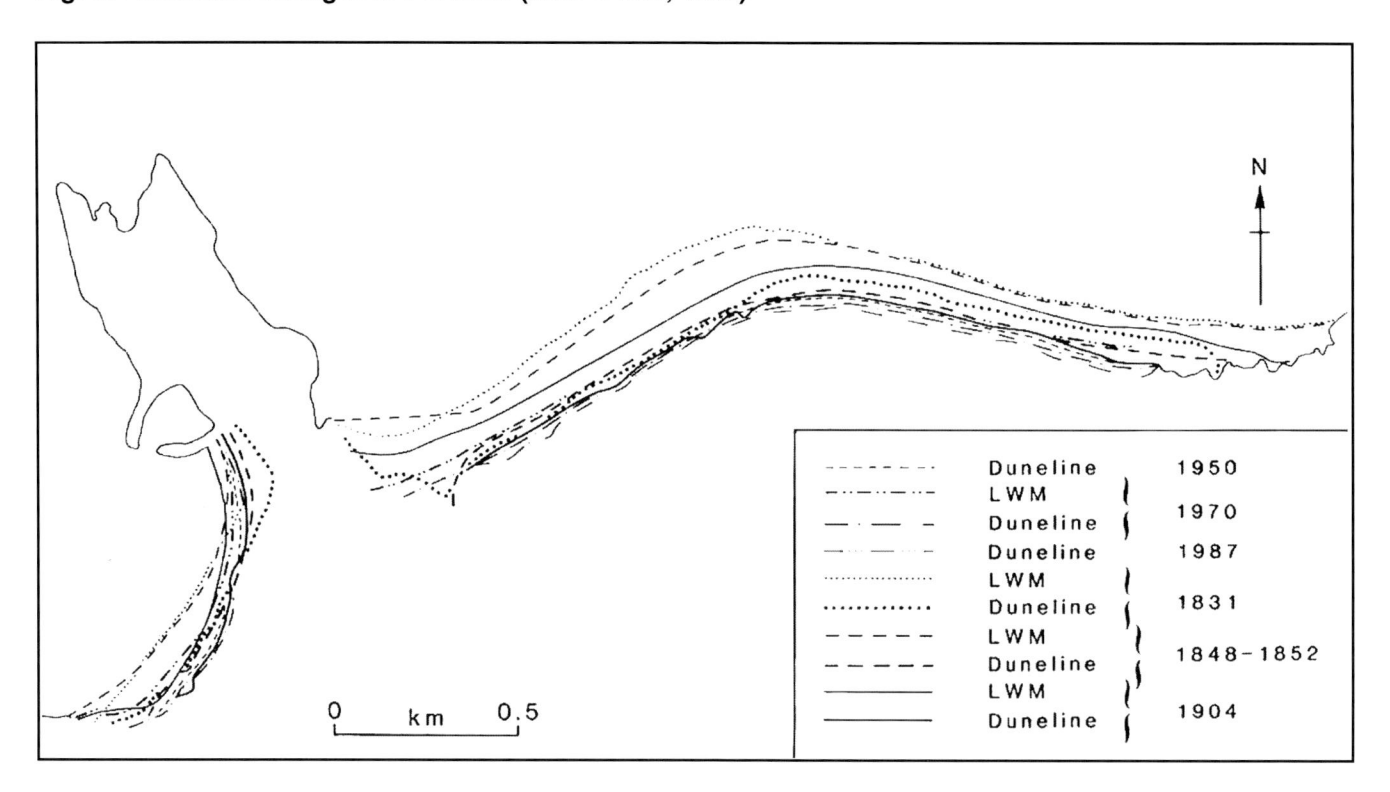

-------	Duneline	1950
---·--·---	LWM	1970
— · — · —	Duneline	
—··—··—	Duneline	1987
············	LWM	
············	Duneline	1831
– – – –	LWM	1848-1852
– – – –	Duneline	
————	LWM	1904
————	Duneline	

up sediment deposits into a coastal bulge of dune forms, particularly during the past period of lower sea-level. The most vulnerable wave attack direction to the foredune system is from the northeast, however, the occurrence of waves from that direction is extremely limited. Waves may however, refract around the eastern side of the Skerries and affect the Whiterocks area of the coast. Much more detailed high-resolution wave refraction analysis is required to establish this further.

In terms of its natural geomorphology and sediment supply the sand dune system here appears to be in a state of general equilibrium, where the dune system has probably reached its maximum seaward extent, with any fresh dune building limited to isolated areas. Any sediment build up would most likely occur on the western regions of the site (closer to Portrush), existing only for a short seasonal period. This scenario of general coastal stability in the local area is supported further by the work of Oldfield *et al.* (1973), Carter (1975b, c) and Carter and Bartlett (1988).

While interactions between the fixed dune and the adjacent beach are limited, there are many locations where internal dune dynamics have led to reworking of fixed dunes via the formation of blowouts. The surface of the rear fixed dune has been extensively stabilised by natural vegetation succession and in recent years by the presence of a

High Energy Coasts

Fig. 88: The beach at Portballintrae showing present and former low water mark. The grading of the remaining sediment is illustrated, as is the pier believed to be responsible for the erosion of the beach (after Carter, 1991b)

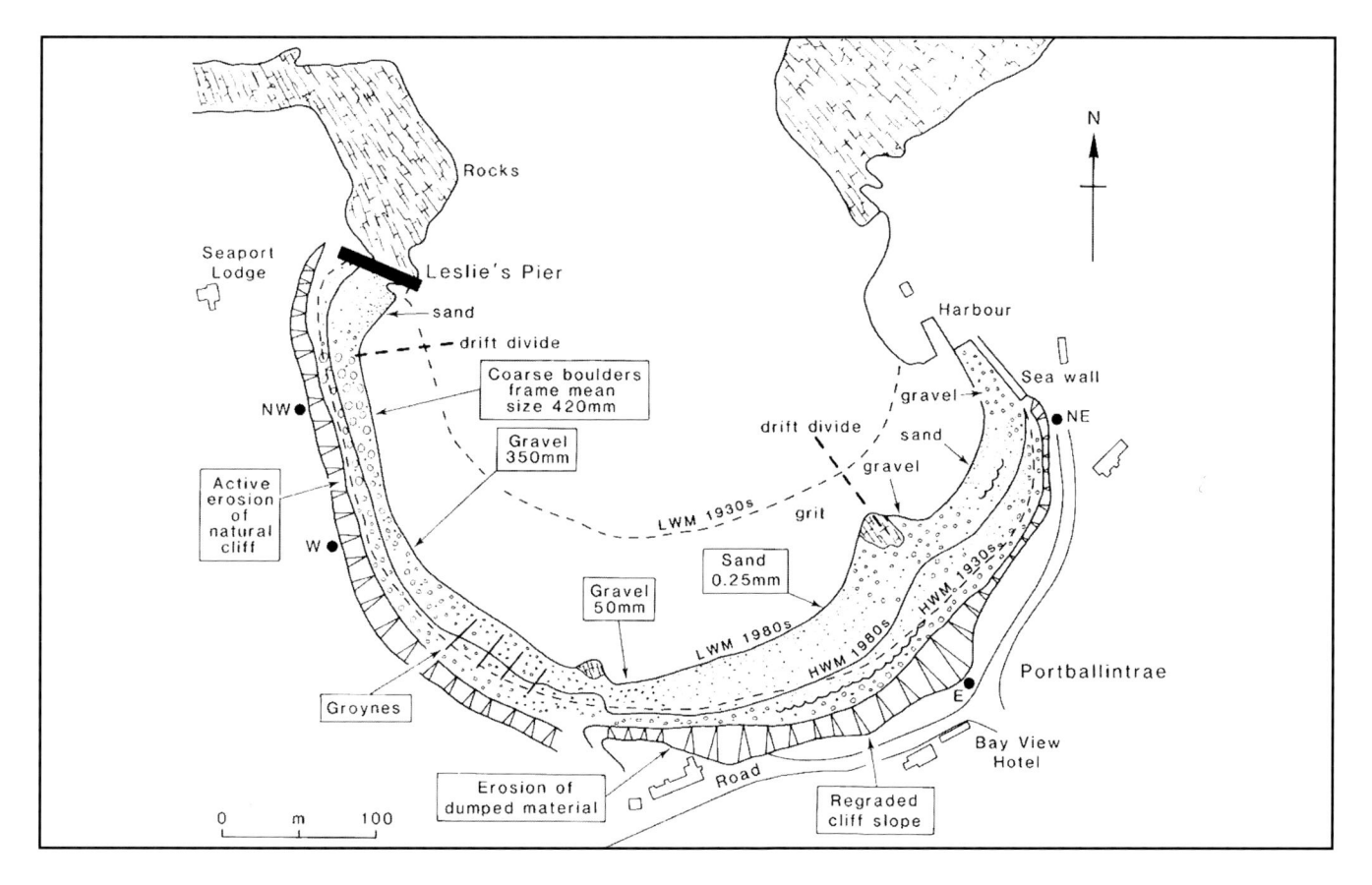

local golf course. Sediment movement is today influenced largely by both anthropogenic and natural processes. The former is restricted to the effect of trampling and subsequent destabilisation of the foredune vegetation which in turn enhances the potential for wind erosion. Sediment reworking and movement occurs on a seasonal regime whereby during the winter period of higher energy events sediment is stripped from the back shore and deposition takes place in the form of nearshore bars, inter-dispersed with rip currents. Sediment is also formed into swash bars in the spring and summer in the nearshore region, with higher elevation mounds exposed to wind transport activity feeding the backshore. Wind action is largely limited to the drier back beach and foredune face region and depending on wind direction, can occur alongshore and/or onshore. It is likely that movement of sand by alongshore winds would lead to deposition of dune forms of more significance due to a longer drier fetch area over which the transport takes place and therefore much more sediment can be transported. During onshore winds however, less dry sediment is available with a significant portion of the beach exposed to the either the water table and/or wetted sand from wave action. It has been shown that around 75% of the winds in the area are actually blowing offshore which will limit the potential of wind blown sand potential (Wilcock and Carter, 1977).

Human pressure is largely focused at the main access points to the beach system, namely the Portrush town car park and at sporadic points along the beach which is manifested as human trampling pressure. Previous attempts at management of the site through brushwood installation and sand fencing have met with mixed results with the main problem being one of lack of continuity after initial management schemes have been set in motion. Significant pedestrian erosion from trampling pressures is present on the site near the large access car park as well as from the beach areas. So far, the provision of pathways has not been implemented on the site and the consequences are evident in the degree of erosion present at certain locations.

Portballintrae

Portballintrae is one of the most celebrated examples of beach loss in Northern Ireland (Carter, 1991b). A former wide intertidal sandy beach backed by a supratidal gravel beach has now all but disappeared (Fig. 88). Part of the loss was due to removal of sand and gravel for agricultural purposes but the major influence on beach loss was identified by Carter (1991b) as a small pier in the north west corner of the bay, built in 1895. This pier is believed to have altered the incoming wave patterns such that a strong longshore current was set up that drove sediment toward the centre of the bay from whence it moved offshore to be lost from the sediment system. The remaining gravel beach has become graded in response to variations in longshore wave energy. The coarsest gravel occurs near the northwest corner and becomes progressively finer toward the centre of the bay. The loss of the sand beach has resulted in increased wave energy at the rear of the beach and consequent cliff erosion in the unconsolidated Quaternary sediments.

Attempts to address the erosion problem have been hampered by diversity in opinion regarding the causes of the erosion problem, by an apparent lack of financial support for coastal defences, and by the lack of a co-ordinated approach to coastal management in Northern Ireland. An interesting by-product of the erosion is that it exposed an important geological section in the Quaternary sediments that records a high sea level during the last deglaciation (McCabe *et al.*, 1994). The site now has protection as an ASSI and cannot be obliterated by a coastal defence structure.

Runkerry beach

Derek Jackson

Runkerry Strand, located on the north coast (Co Antrim) of Northern Ireland (Irish grid reference C935425), consists of a 1.2 km long beach which is oriented southeast-northwest direction (Fig. 89). The beach system is bounded by two tertiary basalt headlands at each end of the embayment, with the River Bush discharging into the southern section. Mature, stable dune forms are located inland from the beach but are significantly eroded and scarped close to the shore by natural wave attack and human trampling. Sand dunes located at the beach-dune intersection are largely in an erosional phase with little or no fresh aeolian sediment supply feeding into them. The dunes rest on significant thicknesses of glacial till deposited during the last glaciation at the site. The pre-Pleistocene basement comprises Mesozoic chalk which underlies Tertiary volcanics (mainly basalt) dominated by east-west structural control (Wilson and Manning, 1978). During the Pleistocene the area was extensively glaciated by both south and north-south-moving ice sheets. Evidence of at least two episodes of glaciation may be inferred form boulder outcrops around the bay (Stephens *et al.*, 1975).

After the dissolution of the ice sheets, sea-level fell below present datum at around 12,000 BP and returned to present levels following the early Holocene (7000 BP). The primary gravel storm beach sedimentation is probably associated with the transgressive stage of RSL while the dunes may have developed somewhat later as a response to slowly falling sea-levels, induced by continuing isostatic uplift into the middle Holocene period (6000-4000 BP). Beach sediment is bounded between the basaltic headlands and is made up of transgressive marine sand overlying a gravel framework with an extensive, vegetated dune field (extending for several kilometers) landward of the beach. In terms of grain size, little spatial variation exists along the beach, representing a single source population of beach sand. Mean sediment size at the beach is approximately 0.17 mm. Most of the sediment in the system is stored within the dunes and beach dynamics can be said to be operating in a sediment deficit environment.

Wave conditions and beach morphodynamics

The beach is located within a high energy, swell wave-dominated environment under a micro-tidal regime (mean spring tidal range of 1.54 m), and represents one of the highest energy beach systems along this stretch of coast. Atlantic swell waves have a modal approach direction of 280° when travelling through the Malin Sea but undergo considerable refraction before reaching the Runkerry site. Previous work on annual wave data 20 km offshore has shown a typical modal significant wave height (Hs) of 0.45m and modal zero crossing period (Tz) of about 8.5 s (Carter, 1991b).

Fig. 89: Location of the Runkerry beach system, north Antrim high energy coastline

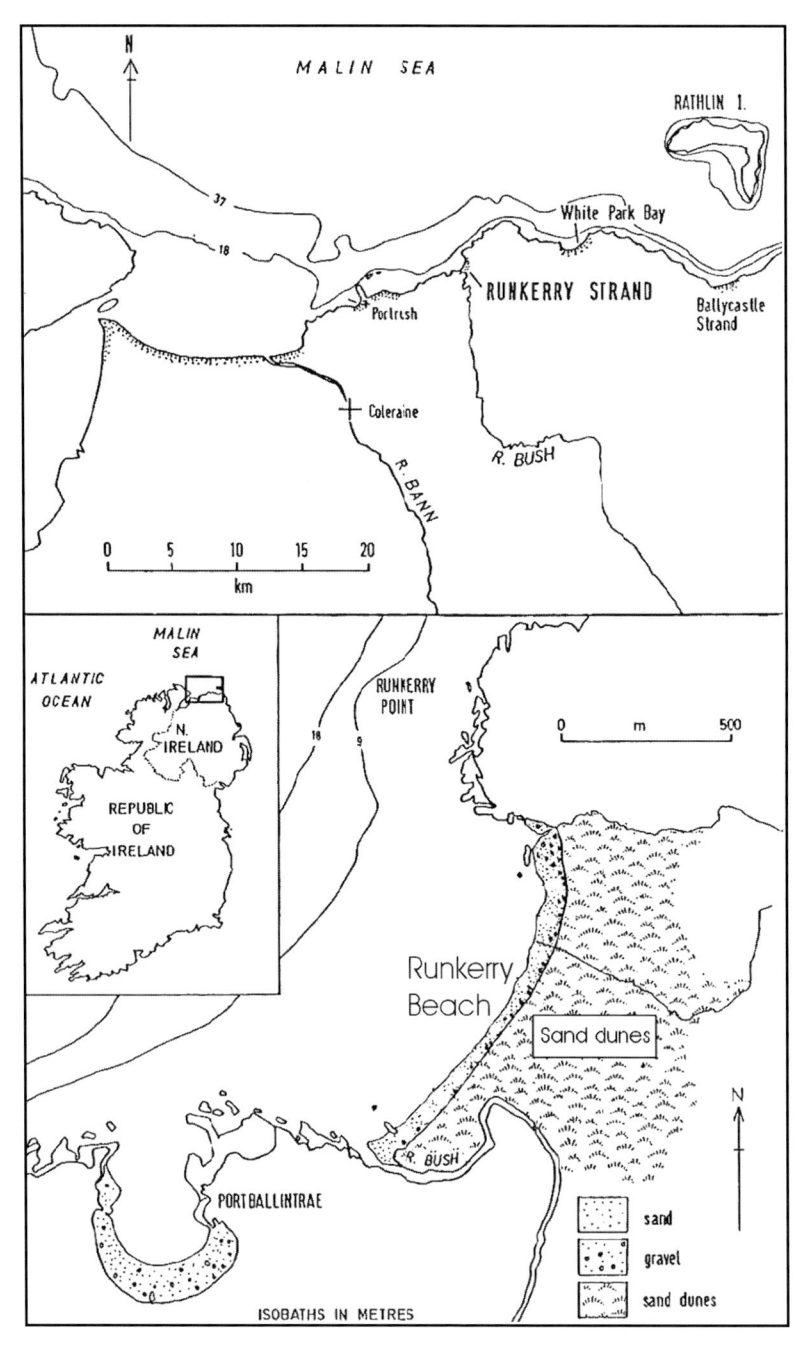

Nearshore modification of waves at Runkerry is largely dictated by the seasonal adjustments to the beach and nearshore areas that undergo dramatic morphological alteration throughout an annual time frame. Previous profile studies at the site (Shaw, 1981, 1985; Malvarez et al., 1995) have shown a general beach level reduction in volume (covering the inter- and supra-tidal area) during the winter months between November to February, and then a beach rebuilding phase occurring between June to early November. The scale of beach level changes also varies considerably along the beach. This is probably due to the presence of local features such as the emerging River Bush, and isolated rock outcrops affecting wave refraction patterns and energy delivery to the shore.

Malvarez et al., (1995) have shown, using the wave propagation model HISWA (Holthuijsen et al., 1989), that deep-water wave direction is largely insignificant at the site, with wave approaches from a north, northwest and west direction having close similarity in terms of their energy dissipation magnitude and direction. This demonstrates almost complete wave refraction within the bay with a higher significance attached to wave height and period parameters for beach morphodynamics.

Under median, low wave conditions (H = 2 m, T = 8 s) low values of wave energy are predicted in the northern section of the bay. In this section waves break offshore on submerged rocks and then reform again before breaking with lower energy at the beach. Rip currents are also generated during median wave conditions along the beach, helping to remove and transport significant amounts of sediment into the offshore zone in nearshore bar formations.

Storm wave conditions (high waves of H = 5 m, T = 12 s) produce significant wave-bottom interaction further offshore manifesting in a concentration of wave energy in the southern part of the bay. This is accompanied by a reduction of final wave energy dissipation through wave breaking events occurring further offshore away from the beach to give energy delivery levels of similar magnitude to median conditions (100-200 W m^{-2}).

In the central section of the bay, bathymetry is essentially smooth to slightly concave and results in wave energy dissipation occurring over a wide surf zone. This is indicated by a broad peak in energy dissipation (600 W m^{-2}) reducing to 200 W m^{-2} at the shoreline.

In the northern section of the bay the bathymetry is strongly influenced the presence of rock outcrops. The nearshore profile is steep and much of the energy is dissipated as waves traverse the rock outcrops. Energy dissipation occurs in three distinctive peaks, diminishing in magnitude to around 100 W m^{-2} as the shoreline is approached.

In terms of energy delivery to the shore, the beach can be described in three sections. The northern part, being more sheltered during high wave energy events; the middle section as a receiver of high energy but with large energy dissipation occurring in a broad surf zone; and the southern section as a receiver of reformed waves dissipating their energy across a narrow surf zone close to the shore.

The Volcanology of the Tertiary Lavas of the Giant's Causeway, Co. Antrim

Paul Lyle

Introduction

The northward extension of the Atlantic Ocean during the Tertiary Period some 60 million years ago was marked in northeast Ireland by extensive volcanic activity similar to that currently occurring in Iceland. The remnants of this volcanic episode are preserved as the basalts of the Antrim Plateau (Wilson and Manning, 1978; Lyle, 1996). These are dark fine-grained rocks that erupted from elongate cracks or fissures in the earth's crust and gradually covered the whole area. The volcanism appears to have occurred in two main phases producing the Lower Basalt Formation and the Upper Basalt Formation with a long interval between allowing the production of a thick soil horizon, the Interbasaltic Formation (Lyle, 1996, 2000). These soils are described as laterite and are typically found today in wet tropical areas. They are rich in iron and aluminium and are often bright red in colour. Since the climate at the time of eruption of the basalts appears to have been warm temperate rather than tropical it may be that an increased heat flow associated with the igneous activity may have enhanced the weathering of the basalt surface. While volcanic activity over much of Antrim ceased during the Interbasaltic period, localized activity in north Antrim produced the lavas of the Giant's Causeway area (Fig. 90). The Causeway lavas erupted on to the weathered surface of the Lower Basalts, the Port na Spaniagh Laterite, and were then weathered themselves to form the Ballylagan Laterite as activity again waned before re-starting at the beginning of Upper Basalt times. The Causeway flows are quite different in character from the earlier Lower Basalts or the succeeding Upper Basalts. They are generally much thicker, around 30 m thick and locally up to 100 m thick, and are characteristically columnar, often with remarkably regular hexagonal cross-sections.

Fig. 90: The statigraphy of the Antrim Lava Group in north Antrim

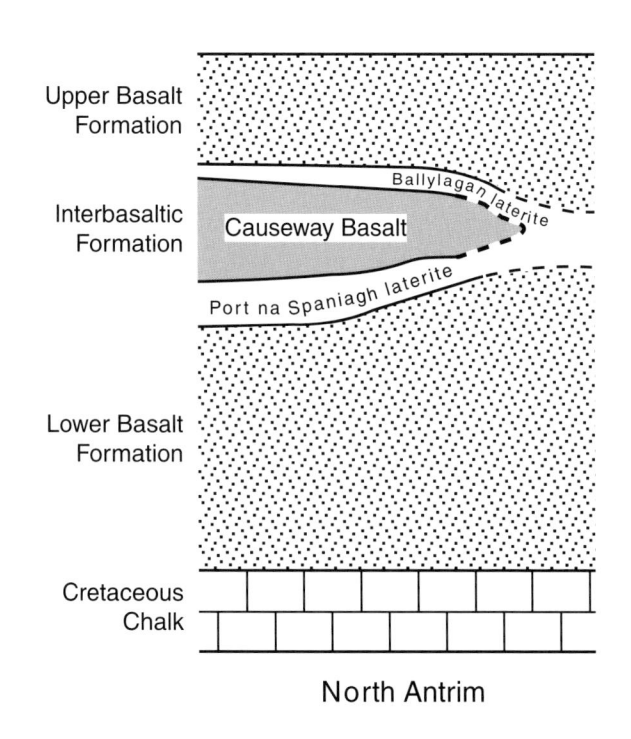

Locality 1

The first locality is situated to the right of the path which leads down from the Visitors' Centre to the Causeway. The outcrop shows the bright red laterite layer (the Port na Spaniagh laterite) that marks the top of the Lower Basalts and the base of the Causeway Basalts (Fig. 90). The Lower Basalts are exposed seawards in the cliffs below the Causeway Hotel. The laterite slopes steeply down towards the Causeway and marks the side of a wide river valley that was filled by this first flow (Fig. 91). *En route* downhill to the Causeway the road passes a fine example of spheroidal weathering in the Lower Basalts. Here weathering of the basalt has produced rounded blocks with a concentric layering sometimes referred to as "onion-weathering".

Locality 2: The Grand Causeway

The Grand Causeway (see Fig. 91) is the largest of the three promontories which make up the Giant's Causeway and consists almost entirely of regular, vertical columns, many of which are 6-sided. The columnar structure of the Causeway flows can be sub-divided into a lower regular section called the colonnade and an upper, more irregular and often curved section called the entablature. These terms are based on classical architecture and were first used by S.I. Tomkeieff, a Russian geologist who described the Causeway columnar basalts in 1940. The terms are now used to describe similar occurrences of columnar basalts around the world. Recent workers on the Columbia River Plateau in the USA have modified the terminology slightly (Long and Wood, 1986) (Fig. 92). The columns are caused by the formation of contraction joints as the lava cools. Lava flows such as these are erupted at temperatures of around 1100°C and lose heat very rapidly to their surroundings, predominantly through their top and bottom surfaces. Thermal contraction produces sets of roughly parallel joints or fractures at right angles to the cooling surfaces and these joints, moving inwards towards the centre of the flow as it solidifies, takes the form of a cooling front (Fig. 93a). Cracks are started at many points on the surface of this cooling front and three-pronged cracks at angles of about 120° occur at each of these points. As these cracks propagate they intersect to form irregular polygons of 3-7 sides (Fig. 93b). With continued cooling these polygonal cracks will move inwards to form polygonal columns, roughly at right angles to the horizontal cooling surfaces (Fig. 93c). Contraction of the columns along their length produces the characteristic "ball and socket" joints that divide the columns horizontally (Fig. 93d). The Causeway is the colonnade of the first flow of the Causeway basalts that filled the river valley on the Lower Basalt surface.

Locality 3: The Giant's Organ

The "organ pipes" here are the colonnade columns of the first flow of the Causeway basalts and above this can be seen the very sharp contact with the upper columnar zone, the entablature. There is evidence that this type of complex jointing is the result of modification of the cooling pattern of the hot flow interior by the influx of water. The river valley on the Lower Basalt surface (Fig. 91) was filled by the first flow of the Causeway basalts that displaced the water, forming widespread, temporary lakes on the flow surface. Early-formed fractures called master joints on the lava surface allowed this water to pass down into the interior of the flow. The effect is to speed up the cooling in the upper part of the flow and to form the columns of the entablature with narrow, curved columns growing rapidly

High Energy Coasts

Fig. 91: Geological map and cross-section of the Giant's Causeway locality

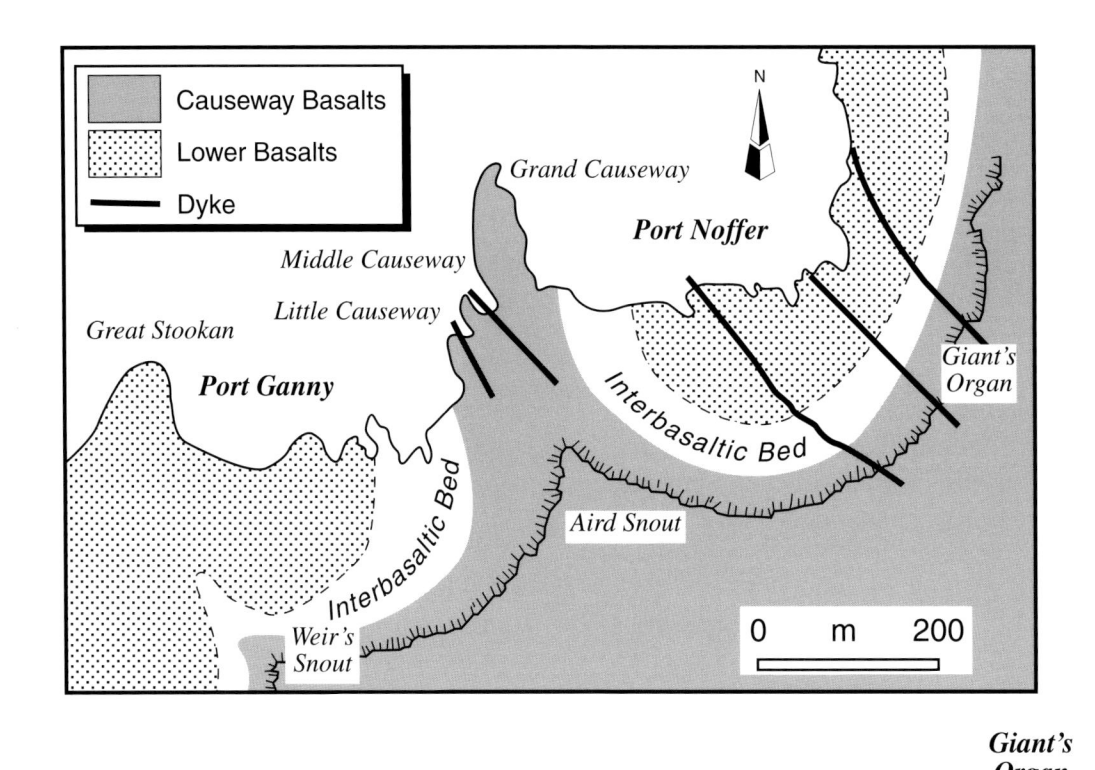

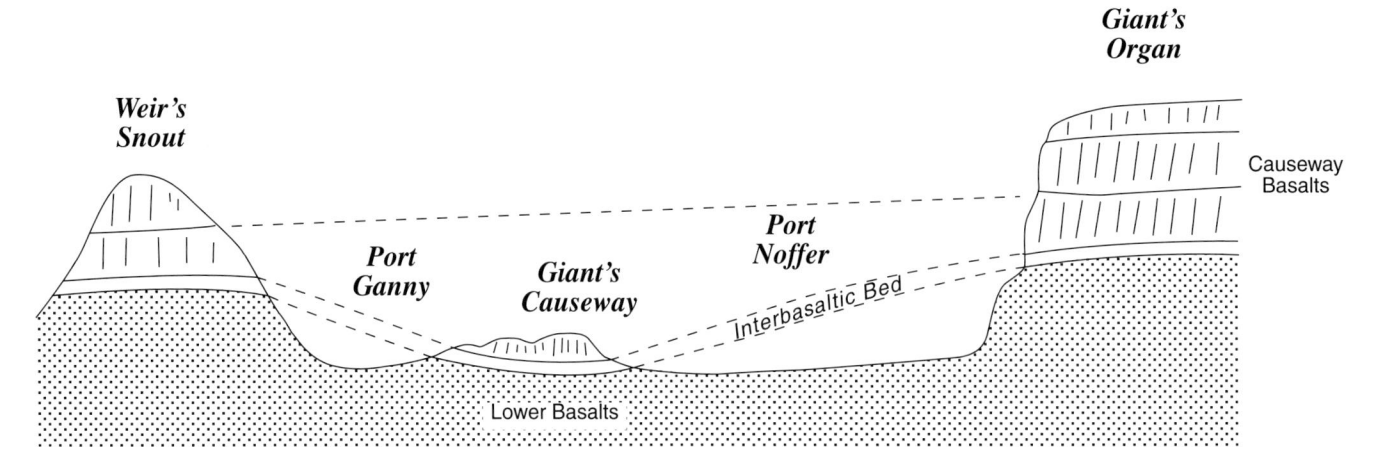

Fig. 92: Subdivisions of columnar basalt flows and their origin in classical architecture

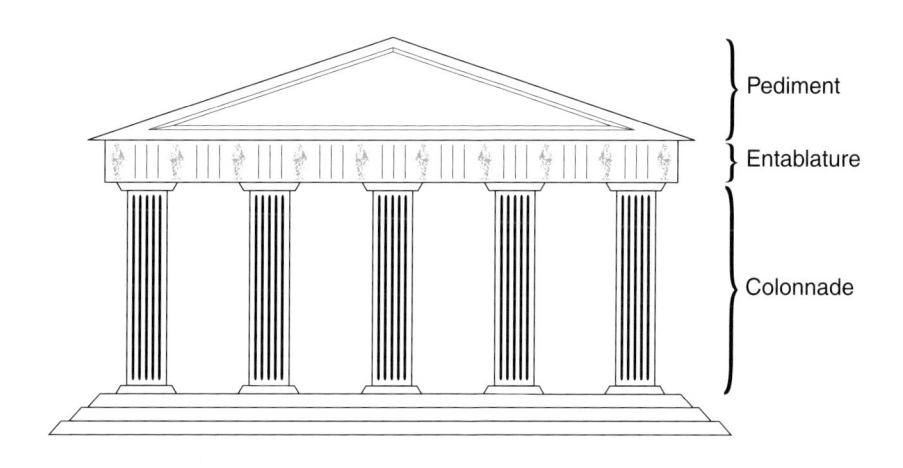

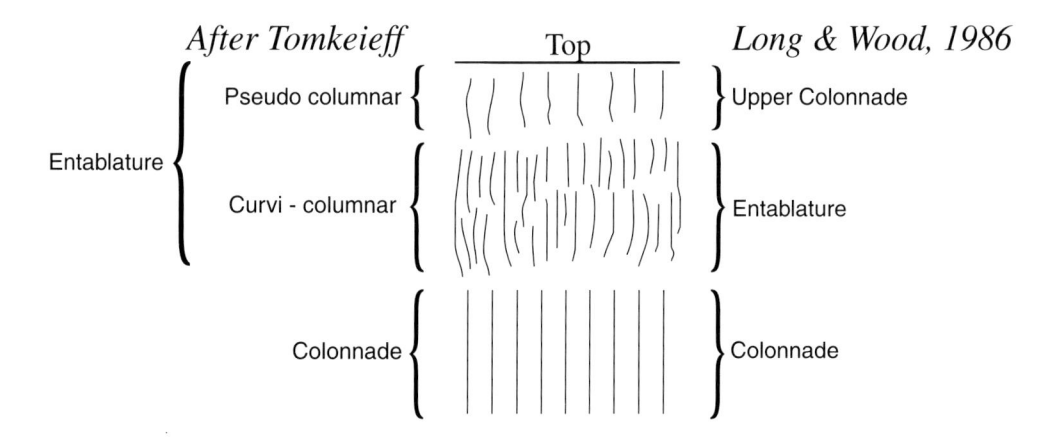

downwards and the more regular columns of the colonnade growing upwards from the base, at a slower rate. The entablature/colonnade contact seen in the Giant's Organ represents the meeting of the upward moving colonnade cooling front and the downward moving entablature cooling front (Fig. 94).

Locality 4

The path east from the Giant's Organ is at the level of the Interbasaltic laterite and this allows the weathered Lower Basalt surface to be easily examined. The large rounded patches known as the "Giant's Eyes" are further examples of spheroidal weathering, in this case the basalt is almost completely altered to laterite. In other areas of Antrim this laterite horizon has been a source of both aluminium and iron ores. Just around the headland to the east a narrow wall of basalt, a dyke, can be seen cutting through the basalts from sea level to the top of the cliff. The dyke may well have acted as a feeder or conduit for the lavas on the surface.

Site management of the Giant's Causeway area

The status of the Giant's Causeway as a World Heritage Site means it attracts visitors in considerable numbers and this presents formidable site management problems. The current closure of the lower cliff path to the east along the cliffs has resulted in a serious loss of access for geologists and geomorphologists, as well as those members of the public who are inclined to walk further than the Causeway and the Giant's Organ. Some significant exposures which illustrate key aspects of the volcanology of the Antrim basalts are presently unavailable for examination.

The dynamics of coastal cliff geomorphology and the construction of the cliff path along the softer Interbasaltic laterites sandwiched between the lavas of the Lower Basalts and the Causeway Tholeiites have resulted in a situation where frequent and severe landslips and rock falls occur. This meant that safe access along the lower path could no longer be guaranteed and so the path was closed. The policy of those responsible for the Causeway Coast appears to rule out the possibility of engineering solutions to these access problems.

Fig. 93: (a) Horizontal cooling surfaces in a lava flow lead to the formation of vertical parallel columnar joints. (b) showing the effect of intersecting cracks forming at 120° to each other forming irregular polygons. (c) formation of columnar pattern as solidification proceeds and the cooling cracks more inwards. (d) cooling contraction along the length at the columns forms the 'ball and socket' joints which divide the vertical columns horizontally

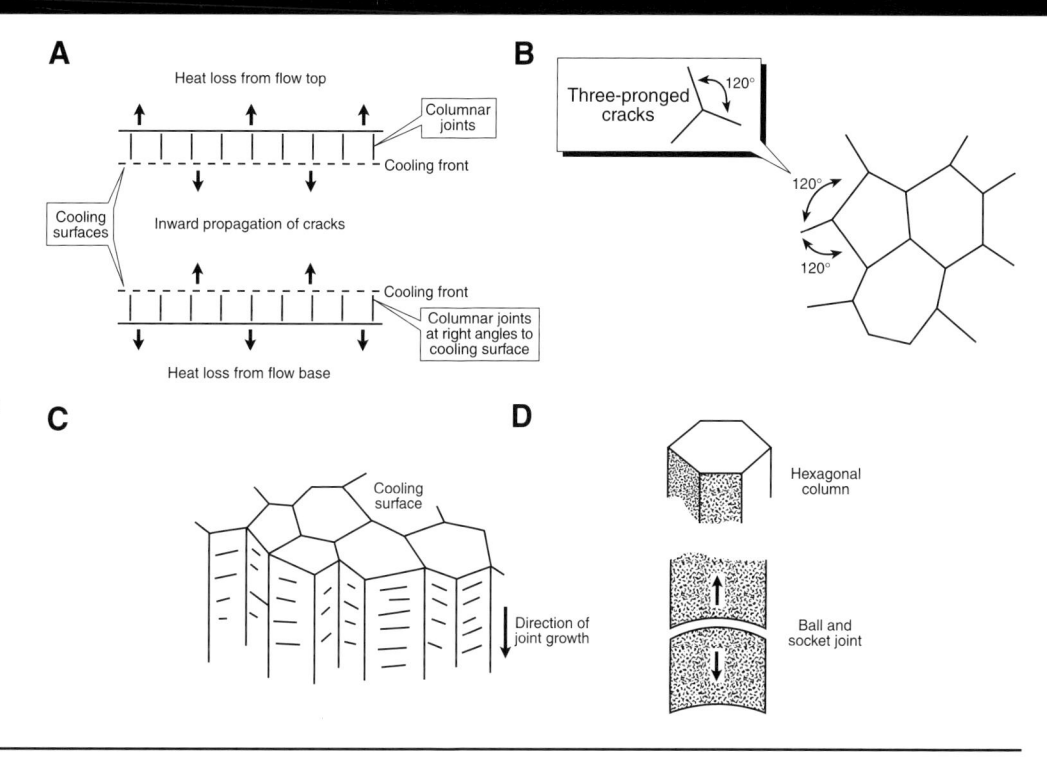

Fig. 94: The formation of multi-tiered columnar basalt flows due to the flooding of the earlier surface after cooling

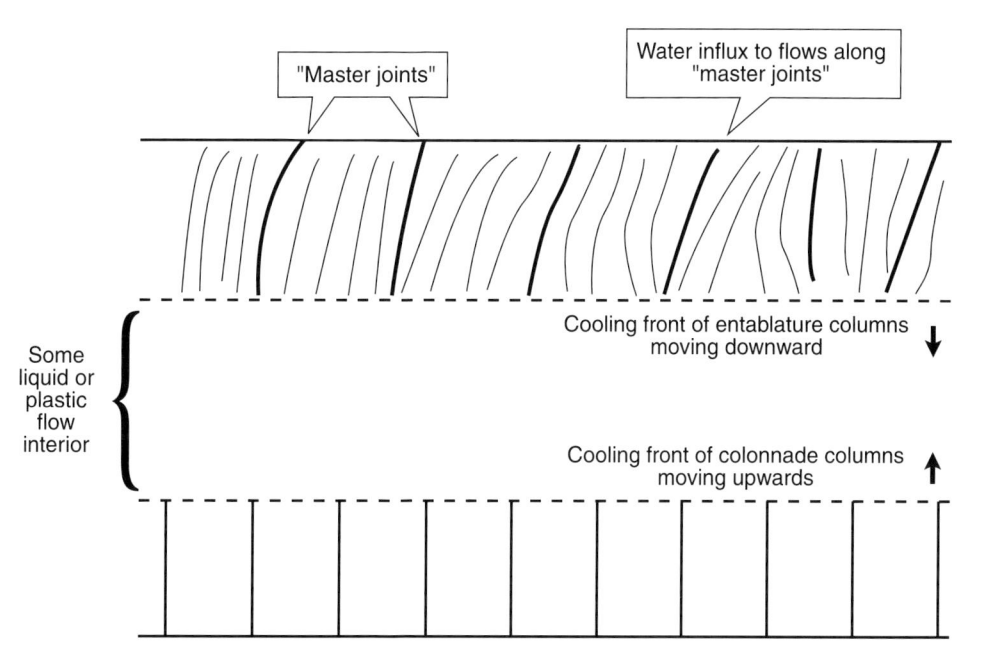

Coastal habitats

Alan Cooper

Regional context

Much of the north coast (Fig. 95) has formal conservation status. For example, the National Trust owns large areas, the Giant's Causeway is a World Heritage Site, cliffs on Rathlin island are a Special Protection Area for birds, the Magilligan dune system, the River Bann estuary and the North Antrim Coast are Special Areas of Conservation and most of the Co Antrim Coast is designated an Area of Outstanding Natural Beauty.

Regionally important seminatural habitats adjacent to the coast but not dependent on coastal processes are blanket bog, heath and broadleaf woodland. Blanket bog, of which Ireland and Scotland hold almost the entire resource of the European Union, covers much of the upland basalt plateau of north Co Londonderry and Co Antrim. Ancient hazel woods (*Corylus avellana*) are a feature of steep scarps in the Antrim Glens, with oak woods (*Quercus petraea*) in the more northerly Glenshesk.

Where physical constraints do not limit access to land, intensive grassland agriculture based on small family farms with beef, sheep and dairy cattle, predominates. Ryegrass leys and pasture (*Lolium perenne*) are the main grassland types and transitions to coastal seminatural vegetation are usually abrupt. Field boundaries are mainly hawthorn hedges (*Crataegus monogyna*), with earth banks (often with gorse - *Ulex europaeus*) more frequent in the uplands and along the coast. Further details of ecological environments and habitats are given in Barne *et al.* (1997), Cooper *et al.* (1997) and Northern Ireland Biodiversity Group (2000).

Habitats

Cliffs and cliff-top vegetation

Cliff and cliff-top vegetation of the basalt and chalk cliffs of northern and eastern County Antrim vary markedly, even over short distances, changing in response to micro-topography and exposure. The main habitats are bare ground, lichen-covered rock in the sea-spray zone, rock crevice and cliff ledge vegetation, maritime grassland, maritime heath, perched saltmarsh and flush vegetation. Seepages and flushes associated with cliffs, rock outcrops and raised beaches can be particularly species-rich.

Wind-pruned dwarf-gorse heath (*Ulex gallii* and *Calluna vulgaris*) is well-developed on Rathlin Island. Species-rich maritime grassland dominated by red fescue-grass (*Festuca rubra*) is frequent over cliffs and headlands throughout the coastline. It is characterised by and thrift (*Armeria maritima*), spring squill (*Scilla verna*), wild thyme (*Thymus praecox*) and bird's-foot trefoil (*Lotus corniculatus*).

Rarities of the basalt cliffs are rose-root (*Sedum rosea*) and rock samphire (*Crithmum maritimum*). Inland cliffs influenced by sea-spray at Binevenagh, County Londonderry support the arctic-alpines, cushion pink (*Silene acaulis*) and purple saxifrage (*Saxifraga oppositifolia*). Near Torr head and

Fig. 95: Location of places named in the text

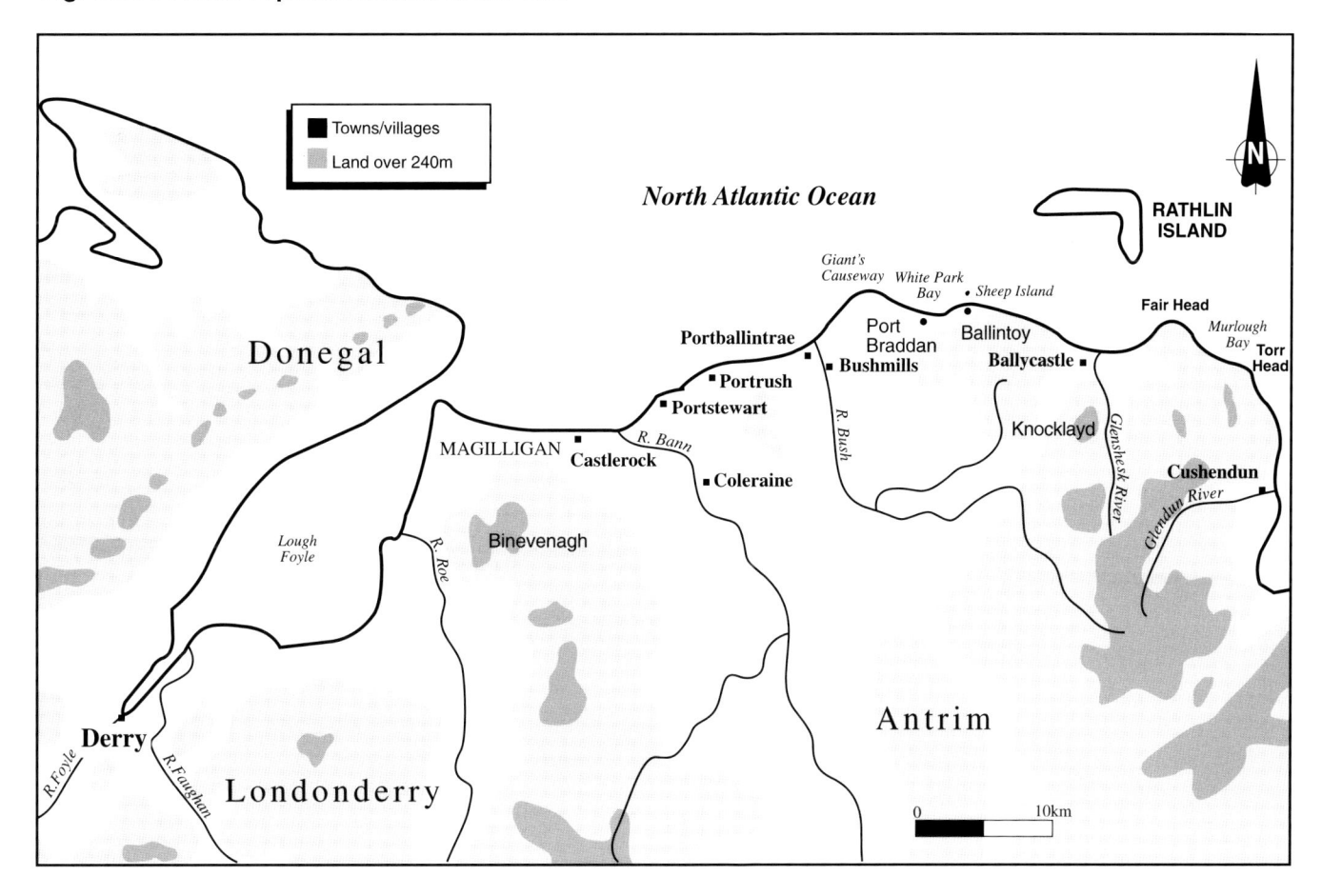

Murlough Bay on the north Antrim coast yellow mountain saxifrage (*Saxifraga aizoides*) and smooth lady's-mantle (*Alchemilla glabra*) occur on old red sandstone cliffs.

Important sea-bird colonies of guillemot (*Urla aalgae*), kittewake (*Rissa tridactyla*) and razorbill (*Alca torda*) occur on the north coast, with the largest colony of Northern European cormorant (*Phalacrocorax carbo carbo*) in Northern Ireland occurs at Sheep Island.

Sand dunes

There are large calcareous sand dune systems from Magilligan Point to Portstewart and at White park Bay. The Magilligan dune system is a Special Area of Conservation under the EC Habitats Directive. It shows a typical spatial sequence from fore-dunes to dune ridge grassland, with dune-plain grassland and dune-slack mosaics inland. Unlike the west of Ireland, extensive machair sand-plains are not a feature of the north coast.

Characteristic species of the fore-dunes and mobile dunes are sand couch-grass (*Elymus farctus*) and marram grass (*Ammophila arenaria*) Closely-grazed dune grassland is species-rich and is characterised by red fescue-grass (*Festuca rubra*), bird's-foot trefoil (*Lotus corniculatus*) and lady's bedstraw (*Galium verum*) indicative of calcareous sand. Dune slack is characterised by creeping willow (*Salix repens*) and common sedge (*Carex nigra*).

Rare species are the smooth cat's-ear (*Hypochoeris glabra*) and white orchid (Pseudorchis albida). Other protected species are bee orchid (*Ophrys apifera*) in dry calcareous sites and marsh helleborine (*Epipactus palustris*) in dune-slack. The dune systems also support a large proportion of the butterfly, moth, bee, ant and wasp fauna of Northern Ireland. Butterflies include the grayling (*Hipparchia semele*), the dark-green fritillary (*Argynnis aglaja*) and the marsh fritillary (*Eurodryas aurinia*).

Whilst many of the dune systems are designated as National Nature Reserves and Areas of Special Scientific Interest or are owned by the National Trust, there are still considerable recreation, golfing, military training and sand excavation pressures. Dune vegetation, in particular at Portstewart, has been damaged by recreational use and sand removal. Public dune protection schemes to counteract erosion have been organised by local authorities at Benone and Portstewart but the general public may still drive their cars onto the beach. The dune systems at Benone, Castlerock, Portstewart and Portrush have golf courses that have resulted in dune habitat loss.

There are also threats from shrub colonisation. Sea buckthorn (*Hippophae rhamnoides*) was widely planted to stabilise sand in the past resulting in considerable loss of dune grassland. At Portstewart the National Trust has implemented control measures.

Most of the dunes have a history of grazing by cattle but where this has stopped, scrub invasion and dominance by rank grasses has reduced species diversity. At Magilligan large areas of the dunes are used for military training and remain ungrazed. Light cattle grazing has been introduced at White Park Bay and at Portstewart a sheep-grazing regime has been introduced by the National Trust.

Vegetated shingle and shorelines

Shingle habitats associated with raised beaches are a feature of the north coast. The vegetation varies from pioneer species to prostrate scrub with blackthorn (*Prunus spinosa*) or burnet rose (*Rosa pimpinellifolia*). Oyster plant (*Mertensia maritima*), a species at the southern limit of its European distribution and sea-kale (*Crambe maritima*), a species at the northern limit of its distribution occur at a small number of open-habitat locations.

Some sites are protected as Areas of Special Scientific Interest but at many sites there are high levels of recreation disturbance. Damage from mineral extraction has also occurred and at other sites scrub encroachment is active where agricultural grazing has been abandoned.

Coastal lagoons

These wetland habitats occur around Lough Foyle as a result of land being enclosed behind sea embankments or coastal defence back-drains. Typically the vegetation includes common reed (*Phragmites australis*), grey club-rush (*Schoenoplectus tabernaemontani*), green algae (*Chaetomorpha, Enteromorpha* and *Ulva*) and tasselweeds (*Ruppia* spp.).

Wet grasslands

Wet grassland habitats are important feeding habitats for waders such as curlew (*Numenius arquata*), snipe (*Gallinago gallinago*) and wildfowl such as greylag goose (*Anser anser*), wigeon (*Anas penelope*), teal (*Anas crecca*) and shoveler (*Anas clypeata*).

Coastal grazing marsh and wet grassland adjacent to estuaries are intensively managed for agricultural production. The main grasses are perennial ryegrass (*Lolium perenne*), rough meadow-grass (*Poa trivialis*) and creeping bent (*Agrostis stolonifera*). Large areas of wet grassland occur on flat, drained polder-lands between the River Roe and River Faughan estuaries and behind the Magilligan dune system on the eastern shores of Lough Foyle. They are drained by brackish or freshwater (often eutrophic) ditches, where plant community interest is greater.

Unimproved seminatural grassland habitats are fragmentary along the back edge of saltmarshes and dune systems where they can grade into fen or swamp communities characterised by sea club-rush (*Scirpus maritimus*), grey club-rush (*Schoenoplectus tabernaemontani*), common spike-rush (*Eleocharis palustris*) or bottle sedge (*Carex rostrata*). Transitions to mire vegetation, characterised by sharp-flowered rush (*Juncus acutiflorus*) or purple moor-grass (*Molinia caerulea*) also occur.

Saltmarsh

This is a scarce habitat in Northern Ireland, usually occurring as a marginal fringe around sea-lough estuaries. The most extensive areas on the north coast are in estuaries of the River Roe, Lough Foyle and the River Bann.

A typical saltmarsh zonation in the region grades from low marsh with saltmarsh grass (*Puccinellia maritima*) and glasswort (*Salicornia maritima*), to mid-marsh, with saltmarsh grass, sea milkwort (*Glaux maritima*), sea lavender (*Limonium vulgare*) and thrift (*Armeria maritima*). The upper marsh is dominated by red fescue-grass (*Festuca rubra*) and sea rush (*Juncus gerardii*). Common couch-grass (*Elymus repens*) typically terminates the upper saltmarsh.

Saltmarsh of the River Roe estuary shows zonation from low saltmarsh to mid-upper saltmarsh turf with red fescue-grass and sea-rush (*Juncus maritimus*). Similar communities occur in the River Bann estuary where there are transitions to fen and rush pasture. Beds of the narrow-leaved eelgrass (*Zostera angustifolia*) occur on mud-flats in Lough Foyle, where they are a food supply for grazing wildfowl in winter.

Common cord-grass (*Spartina anglica*) was introduced to Northern Ireland in the 1940s and is now extensive and spreading over mud-flats, threatening bird feeding habitat. It is found in Lough Foyle, where experimental control measures are being researched.

Small perched saltmarsh communities occur behind raised beaches and sheltered rock platforms of the north Antrim coast, usually flushed with cliff seepage. Plant species with geographically restricted distributions are frequent in these habitats, which are often species-rich.

Many saltmarsh sites have been designated as either National Nature reserves or Areas of Special Scientific Interest. Grazing is extensive on Lough Foyle saltmarsh. In the River Roe estuary, sheep-grazing is under license from the Environment and Heritage Service (EHS) of the Department of the

Environment for Northern Ireland. The National Trust also has grazing agreements on River Bann estuarine saltmarsh. Grazing maintains well-defined zonational vegetation sequences.

The landward boundaries of the saltmarshes are usually fixed by agricultural grassland and often the seaward edge is eroding, so that sea-level rise through global warming is likely to reduce the area. Currently there is seaward edge erosion of saltmarsh at Lough Foyle.

Sites

Giant's Causeway

The Causeway area is notable for its maritime cliff grassland, rock ledge and crevice vegetation, species-rich grassland over basalt and chalk with kidney vetch and spring squill. Maritime heath occurs at some cliff-top locations. There is perched saltmarsh and species-rich flush vegetation at the shore. Notable plant species include the oyster plant (*Mertensia maritima*) on shingle beaches and the saltmarsh flat-sedge (*Blysmus rufus*) in perched saltmarsh. There are significant populations of breeding fulmar (*Fulmaris glacialis*) and black guillemot and breeding chough (*Pyrrhocorax pyrrhocorax*).

Bann Estuary

There is a complex mosaic of habitat types associated with the dune systems of Castlerock and Portstewart. These include embryo dunes with sand couch (*Elymus farctus*) and extensive areas of white dune dominated by marram. The oldest dunes consist of a short-grazed sward with the rare shepherd's cress (*Teesdalia nudicaulis*). Saltmarsh and inland, rich-fen communities also occur, with reedbeds dominated by common reed (*Phragmites australis*) frequent along tidal parts of the River Bann. The estuary is used by significant numbers of waders and wildfowl and is important for breeding species including shelduck, redshank, snipe and lapwing.

Lough Foyle

Lough Foyle comprises a large shallow sea lough which includes the estuaries of the rivers Foyle, Faughan and Roe.

Narrow-leaved eelgrass (*Zostera angustifolia*) and dwarf eelgrass (*Z. noltii*) are extensive on the estuarine sediments. Stands of saltmarsh vegetation occur along parts of the foreshore, despite extensive reclamation in the past. The low-marsh consists of a community dominated by common saltmarsh-grass which is replaced by a mid-marsh community, characterised by red fescue and sea rush. Localised stands of sea club-rush and common reed also occur. The upper-marsh is dominated by common couch (*Elymus repens*). On parts of the intertidal sand and mudflats the low-marsh communities are replaced by extensive stands of the introduced common cord-grass. Brackish dykes behind the shore support a maritime aquatic and swamp vegetation, including the reflexed saltmarsh-grass (*Puccinellia distans*) and spiral tasselweed (*Ruppia cirrhosa*).

The site regularly supports internationally important numbers of whooper swan (*Cygnus cygnus*), light-bellied brent goose (*Branta bernicla hrota*) and bar-tailed godwit (*Limosa lapponica*). There are extensive beds of common mussel (*Mytilus edulis*) in the estuary. The green leaf worm (*Eulalia viridis*), a polychaete, is a common associate. In places there are large populations of the bivalves sand gaper (*Mya arenaria*) and peppery furrow shell (*Scrobicularia plana*). Important populations of Atlantic salmon (*Salmo salar*) migrate through the system.

Rathlin Island

Mosaics of dwarf heath with western gorse (at the limit of its northern distribution in Europe), acid grassland, flushes and wetland communities with maritime influence are extensive. There are substantial areas of species-rich grasslands large orchid populations. The only known locality of Pyramidal Bugle in Northern Ireland occurs on Rathlin Island.

Rathlin Island supports nationally important numbers of peregrine falcon (*Falco peregrinus*). Chough has bred recently on the site. The site supports internationally important breeding numbers of the migratory species, razorbill (*Alca torda*), guillemot and kittiwake and regularly supports breeding Manx shearwater (*Puffinus puffinus*). Between early May to mid July, the cliffs and rocky islands have large numbers of breeding seabirds. Peregrine falcons, buzzards and ravens also build nests on cliff ledges.

There are exceptionally well-developed marine communities, especially on the northern coast, where steep cliffs reach their greatest depth in Northern Ireland.

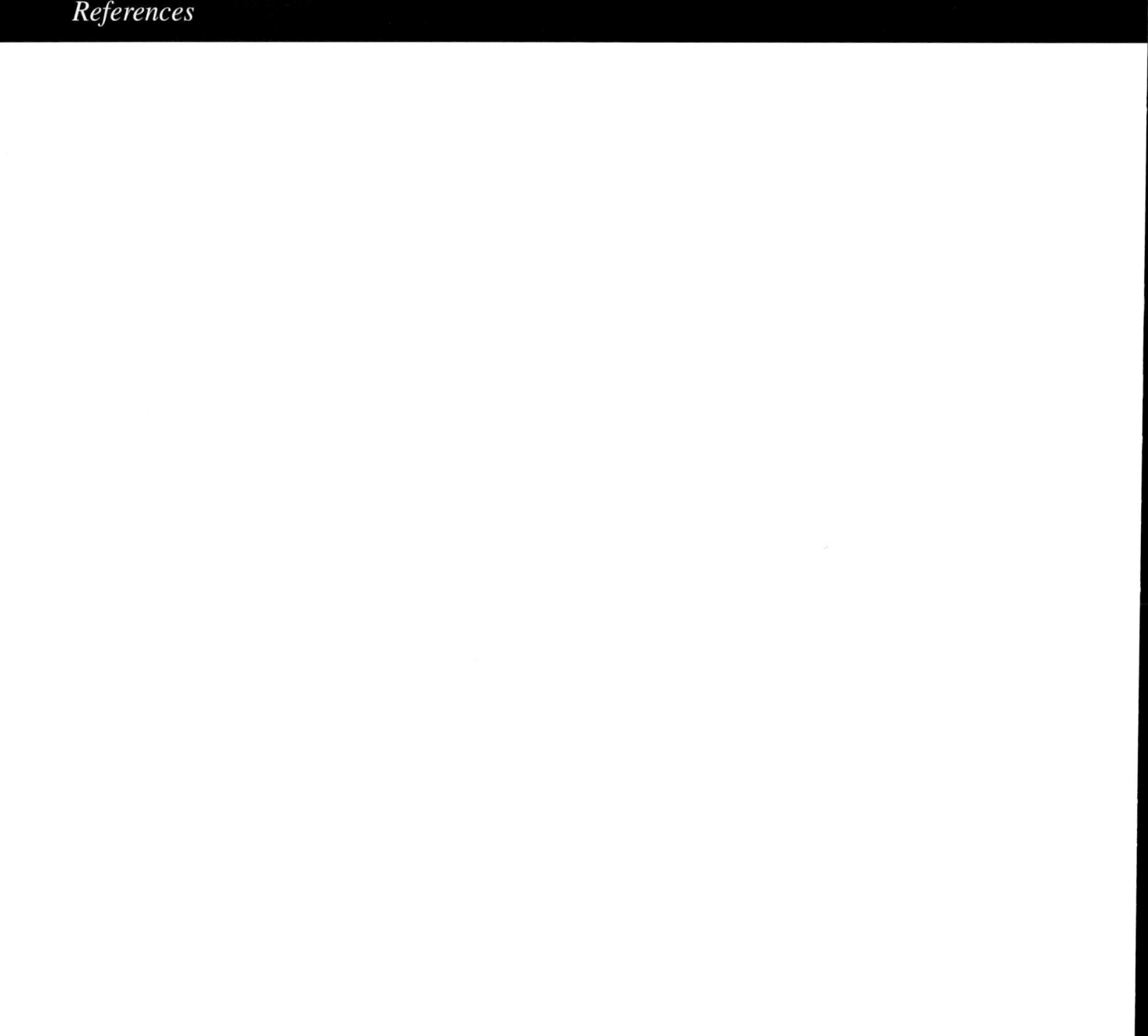

References

Aagaard, T., Nielsen, J. and Greenwood, B. 1998. Suspended sediment transport and nearshore bar formation on a shallow intermediate-state beach. *Marine Geology*, 148, 203-225.

Andrews, J.T., King, C.A.M. and Stuiver, M. 1973. Holocene sea level changes, Cumberland coast, northwest England: eustatic and glacioisostatic movements. *Geologie en Mijnbouw*, 52, 1-12.

Atkins, W.S. 1997. Landuse, infrastructure and coastal defence. *In*: Barne, J.H., Robson, C.F., Kaznowska, S.S., Doody, J.P., Davidson, N.C. and Buck, A.L. (eds) *Coasts and seas of the United Kingdom.* Joint Nature Conservation Committee, Peterborough, Region 17, Northern Ireland, 163-172.

Austin, W.E.N. and McCarroll, D. 1992. Foraminifera from the Irish Sea glacigenic deposits at Aberdaron, western Lleyn, North Wales: palaeoenvironmental implications. *Journal of Quaternary Science*, 7, 311-317.

Barne, J.H., Robson, C.F., Kaznowska, S.S., Doody, J.P., Davidson, N.C. and Buck, A.L. (eds) 1997. *Coasts and Seas of the United Kingdom. Region 17. Northern Ireland.* JNCC, Peterborough.

Bazley, R.A.B., Brandon, A. and Arthurs, J.W. 1997. *Geology of the country around Limavady and Londonderry.* Geological Survey of Northern Ireland Technical Report GSNI/97/1.

Belderson, R.H. 1964. Holocene sedimentation in the western half of the Irish Sea. *Marine Geology*, 2, 147-163.

Bell, A. 1891. Notes upon the marine accumulations in Largo Bay, Fife, and at Portrush, County Antrim. *Proceedings of the Royal Physical Society, Edinburgh*, 10, 290-297.

Björck, S., Walker, M.J.C., Cwynar, L.C., Johnsen, S., Knudsen, K.-L., Lowe, J.J., Wohlfarth, B. and INTIMATE Members. 1998. An event stratigraphy for the Last Termination in the North Atlantic region based on the Greenland ice-core record: a proposal by the INTIMATE group. *Journal of Quaternary Science*, 13, 283-292.

Boulton, G.S., Smith, G.D., Jones, A.S. and Newsome, J. 1985. Glacial geology and glaciology of the last mid-latitude ice sheets. *Journal of the Geological Society of London*, 142, 447-474.

Bowen, D.Q. (ed.) 1999. *A revised correlation of Quaternary deposits in the British Isles.* Geological Society Special Report 23, Geological Society, London. 174pp.

Bowen, D.Q., Phillips, F.M., McCabe, A.M., Knutz, P.C. and Sykes, G.A. 2002. New data for the Last Glacial Maximum in Great Britain and Ireland. *Quaternary Science Reviews*, 21, 89-101.

Bradshaw, P., Carter, R.W.G. and Eastwood, D.A.E. 1991. *Sand removal from beaches on the NE coast of Ireland.* DoE Report, Belfast.

Breen, C. 1996. Maritime archaeology in Northern Ireland: an interim statement. *International Journal of Nautical Archaeology*, 25, 55-65

References

Carter, R.W.G. 1972. *The coastal geomorphology of the Magilligan Foreland.* Unpublished DPhil thesis, New University of Ulster.

Carter, R.W.G. 1975a. The origin of the Magilligan shell mounds. *Irish Naturalists' Journal*, 18, 184-187.

Carter, R.W.G. 1975b. Recent changes in the coastal geomorphology of the Magilligan Foreland, Co. Londonderry. *Proceedings of the Royal Irish Academy*, 75B, 469-497.

Carter, R.W.G. 1975c. The effect of humans on the coastline of Co. Antrim and Co. Londonderry. *Irish Geography*, 8, 72-85.

Carter, R.W.G. 1979. Recent progradation of the Magilligan Foreland, Co. Londonderry, Northern Ireland. *In*: Guilcher, A. (ed) *Les Côtes Atlantiques de L'Europe*. CNEXO, Actes de Colloques, Brest, 9, 17-27.

Carter, R.W.G. 1980. Human activities and geomorphic processes: the example of recreation pressure on the Northern Ireland coast. *Zeitschrift fur Geomorphogie, N.F.*, 34, 155-164.

Carter, R.W.G. 1982a. Sea level changes in Northern Ireland. *Proceedings of the Geologists' Association*, 93, 7-23.

Carter, R.W.G. 1982b. Recent variations in sea-level on the north and east coasts of Ireland and associated shoreline response. *Proceedings of the Royal Irish Academy*, 82B, 177-187.

Carter, R.W.G. 1983. Raised coastal landforms as products of modern process variations, and their relevance in eustatic sea-level studies: examples from eastern Ireland. *Boreas*, 12, 167-182.

Carter, R.W.G. 1986. The morphodynamics of beach-ridge formation: Magilligan, Northern Ireland. *Marine Geology*, 73, 191-214.

Carter, R.W.G. 1988. *Coastal Environments.* Academic Press, London.

Carter, R.W.G. 1988a. Man's response to change in the coastal zone of Ireland. *In*: Ruddle, K., Morgan, W.B. and Pfafflin, J.R. (eds) *The coastal zone: man's response to change*. Harwood, Chur, 127-164.

Carter, R.W.G. 1989. The resources and management of Irish coastal waters. *In*: Carter, R.W.G. and Parker, A.J. (eds) *Ireland: geographical perspectives*. Routledge, London, 391-419.

Carter, R.W.G. 1990. Coastal processes in relation to geographic setting, with special reference to Europe. *Senckenbergiana Maritima*, 21, 1-23.

Carter, R.W.G. 1991a. Near-future sea level impacts on coastal dune landscapes. *Landscape Ecology*, 6, 29-39.

Carter, R.W.G. 1991b. *Shifting sands: a study of the coast of Northern Ireland from Magilligan to Larne.* Countryside and Wildlife Research Series No. 2, HMSO, Belfast.

Carter, R.W.G. 1993. Age, origin and significance of the raised gravel barrier at Church Bay, Rathlin Island, County Antrim. *Irish Geography*, 26, 141-146.

Carter, R.W.G. and Bartlett, D.J. 1988. *Coast Erosion and Management in the Glens of Antrim and the Causeway Coast Areas of Outstanding Natural Beauty.* Department of the Environment, Northern Ireland. 152pp.

Carter, R.W.G. and Bartlett, D.J. 1990. Coastal erosion in Northern Ireland – Part 1: Sand beaches, dunes and river mouths. *Irish Geography*, 23, 1-16.

Carter, R.G.W., Devoy, R.J.N. and Shaw, J. 1989. Late Holocene sea levels in Ireland. *Journal of Quaternary Science*, 4, 7-24.

Carter, R.W.G., Eastwood, D.A. and Bradshaw, P. 1992. Small scale sediment removal from beaches in Northern Ireland: environmental impact, community perception and conservation management. *Aquatic Conservation and Freshwater Ecosystems*, 2, 95-113.

Carter, R.W.G., Eastwood, D.A. and Pollard, H.J. 1993. Man's impact on the coast of Ireland. *In*: Wong, P.P. (eds) *Tourism vs Environment: The case for coastal areas.* Kluwer Academic Publishers, Netherlands, 211-224.

Carter, R.W.G., Johnston, T.W., McKenna, J. and Orford, J.D. 1987. Sea-level, sediment supply and coastal changes: examples from the coast of Ireland. *Progress in Oceanography*, 18, 79-101.

Carter, R.W.G., Lowry, P. and Stone G.W. 1982. Sub-tidal ebb-shoal control of shoreline erosion via wave refraction, Magilligan Foreland, Northern Ireland. *Marine Geology*, 48, M17-M25.

Carter, R.W.G. and Mulrennan, M. 1985. *The coasts of Co. Dublin.* Field Guide No 1., Geographical Society of Ireland, Dublin.

Carter, R.W.G. and Orford, J.D. 1988. Ireland. *In*: Walker, H.J. (ed) *Artificial Structures and Shorelines.* Kluwer Academic Publishers, Berlin. 155-164.

Carter, R.W.G. and Stone, G.W. 1989. Mechanisms associated with the erosion of sand dune cliffs, Magilligan, Northern Ireland. *Earth Surface Processes and Landforms*, 14, 1-10.

Carter, R.W.G. and Wilson, P. 1993. Aeolian processes and deposits in northwest Ireland. *In*: Pye, K. (ed) *The Dynamics and Environmental Context of Aeolian Sedimentary Systems.* Geological Society, London, Special Publication, 72, 173-190.

Carter, R.W.G. and Wilson, P. 1990. The geomorphological, ecological and pedological development of coastal foredunes at Magilligan Point, Northern Ireland. *In*: Nordstrom, K.F., Psuty, N.P. and Carter, R.W.G. (eds) *Coastal dunes: form and process.* Wiley, Chichester, 129-157.

Carter, R.W.G. and Wilson, P. 1990a. Portstewart Strand and the Bann estuary. *In*: Wilson, P. (ed) *A guide to the sand dunes of Ireland.* European Union for Dune Conservation and Coastal Management, Leiden, 18-41.

References

Case, H.J., Dimbleby, G.W., Mitchell, G.F., Morrison, M.E.S. and Proudfoot, V.B. 1969. Land use in Goodland Townland, Co. Antrim, from Neolithic times until today. *Journal of the Royal Society of Antiquaries of Ireland*, 99, 39-53.

Chapman, V.J. 1970. *Seaweeds and their uses*. Methuen, London (2nd edition).

Charlesworth, J.K. 1924. The glacial geology of the north-west of Ireland. *Proceedings of the Royal Irish Academy*, 36B, 174-314.

Charlesworth, J.K. 1939. Some observations on the glaciation of north-east Ireland. *Proceedings of the Royal Irish Academy*, 45B: 255-295.

Charlesworth, J.K. 1963. Some observations on the Irish Pleistocene. *Proceedings of the Royal Irish Academy*, 62B: 295-322.

Charlesworth, J.K. 1973. Stages in the dissolution of the late ice sheet in the Irish Sea region. *Proceedings of the Royal Irish Academy*, 73B, 79-86.

Childe, V.G. 1936. A promontory fort on the Antrim coast. *Antiquity Journal*, 16, 179-198.

Coffey, G. and Praeger, R.L. 1904. The Antrim raised beach: a contribution to the Neolithic history of the north of Ireland. *Proceedings of the Royal Irish Academy*, 25C, 143-200.

Colhoun, E.A. 1970. On the nature of the glaciations and final deglaciation of the Sperrin Mountains and adjacent areas in the North of Ireland. *Irish Geography*, 6, 162-185.

Colhoun, E.A. 1971. The glacial stratigraphy of the Sperrin Mountains and its relation to the glacial stratigraphy of north-west Ireland. *Proceedings of the Royal Irish Academy*, 71B, 37-52.

Colhoun, E.A., Dickson, J.H., McCabe, A.M. and Shotton, F.W. 1972. A Middle Midlandian freshwater series at Derryvree, Maguiresbridge, County Fermanagh, Northern Ireland. *Proceedings of the Royal Society of London, Series B*, 180, 273-292.

Colhoun, E.A., Ryder, A.T. and Stephens, N. 1973. ^{14}C age of an oak-hazel forest bed at Drumskellan, Co. Donegal, and its relation to Late Midlandian and Littletonian raised beaches. *Irish Naturalists' Journal*, 17, 321-327.

Collins, A.E.P. 1977. A sand-dune site at the White Rocks, County Antrim. *Ulster Journal of Archaeology*, 40, 21-26.

Conroy, M.J. and Mitchell, G.F. 1971. The age of Irish plaggen soils. *In*: Yaalon, D. H. (eds) *Palaeopedology: origin, dating and nature of palaeosols*. Israel Universities Press, 129-137.

Cooper, A., Murray, R. and McCann, T. 1997. *The Northern Ireland Countryside Survey: summary report and application to rural decision making*. Environment and Heritage Service, Department of the Environment for Northern Ireland, Belfast.

Cooper, J.A.G., Kelley, J.T. and Belknap, D.F. 1998. New seismic stratigraphic and side scan sonar evidence for a sea level lowstand off the north coast of Ireland: a preliminary appraisal. *Journal of Coastal Research*, Special Issue 26, 129-133.

Cooper, J.A.G., Kelley, J.T., Belknap, D.F., Quinn, R. and McKenna, J. 2002. Seismic stratigraphic evidence for a sea level lowstand at 30-35 m off the north Irish Coast. *Marine Geology*, in press.

Cooper, J.A.G. and Orford, J.D. 1998. Hurricanes as agents of mesoscale coastal change in western Britain and Ireland. *Journal of Coastal Research*, SI 26 (ICS Proceedings), 123-128.

Crawford, W.H. 1980. Drapers and Bleachers in early the Ulster linen Industry. *In*: Cullen, L.M. and Butel, P. (eds) *Négoce et Industrie en France et en Irlande aux XVIIIe et XIXe Siècles*. Franco-Irish Symposium on Social and Economic History. Éditions du National de la Recherche Scientifique, Paris, 113-119.

Cruickshank, J. 1980. Buried, relict soils at Murlough sand dunes, Dundrum, Co. Down. *Irish Naturalists' Journal*, 20, 21-30.

Curtis, T.G.F. 1991. A site inventory of the sandy coasts of Ireland. *In*: Quigley, M. (ed) *A guide to the sand dunes of Ireland*. EUDC, Leiden, 6-17.

Dardis, G.F. 1986. Late Pleistocene glacial lakes in south-central Ulster, Northern Ireland. *Irish Journal of Earth Sciences*, 7, 133-144.

Dardis, G.F. and McCabe, A.M. 1983. Facies of subglacial channel sedimentation in late-Pleistocene drumlins, Northern Ireland. *Boreas*, 12, 263-278.

Dardis, G.F., McCabe, A.M. and Mitchell, W.I. 1984. Characteristics and origins of lee-side stratification sequences in late Pleistocene drumlins, Northern Ireland. *Earth Surface Processes and Landforms*, 9, 409-424.

Davies, G.L.H. and Stephens, N. 1978. *Ireland*. Methuen, London. 250pp.

Dawson, J. 1835. *Ordnance Survey field memoir for the parish of Tamlaghtard or Magilligan, Co. Londonderry*. Dublin.

Devoy, R.J.N. 1992. Questions of coastal protection and the human response to sea-level rise in Ireland and Britain. *Irish Geography*, 25, 1-22.

Dresser, P.Q., Smith, A.G. and Pearson, G.W. 1973. Radiocarbon dating of the raised beach at Woodgrange, Co. Down. *Proceedings of the Royal Irish Academy*, 73B, 53-56.

Dwerryhouse, A.R. 1923. The glaciation of north-eastern Ireland. *Quarterly Journal of the Geological Society*, 79, 352-421.

European Commission. 1999. *Towards a European Integrated Coastal Zone Management Strategy: General principles and policy options*. EU Demonstration Programme on Integrated Management in Coastal Zones 199-1999, 5-91.

References

Evans, E.E. 1967. *Mourne Country - Landscape and Life in South Down*, Dundalgan Press Ltd.

Eyles, N. and McCabe, A.M. 1989. The Late Devensian (<22,000 BP) Irish Sea Basin: The sedimentary record of a collapsed ice sheet margin. *Quaternary Science Reviews*, 8, 307-351.

Ferguson and McIlveen. 1997. *Royal County Down Golf Club - Coastal Erosion*. (Unpublished report) November 1997.

Fisher, N. 1935. Locally extinct marine mollusca at Portstewart. *Journal of Conchology*, 20, 117-126.

Forbes, D.L., Taylor, R.B., Shaw, J., Orford, J.D. and Carter, R.W.G. 1990. Development and instability of barrier beaches on the Atlantic coast of Nova Scotia. *Proceedings of the Canadian Coastal Conference, '90, 83-98.*

Fyfe, J.A., Long, D. and Evans, D. 1993. *United Kingdom offshore regional report: the geology of the Hebrides-Malin sea area*. HMSO, London, for the British Geological Survey.

Gardner, J. and Elliott, M. 2001. *UK Biodiversity Action Plan Native Oyster Species Information Review*. Final Report English Nature. ICES Report Z123-F-2001. Institute of Estuarine and Coastal Studies, University of Hull, 157pp.

Godfrey, E.S. 1975. *The Development of English glass making, 1560-1640*. University of North Carolina Press.

Gray, W. 1879. The character and distribution of the rudely-worked flints of the north of Ireland, chiefly in Antrim and Down. *Journal of the Royal Historical and Archaeological Association of Ireland*, 5 (4th series), 109-143.

Gray, W. 1884. Comlechs in counties of Down and Antrim. *Journal of the Royal Historical and Archaeological Association of Ireland*, 6 (4th series), 354-367.

Gray, W. 1888. Rough flint celts of the County Antrim. *Journal of the Royal Historical and Archaeological Association of Ireland*, 8 (4th series), 505-506.

Griffiths, A.E. and Wilson, H.E. 1982. *Geology of the country around Carrickfergus and Bangor*. Geological Survey of Northern Ireland, HMSO, Belfast.

Gwynn, A. and Hadcock, R. N. 1988. *Medieval Religious Houses, Ireland*. Dublin (Irish Academic Press, reprint of 1970 edition).

Hamilton, A.C. and Carter, R.W.G. 1983. A mid-Holocene moss bed from eolian dune sands near Articlave, Co. Londonderry. *Irish Naturalists' Journal*, 21, 73-75.

Harper, D. 1974. Kelp burning in the Glens. *The Glynns, Journal of the Glens of Antrim Historical Society*.

Hassé, L. 1890. Objects from the sandhills at Portstewart and Grangemore, and their antiquity. *Proceedings and Papers of the Royal Society of Antiquaries of Ireland*, 1 (5th series), 130-138.

Haynes, J.R., McCabe, A.M. and Eyles, N. 1995. Microfaunas from late Devensian glaciomarine deposits in the Irish Sea Basin. *Irish Journal of Earth Sciences*, 14, 81-103.

Hein, F.J. 1982. Depositional mechanisms of deep-sea coarse clastic sediments, Cap Etrangé Formation, Québec. *Canadian Journal of Earth Sciences*, 19, 267-287

Hewson, L.M. 1934. Notes on Irish sandhills. *The Journal of the Royal Society of Antiquaries of Ireland*, 4 (7th series), 231-244.

Hill, A.R. and Prior, D.B. 1968. Directions of ice movement in north-east Ireland. *Proceedings of the Royal Irish Academy,* 66B, 71-84.

Hoare, P.G. 1991. Pre-Midlandian glacial deposits in Ireland. *In*: Ehlers, J., Gibbard, P.L. and Rose, J. (eds) *Glacial deposits in Great Britain and Ireland. Balkema, Rotterdam.* 37-45.

Hunter, L.E., Powell, R.D. and Smith, G.W. 1996. Facies architecture and grounding-line fan processes of morainal banks during the deglaciation of coastal Maine. *Bulletin of the Geological Society of America*, 108, 1022-1038.

Hobson, M. & F. 1907. Some rude stone monuments in Antrim and Down. *Ulster Journal of Archaeology*, 13, 84-89.

Holthuijsen, L.H., Booij, N. and Herbers, T.H.C. 1989. A prediction model for stationary, short-crested waves in shallow water with ambient currents. *Coastal Engineering*, 13, 23-54.

Innes, R. 1794. An account of the great variety of plants, shell-sones, and many other curiosities in the parish of Magilligan in the County of Londonderry in Ireland; together with a curious account of the forming the land, being formerly under water. *Anthologia Hibernica*, 3, 116-120.

Jackson, D.I., Jackson, A.A., Evans, D., Wingfield, R.T.R., Barnes, R.P. and Arthurs, M.J. 1995. *United Kingdom offshore regional report: the geology of the Irish Sea.* HMSO, London.

Jackson, J.W. 1933. Preliminary report on excavations at the caves of Ballintoy, Co. Antrim. *Irish Naturalists' Journal*, 4, 230-235.

Jackson, J.W. 1934. Further excavations at Ballintoy caves, Co. Antrim. *Irish Naturalists' Journal* 5, 104-114.

Jackson, J.W. 1936. Excavations at Ballintoy caves, Co. Antrim. Third report. *Irish Naturalists' Journal*, 6, 31-42.

Jackson, J.W. 1938. Excavations at Ballintoy caves, Co. Antrim. Fourth report. *Irish Naturalists' Journal*, 7, 107-112.

References

Jessen, K. 1949. Studies in late-Quaternary deposits and flora-history of Ireland. *Proceedings of the Royal Irish Academy*, 52B, 85-290.

Kilroe, J.R. 1913. Outline of geological observations in north-west Londonderry collected during the progress of revising work. *Proceedings of the Belfast Naturalists' Field Club*, 6, 634-663.

Knight, J. 2001. Glaciomarine deposition around the Irish Sea Basin: some problems and solutions. *Journal of Quaternary Science*, 16, 405-418.

Knight, J. Submitted. Evaluating controls on ice dynamics in the north-east Atlantic using an event stratigraphy approach. *Quaternary International*.

Knight, J., Coxon, P., McCabe, A.M., McCarron, S.G., in press. Pleistocene glaciations in Ireland. *In*: Ehlers, J., Gibbard, P.L. (eds.), *Chronology and extent of world glaciations*. Wiley, London.

Knight, J. and McCabe, A.M. 1997. Identification and significance of ice flow-transverse subglacial ridges (Rogen moraines) in north central Ireland. *Journal of Quaternary Science*, 12, 219-224.

Knight, J., McCarron, S.G. and McCabe, A.M. 1999. Landform modification by palaeo-ice streams in east central Ireland. *Annals of Glaciology*, 28, 161-167.

Knight, P.J. and Howarth, M.J. 1999. The flow through the north channel of the Irish Sea. *Continental Shelf Research*, 19, 693-716.

Knowles, W.J. 1878. Flint implements and associated remains found near Ballintoy, Co. Antrim. *Journal of the Anthropological Institute*, 7, 202-205.

Knowles, W.J. 1885. Whitepark Bay, Co. Antrim. *Journal of the Royal Historical and Archaeological Association of Ireland*, 7 (4th series), 104-125.

Knowles, W.J. 1887. The prehistoric sites of Portstewart, County Londonderry. *Journal of the Royal Historical and Archaeological Association of Ireland*, 8 (4th series), 221-237.

Knowles, W.J. 1889. Report on the prehistoric remains from the sand-hills of the coast of Ireland. *Proceedings of the Royal Irish Academy*, 17, 173-187.

Knowles, W.J. 1891. Second report on the prehistoric remains from the sandhills of the coast of Ireland. *Proceedings of the Royal Irish Academy*, 17, 612-625.

Knowles, W.J. 1895. The third report on the prehistoric remains from the sandhills of the coast of Ireland. *Proceedings of the Royal Irish Academy*, 19, 650-663.

Knowles, W.J. 1901. The fourth report on the prehistoric remains from the sandhills of the coast of Ireland. *Proceedings of the Royal Irish Academy*, 22, 331-389.

Komar, P.D. 1976. *Beach processes and sedimentation*. Prentice Hall Inc, New Jersey.

References

Kroon, D., Austin, W.E.N., Chapman, M.R. and Ganssen, G. 1997. Deglacial surface circulation changes in the northeastern Atlantic: Temperature and salinity records off NW Scotland on a century scale. *Paleoceanography*, 12, 755-763.

Kroon, D., Shimmield, G., Austin, W.E.N., Derrick, S., Knutz, P. and Shimmield, T. 2000. Century- to millennial-scale sedimentological-geochemical records of glacial-Holocene sediment variations from the Barra Fan (NE Atlantic). *Journal of the Geological Society*, 157, 643-653.

Lamb, H.H. 1995. *Climate, history and the modern world*. Routledge, London.

Lambeck, K. 1995. Late Devensian and Holocene shorelines of the British Isles and North Sea from models of glacio-hydro-isostatic rebound. *Journal of the Geological Society*, 152, 437-448.

Lambeck, K. 1996. Glaciation and sea-level change for Ireland and the Irish Sea since Late Devensian/Midlandian times. *Journal of the Geological Society*, 153, 853-872.

Lambeck, K. and Purcell, A.P. 2001. Sea-level change in the Irish Sea since the Last Glacial Maximum: constraints from isostatic modelling. *Journal of Quaternary Science*, 16, 497-506.

Lawlor, D.P. 2000. *Inner shelf sedimentology off the North Coast of Northern Ireland*. Unpublished DPhil Thesis, University of Ulster.

Lewis, S. 1837. *A topographical dictionary of Ireland*. Volume II (H-Z). London.

Long, P.E. and Wood, B.J. 1986. Structures, textures and cooling histories of Columbia River basalt flows. *Geological Society of America Bulletin*, 97, 1144-1155.

Lowe, D.R. 1982. Sediment gravity flows. II. Depositional models with special reference to the deposits of high-density turbidity currents. *Journal of Sedimentary Petrology*, 52, 279-297.

Lowry, P. 1982. *Form and process of an estuarine washover barrier, Carrickhue, County Londonderry, Northern Ireland*. Unpublished MPhil Thesis, New University of Ulster.

Lyle, P. 2000. The eruption environment of multi-tiered columnar basalt lava flows. *Journal of the Geological Society*, 157, 715-722.

Lyle, P. 1996. *A Geological Guide to the Causeway Coast*. Environment and Heritage Service, DOE (NI). W&G Baird, Belfast.

MacMillan, N.F. 1957. Quaternary deposits around Lough Foyle. *Proceedings of the Royal Irish Academy*, 58B, 185-205.

Mallory, J.P., McCormick, F., Wilson, P., Henderson, J., Goddard, A. and Crone, F.J. 1988. Excavations at Ballymulholland, Magilligan Foreland, Co. Londonderry. *Ulster Journal of Archaeology*, 51, 103-114.

Mallory, J.P. and McNeill, T.E. 1991. *The archaeology of Ulster from colonization to plantation*. The Institute of Irish Studies, The Queen's University of Belfast.

References

Mallory, J.P. and Woodman, P.C. 1984. Oughtymore: an Early Christian shell midden. *Ulster Journal of Archaeology*, 47, 51-62.

Malvarez, G.C., McCloskey, J., McLaughlin, S. and Cooper, J.A.G. 1995. *Formulation of a sensitivity index based on wave-sediment interaction*. Final report to Forbairt, ECOPRO project (EC research project).

Manning, P.I., Robbie, J.A. and Wilson, H.E. 1970. *Geology of Belfast and the Lagan Valley*. Memoirs of the Geological Survey, HMSO, Belfast.

May, A. McL. 1934. Excavations in caves at Port Braddon, County Antrim. *Irish Naturalists' Journal*, 5, 56-58.

May, A. McL. and Batty, J. 1948. The sandhill cultures of the River Bann estuary, Co. Londonderry. *Journal of the Royal Society of Antiquaries of Ireland*, 78, 130-156.

McCabe, A.M. 1985. Glacial geomorphology. *In*: K.J. Edwards and W.P. Warren (eds) *The Quaternary History of Ireland*. Academic Press, London. 67-93.

McCabe, A.M. 1987. Quaternary deposits and glacial stratigraphy in Ireland. *Quaternary Science Reviews*, 6, 259-299.

McCabe, A.M. 1993. The 1992 Farrington Lecture: Drumlin bedforms and related ice-marginal depositional systems in Ireland. *Irish Geography*, 26, 22-44.

McCabe, A.M. 1996. Dating and rhythmicity from the last deglacial cycle in the British Isles. *Journal of the Geological Society*, 153, 499-502.

McCabe, A.M. 1997. Geological constraints on geophysical models of relative sea-level change during deglaciation of the western Irish Sea Basin. *Journal of the Geological Society*, 154, 601-604.

McCabe, A.M. 1999. Ireland. *In*: Bowen, D.Q. (ed) *A revised correlation of Quaternary deposits in the British Isles*. Geological Society Special Report 23, Geological Society, London, 115-124.

McCabe, A.M., Carter, R.W.G. and Haynes, J.R. 1994. A shallow marine emergent sequence from the northwestern sector of the last British ice sheet, Portballintrae, Northern Ireland. *Marine Geology*, 117, 19-34.

McCabe, A.M. and Clark, P.U. 1998. Ice-sheet variability around the North Atlantic Ocean during the last deglaciation. *Nature*, 392, 373-377.

McCabe, A.M. and Dardis, G.F. 1989. A geological view of drumlins in Ireland. *Quaternary Science Reviews*, 8, 169-177.

McCabe, A.M., Dardis, G.F. and Hanvey, P.M. 1984. Sedimentology of a late Pleistocene submarine-moraine complex, County Down, Northern Ireland. *Journal of Sedimentary Petrology*, 54, 716-730.

McCabe, A.M., Dardis, G.F. and Hanvey, P.M. 1987. Sedimentation at the margins of a late Pleistocene ice-lobe terminating in shallow marine environments, Dundalk Bay, eastern Ireland. *Sedimentology*, 34, 473-493.

McCabe, A.M. and Eyles, N. 1988. Sedimentology of an ice-contact glaciomarine delta, Carey Valley, Northern Ireland. *Sedimentary Geology*, 59, 1-14.

McCabe, A.M. and Haynes, J.R. 1996. A late Pleistocene intertidal boulder pavement from an isostatically emergent coast, Dundalk Bay, eastern Ireland. *Earth Surface Processes and Landforms*, 21, 555-572.

McCabe, A.M., Haynes, J.R. and MacMillan, N.F. 1986. Late-Pleistocene tidewater glaciers and glaciomarine sequences from north County Mayo, Republic of Ireland. *Journal of Quaternary Science*, 1, 73-84.

McCabe, A.M., Knight, J. and McCarron, S. 1998. Evidence for Heinrich event 1 in the British Isles. *Journal of Quaternary Science*, 13, 549-568.

McCabe, A.M., Knight, J. and McCarron, S.G. 1999. Ice flows and glacial bedforms in north central Ireland: a record of rapid environmental change during the last glacial termination. *Journal of the Geological Society*, 156, 63-72.

McCarron, S.G. 2001. *Late Devensian glaciation of the north of Ireland*. Unpublished DPhil Thesis, University of Ulster. 319pp.

McCauley, M. 1997. History and archaeology. *In:* Barne, J.H., Robson, C.F., Kaznowska, S.S., Doody, J.P., Davidson, N.C. and Buck, A.L. (eds) *Coasts and seas of the United Kingdom*. Joint Nature Conservation Committee, Peterborough, Region 17, Northern Ireland, 133-144.

McErlean, T., McConkey, R. and Forsythe, W. (eds) 2002. *The maritime cultural landscape of Strangford Lough*. Blackstaff Press, Belfast.

McGourty, J. and Wilson, P. 2000. Investigating the internal structure of Holocene coastal sand dunes using ground-penetrating radar: example from the north coast of Northern Ireland. *In*: Noon, D.A., Stickley, G.F. and Longstaff, D. (eds) *Proceedings of the Eighth International Conference on Ground Penetrating Radar*. SPIE - The International Society for Optical Engineering, Washington, 4084, 14-19.

McKelvey F.B. and Andrew T.E. 1996. The present status of the oyster fishery of Lough Foyle. *In:* Reynolds, J.D. (ed) *The conservation of aquatic ecosystems*. Royal Irish Academy, Dublin, 167-170.

McKelvey F.B., Andrew T.E. and Cunningham P. 1996. Recruitment potential of native oysters, *Ostrea edulis*, in Lough Foyle. *J.Int. Cons. MER. September* 1993, 21, 10pp.

McKenna, J. 1990. Portballintrae – Port Gorm. *In:* Wilson, P. (ed.) *North Antrim and Londonderry*. Field Guide 13, Irish Association for Quaternary Studies, Dublin, 45-48.

McKenna, J., Carter, R.W.G. and Bartlett, D. 1992. Coast erosion in northeast Ireland: - Part II: Cliffs and shore platforms. *Irish Geography*, 25, 111-128.

McMorris, J.A.V. 1979. *The formation and development of Holocene peat in the dune system at Magilligan, Co. Londonderry*. Unpublished MSc thesis, New University of Ulster.

References

McNeill, T.E. 1983. The stone castles of northern County Antrim. *Ulster Journal of Archaeology*, 46, 101-128.

Merritt, J.W. and Auton, C.A. 2000. An outline of the lithostratigraphy and depositional history of Quaternary deposits in the Sellafield district, west Cumbria. *Proceedings of the Yorkshire Geological Society*, 53, 129-154.

Middleton, G.F. and Hampton, M.A. 1976. Subaqueous sediment transport and deposition by sediment gravity flows. *In*: Stanley, D.G. and Swift, D.J.P (eds) *Marine Sediment Transport and Environmental Management*. Wiley, New York, 197-218.

Mitchell, G.F. 1976. *The Irish landscape*. Collins, London.

Mitchell, G. F. and Stephens, N. 1974. Is there evidence for a Holocene sea-level higher than that of today on the coasts of Ireland? *Colloque Int. Centre National Recherche*, 219, 115-125.

Morrison, M.E.S. and Stephens, N. 1965. A submerged Late Quaternary deposit at Roddans Port on the northeast coast of Ireland. *Philosophical Transactions of the Royal Society of London*, 249B, 221-255.

Murdy J. 2001. *Origins and development of coastal dunes of southeast Co. Down, Northern Ireland*. Unpublished PhD thesis, Queen's University, Belfast, 334pp.

Murphy, M.E. 1980. *Management of sand dunes in the west of Ireland*. Unpublished MSc thesis, New University of Ulster, Coleraine.

Northern Ireland Biodiversity Group. 2000. *Biodiversity in Northern Ireland. Recommendations to Government for a Biodiversity Strategy*. Stationery Office, Belfast.

Oak, H.L. 1984. The boulder beach: a fundamentally distinct sedimentary assemblage. *Annals of the Association of American Geographers*, 74, 71-82.

O'Connor R., Whelan B.J. and Crutchfield, J.A. (with O'Sullivan, A.J.) 1992. *Review of the Irish aquaculture sector and recommendations for its development*. Economic and Social Research Institute, Dublin.

Oldfield, F., Carter, R.W.G., Kitcher, K.J. and Wilcock, F.A. 1973. *Report into the investigation of erosion and accretion on the coastlines of Co. Antrim and Co. Londonderry*. N.I. Ministry of Agriculture, 47pp (unpublished).

Orford, J.D. 1986. Murlough Spit. *In:* McCabe, M. and Hirons, K.R. (eds) *Field guide to south-east Ulster*. Quaternary Research Association, Cambridge, 103-113.

Orford, J.D. 1988. Alternative interpretation of man-induced shoreline changes in Rosslare Bay, southeast Ireland. *Transactions of the Institute of British Geographers*, New Series, 13, 65-78.

Orford, J.D. 1989. Tides, currents and waves in the Irish Sea. *Geographical Society of Ireland, Special Publication*, 3, 18-46.

Orford, J.D. 1992. Littoral processes, sediments, coastal geomorphology and sea-level change: implications for coastal management strategies in Ireland. *In*: Devoy, R.J.N. and O'Mahoney, A. (eds) C*oastal Engineering and Management. REMU Cork*, Occasional Publication No. 2, 29-45.

Orford, J.D. 2001. *Tide gauge determinations of 20th century relative sea-level changes around North-East Ireland*. Unpublished Report for Environment and Heritage Service, Northern Ireland, 11pp.

Orford, J.D. and Carter, R.W.G. 1988. Shelf-coast evolution: an Irish perspective. *In:* Van de Plasche, O. (ed) *Shelf-Coast Interaction*. Vrijie Universitet, Amsterdam, 88-91.

Orford, J.D, Murdy, J. and Wintle, A. (in press) Holocene sea-level highstand beach-ridges with superimposed dunes in north-east Ireland: cause and timing of fine and coarse beach sediment decoupling. *Marine Geology*.

Orme, A.R. 1966. Quaternary changes of sea-level in Ireland. *Transactions of the Institute of British Geographers*, 39, 127-140.

Patterson, W.H. 1896. On a find of worked flint in submerged peat at Portrush, Co. Antrim. *Journal of the Royal Society of Antiquaries of Ireland*, 26, 383-384.

Pendlebury, D.C. and Dobson, M.R. 1976. Sediment and macrofaunal distribution in the eastern Malin Sea, as determined by side-scan sonar and sampling. *Scottish Journal of Geology*, 11, 315-332.

Phillips, F.M., Bowen, D.Q. and Elmore, D. 1996. Surface exposure dating of glacial features in Great Britain using cosmogenic chlorine-36: preliminary results. *Mineralogical Magazine*, 58A, 722-723.

Portlock, J.E. 1843. *Report on the geology of the County of Londonderry and parts of Tyrone and Fermanagh*. HMSO, Dublin. 784pp.

Posamentier, H.W., Allen, G.P. and James, D.P. 1992. High resolution sequence stratigraphy, the East Coulee delta, Alberta. *Journal of Sedimentary Petrology*, 62, 310-317.

Postma, G., Menec, W. and Kleinspehn, K.L. 1988. Large floating clasts in turbidites: a mechanism for their emplacement. *Sedimentary Geology* 58, 47-61.

Praeger, R.L. 1893. Report on the estuarine clays of the north-east of Ireland. *Proceedings of the Royal Irish Academy*, 2 (3rd Series), 212-289.

Praeger, R.L. 1895. Report of the subcommittee to investigate the gravels of Ballyrudder, County Antrim. Belfast Naturalists' Field Club.

Praeger, R.L. 1897. Report upon the raised beaches of the north-east of Ireland, with special reference to their fauna. *Proceedings of the Royal Irish Academy*, 4 (3rd series), 30-54.

Prior, D.B. 1966. Late-glacial and Post-glacial shorelines in north-east Antrim. *Irish Geography*, 5, 173-187.

References

Prior, D.E. 1970. Ice limits in the Cushendun area of northeast Antrim. *In:* Stephens N. and Glasscock, R.E. (eds) *Irish Geographical Studies in Honour of E. Estyn Evans.* Queen's University, Belfast, 59-64.

Proudfoot, V.B. 1958. Problems of soil history. Podzol development at Goodland and Torr Townlands, Co. Antrim, Northern Ireland. *Journal of Soil Science,* 9, 186-198.

Proudfoot, V.B. 1961-62. Further excavations at Larrybane promontory fort, Co. Antrim. *Ulster Journal of Archaeology,* 24-25, 91-115.

Quinn, A.C.M. 1977. *Sand dunes: formation, erosion and management.* An Foras Forbartha, Dublin.

Quinn, R., Cooper, J.A.G. and Williams, B. 2000. Marine geophysical investigation of the inshore coastal waters of Northern Ireland. *International Journal of Nautical Archaeology,* 29, 294-298.

Ramster, J.W. and Hill, H.W. 1969. Current system in the northern Irish Sea. *Nature,* 224, 59-61.

Sampson, G.V. 1802. *Statistical survey of the County of Londonderry.* Dublin.

Shaw, J. 1981. *The morphodynamics of Bushfoot strand, Co. Antrim.* Unpublished MSc thesis, New University of Ulster, Coleraine.

Shaw, J. 1985. Beach morphodynamics of an Atlantic coastal embayment: Runkerry strand, County Antrim. *Irish Geography,* 18, 51-58.

Shaw, J. and Carter, R.W.G. 1980. Late-Midlandian sedimentation and glaciotectonics of the North Antrim End Moraine. *Irish Naturalists' Journal,* 20, 67-69.

Shaw, J. and Carter, R.W.G. 1994. Coastal peats from northwest Ireland: implications for late-Holocene relative sea-level change and shoreline evolution. *Boreas,* 23, 74-91.

Short, A.D. 1991. Macro - meso tidal beach morphodynamics - an overview. *Journal of Coastal Research,* 7, 417-436.

Singh, G. and Smith, A.G. 1973. Post-glacial vegetational history and relative land- and sea-level changes in Lecale, Co. Down. *Proceedings of the Royal Irish Academy,* 73B, 1-51.

Sissons, J.B. 1979. The Loch Lomond Stadial in the British Isles. *Nature,* 280, 199-203.

Smith, A.G., Pearson, G.W. and Pilcher, J.R. 1971. Belfast radiocarbon dates IV. *Radiocarbon,* 13, 450-467.

Stephens, N. 1958. The evolution of the coastline of north-east Ireland. *Advancement of Science,* 56, 389-391.

Stephens, N. 1963. Late-glacial sea levels in northeast Ireland. *Irish Geography,* 4, 345-359.

Stephens N. 1968 Late-glacial and post-glacial shorelines in Ireland and south-west Scotland. *In:* Morrison, R.B. and Wright, H.E., Jr (eds) *Means of Correlation of Quaternary Successions*, Proceedings of the 7th INQUA Congress. University of Utah Press, 437-456.

Stephens, N. 1970. The coastline of Ireland. *In*: Stephens, N. and Glasscock, R.E. (eds) *Irish Geographical Studies in Honour of E. Estyn Evans*. Queen's University, Belfast, 125-145.

Stephens, N., Creighton, J.R. and Hannon, M.A. 1975. The Late Pleistocene period in north eastern Ireland: an Assessment. *Irish Geography*, 8, 1-23.

Stephens, N. and McCabe, A.M. 1977. Late-Pleistocene ice movements and patterns of Late- and Post-glacial shorelines on the coast of Ulster, Ireland. *In*: Kidson, C. and Tooley, M.J. (eds) *Quaternary History of the Irish Sea*. Seel House Press, Liverpool, 179-198.

Stephens, N. and Synge, F.M. 1965. Late-Pleistocene shorelines and drift limits in north Donegal. *Proceedings of the Royal Irish Academy,* 64B, 131-153.

Stewart, S.A. 1897. The Portrush raised beach. *The Irish Naturalist*, 6, 287-290.

Sweeny, J.C. (ed) 1989. *The Irish Sea: a resource at risk.* Geographical Scoiety of Ireland Special Publication 3. Maynooth, Ireland.

Symes, R.G., Egan, F.W. and M'Henry, A. 1888. *Explanatory memoir to accompany sheets 7 and 8 of the maps of the Geological Survey of Ireland*. Geological Survey of Ireland, Dublin.

Synge, F.M. and Stephens, N. 1966. Late- and post-glacial shorelines and ice limits in Argyll and north-east Ulster. *Transactions of the Institute of British Geographers*, 39, 101-125.

Taylor, R.B., Carter, R.W.G., Forbes, D.L. and Orford, J.D. 1986. Beach sedimentation in Ireland: contrasts and similarities with Atlantic Canada. *Current Research 86-B. Geological Survey of Canada*, 55-64.

Thomas, G.S.P. and Kerr, P. 1987. The stratigraphy, sedimentology and palaeontology of the Pleistocene Knocknasilloge Member, Co. Wexford, Ireland. *Geological Journal*, 22, 67-82.

Trenhaile, A.S. 1971. Lithological control of high-water rock ledges in the Vale of Glamorgan, Wales. *Geografiska Annaler*, 53A, 59-69.

Trenhaile, A.S. and Layzell, M.G.J. 1980. Shore platform morphology and tidal-duration distributions in storm wave environments. *In:* McCann, S.B. (ed.) *The Coastline of Canada*. Geological Survey of Canada, Paper 80-10, 207-214.

Trenhaile, A.S. 1987. *The Geomorphology of Rock Coasts*. Clarendon Press, Oxford.

Walker, R.G. 1975. Generalised facies models for resedimented conglomerates of turbidite association. *Bulletin of the Geological Society of America*, 86, 737-748.

Walker, R.G. 1983. Turbidite and associated coarse clastic deposits. *In:* Walker, R.G. (ed) *Facies Models.* Geological Association of Canada, Reprint Series 1, 91-103.

Warren, W.P. 1985. Stratigraphy. *In*: Edwards, K.J. and Warren, W.P. (eds) *The Quaternary History of Ireland*. Academic Press, London, 39-65.

Wells, J. 1997. The 'Errol Beds' and 'Clyde Beds': a note on their equivalents in the Solway Firth. *Quaternary Newsletter,* 83, 21-26.

Westropp, M.S.D. 1920. *Irish Glass*. London.

Wilcock, F.A. 1976. *Dune physiography and the impact of recreation on the north coast of Ireland.* Unpublished D.Phil. thesis, New University of Ulster.

Wilcock, F.A. and Carter, R.W.G. 1977. An environmental approach to the restoration of badly eroded sand dunes. *Biological Conservation*, 77, 279-291.

Williams, W.W. 1960. *Coastal Changes.* London.

Wilson, H.E. 1972. *Regional Geology of Northern Ireland.* HMSO, Belfast.

Wilson, H.E. and Manning, P.I. 1978. *Geology of the Causeway Coast.* Volume 1. Memoirs of the Geological Survey of Northern Ireland, Sheet 7. HMSO, Belfast.

Wilson, H.E. and Robbie, J.A. 1966. *Geology of the country around Ballycastle*. Memoirs of the Geological Survey, HMSO, Belfast.

Wilson, P. 1987. Soil formation on coastal beach and dune sands at Magilligan Point Nature Reserve, Co. Londonderry. *Irish Geography*, 20, 43-49.

Wilson, P. 1991a. Sediment clasts and ventifacts from the north coast of Northern Ireland. *Irish Naturalists' Journal*, 23, 446-450.

Wilson, P. 1991b. Buried soils and coastal aeolian sands at Portstewart, Co. Londonderry, Northern Ireland. *Scottish Geographical Magazine*, 107, 198-202.

Wilson, P. 1994. Characteristics, age and significance of buried podzols in the Grangemore sand dunes, Co. Londonderry. *Irish Naturalists' Journal*, 24, 475-480.

Wilson, P. 1996. Morphological and chemical variations of a buried palaeocatena in late Holocene beach-ridge sands at Magilligan Foreland, Northern Ireland. *Journal of Coastal Research*, 12, 605-611.

Wilson, P. and Bateman, R.M. 1986. Nature and palaeoenvironmental significance of a buried soil sequence from Magilligan Foreland, Northern Ireland. *Boreas*, 15, 137-153.

Wilson, P. and Bateman, R.M. 1987. Pedogenic and geomorphic evolution of a buried dune palaeocatena at Magilligan Foreland, Northern Ireland. *Catena*, 14, 501-517.

Wilson, P. and Braley, S.M. 1997. Development and age structure of Holocene coastal sand dunes at Horn Head, near Dunfanaghy, Co. Donegal. *The Holocene*, 7, 187-197.

Wilson, P. and Farrington, O. 1989. Radiocarbon dating of the Holocene evolution of Magilligan Foreland, Co. Londonderry. *Proceedings of the Royal Irish Academy*, 89B, 1-23.

Wilson, P. and McGourty, J. 1999. Grangemore sand dunes. *In:* Knight, J. (ed) *Lower Bann and adjacent areas*. Field Guide No. 23, Irish Association for Quaternary Studies, Dublin, 40-44.

Wilson, P. and McKenna, J. 1996. Holocene evolution of the River Bann estuary and adjacent coast, Northern Ireland. *Proceedings of the Geologists' Association*, 107, 241-252.

Wintle, A., Clarke, M, Musson, F., Orford, J.D. and Devoy, R.J.N. 1998. Luminescence dating of recent dune formation on Inch Spit, Dingle Bay, southwest Ireland. *The Holocene*, 8, 331-339.

Wright, L.W. 1970. Variation in the level of the cliff/shore platform junction along the south coast of Great Britain. *Marine Geology*, 9, 347-353.

Wright, W.B. 1937. *The Quaternary Ice Age.* 2nd ed. Macmillan, London.

Woodman, P.C. 1978. *The Mesolithic in Ireland: Hunter-Gatherers in an Insular Environment.* British Archaeological Reports, British Series 58, Oxford.

Woodman, P.C. 1985. *Excavations at Mount Sandel 1973-77.* Archaeological Monographs 2, HMSO, Belfast.

Yates, M.J. 1985-86. Ballywoolen: Neolithic and Early Bronze Age settlement. *Unpublished report.*